D0506668

A Picture Book Primer

Kiddiebookland is where we live. . . . It's next to Neverneverville and Peterpanburg. It's that awful place that we've been squeezed into because we're children's book illustrators or children's book writers. Yes, we are! But isn't our work meant for everybody? How infuriating and insulting when serious work is considered only a trifle for the nursery.

—Maurice Sendak, *Caldecott and Co.: Notes on Books and Pictures*

A Picture Book Primer

Understanding and Using Picture Books

Denise I. Matulka

Art by Megan Elizabeth Bergman

Foreword by Susan McCleaf Nespeca

LIBRARIES UNLIMITED

A Member of the Greenwood Publishing Group

Westport, Connecticut • London

Library of Congress Cataloging-in-Publication Data

Matulka, Denise I.

   A picture book primer : understanding and using picture books / Denise I. Matulka.

     p. cm.

   Includes bibliographical references and index.

   ISBN 978-1-59158-441-4 (alk. paper)

   1. Picture books for children. 2. Illustrated children's books. I. Title.

NC965.85.M38 2008

   741.6'42—dc22   2008016754

British Library Cataloguing in Publication Data is available.

Library of Congress Catalog Card Number: 2008016754
ISBN: 978-1-59158-441-4

First published in 2008

Libraries Unlimited, 88 Post Road West, Westport, CT 06881
A Member of the Greenwood Publishing Group, Inc.
www.lu.com

Printed in the United States of America

The paper used in this book complies with the Permanent Paper Standard issued by the National Information Standards Organization (Z39.48–1984).

10 9 8 7 6 5 4 3 2 1

To all kindred spirits who love picture books:
the authors, illustrators, editors, designers, librarians,
critics, scholars, booksellers, and educators

Contents

Foreword

While teaching graduate library school students and discussing picture book art, I am often asked questions such as, "What is gouache?" "How does an illustrator do scratch board?" "How can I tell if this art is computer generated?" Though some students' questions fall in the realm of innocent curiosity, at other times they are agonizing over an annotation assignment I give for every type of class I teach that involves picture books: "Include information in your annotation regarding the illustrations—tell me something about the art. Is it appropriate for and does it complement the text? Why or why not? Is this a picture book, a picture storybook, or an illustrated picture book?"

For the answers to all questions and concerns regarding picture book art, I direct them to Denise Matulka's Web site on picture books. This fine site is a great source of information about types of media, art styles, and techniques. I am delighted to see her wealth of knowledge on picture books incorporated into a book that goes far beyond art techniques, types of media, and visual elements. Here we find a general historical overview of picture books; information on the publishing process, including a great glossary of terms; and a list of various awards given to picture books. The various types of picture books are described—from alphabet books to number books, concept books to toy books including board books, and multicultural to international picture books. There is even an inside look at how the cost of an average picture book is distributed (the author and illustrator only receive around 10 percent in royalties, and the publisher receives only around 50 percent of the price). Particularly enlightening is how the actual illustrations are processed and how this has changed over the years—from color separations in the 1970s to the computer-generated art or digitally enhanced illustrations that are the norm today.

Because early literacy is such a hot topic in libraries today, the author shares how the six early literacy skills children need to have in place before they arrive at school can be strengthened through the use of picture books. And as children's literature enthusiasts know, picture books are not just "for kids anymore": visual literacy is a skill that children of all ages (and adults) can acquire from the study and enjoyment of picture books.

It is difficult to find one set definition of a picture book—authorities on children's literature have made a attempts, and Matulka includes many experts' opinions. However, as a member of the 2008 Caldecott Committee that selected as its winner *The Invention of Hugo Cabret*—a book more than 500 pages long that alternates wordless double-page spreads with text—as the most distinguished American picture book for children published during the preceding year, I have found that even standard definitions from the past may need a contemporary twist; this is a new era for picture books and the creation of the art that accompanies the text.

This basic guide to all facets of picture books will definitely be appreciated by library, literature, education, and art students; librarians and teachers; children's book reviewers; art lovers; and anyone who is an aficionado of picture books.

Sue McCleaf Nespeca
Early Literacy/Children's Literature Consultant, Kid Lit Plus Consulting
author of *Picture Books Plus*

Preface

I cannot recall a time when I haven't read picture books. As a child I read them voraciously—sitting in the reading corner at school every chance I got, dragging home as many as the public library would let me check out. Today, my personal collection consists of over 1,000 hardcover titles. Over time, my favorites, some known and some forgotten, have created a love for picture books that is never sated. Gail E. Haley's *A Story, a Story* (1970) is the first picture book I recall loving and reading again and again. The simple idea of how stories came to the world proved to be pure magic for this reader who cannot get enough of stories.

Another favorite of mine, Robert Barry's *Mr. Willowby's Christmas Tree* (1963), tells the delightful story of a too-big Christmas tree and a cast of characters that saw the potential in what others had thrown away. Here, a simple object—a Christmas tree—has an amazing ability to connect people from different backgrounds. It has recently come back in print, as have many of the older titles.

Now is an exciting time for classic picture books. New generations have an opportunity to read picture books loved and treasured by their parents and grandparents. As a child, I loved everything by Roger Duvoisin, particularly *House of Four Seasons* (1956), a story of a family trying to decide what color to paint their house. I loved the house and the way it changed throughout the book, and I was also introduced to color theory without knowing it.

Then there's *Petunia* (1950), of course, Petunia, whom I loved because she was a silly little goose and I was a silly little girl. The diminutive world of Don Freeman's *Norman the Doorman* (1959) was another favorite. Norman's world, the Majestic Museum of Art, was a ceaseless source of wonder about the possibilities of places people are sometimes too busy to see or take note of, a world independent of ours and just as vibrant.

As an adult I have retained my passion for picture books. I have read picture books as a volunteer, an aunt, a librarian, and a storyteller. In college, wanting to focus on English studies but uninspired by existing opportunities to study nineteenth-century literature or Shakespeare, I took a class called "History of Children's Literature." I was hooked. I wanted more. Unfortunately, the university I attended did not have a formal program to study children's literature. With the help of two fabulous professors, I created an interdisciplinary major. I am the only person to graduate from the University of Nebraska with a degree in children's literature, an integrated studies program that allowed me to combine courses in child development, children's books, reading and language development, and art into a degree. Over time I realized that the picture book was the format within the children's literature field that intrigued me most.

There are many wildly popular picture books that many people are familiar with, books that have sold at least a million copies, including *Chicka Chicka Boom Boom* (1989), *If You Give a Mouse a Cookie* (1985), *The Polar Express* (1985), *Rainbow Fish* (1992), *Where the Wild Things Are* (1963), *Guess How Much I Love You* (1994), and *Everyone Poops* (1993). Then of course there is Dr. Seuss's *Oh! The*

Places You'll Go! (1990), which tops the best seller list anew each May and June during high school and college graduations. *Gallop!* was released in late 2007, just in time for the holiday shopping season. With 800,000 copies in print so far, I am sure it will surpass the one million mark before long. *Pat the Bunny* (1940) and *Goodnight Moon* (1947) have firmly established themselves as the perfect first picture books for babies. Caldecott winners (and honor titles) are guaranteed success because schools and libraries rush to purchase extra copies, which often results in increased sales, as well as a place on the *New York Times'* Children's Best-Sellers list.

The majority of picture books only sell 10,000 copies. Nonetheless, they manage to find their way into the hearts and minds of readers. In many ways these books are perhaps even more special for the lasting impression they make because they have connected with readers in a very specific way. I am sure everyone who loves picture books can quickly generate a list of books that have had a lasting impression on him or her.

While writing this book I hired an artist to create original art. Taking this approach and working with the artist taught me a great deal and really added to the content of the book. It is my sincere hope that this is reflected in the book. Throughout *A Picture Book Primer*, I refer to hundreds of published picture books—over 500, in fact; however, the art used to support terms and definitions is original, illustrations for a book called *Butler and the Fly*. Using images that are drawn from a particular story creates a flow and continuity that would not otherwise have been possible. A full version of the book is included in appendix A. An interactive color version is available at my Web site, www.picturingbooks.com.

Writing this book was a very special project for me. I hope people who love the format but lack the background to truly appreciate all it has to offer learn to look at and appreciate picture books in new and exciting ways. Academia has begun to address the special world of picture books, but often the books and articles are beyond the average reader. After all, scholars write for other scholars, so although wonderful research about picture books is being done, it can be difficult to extract the information readers to need to articulate an opinion. My goal is to open the world of picture books to readers, hopefully in ways I can't even imagine.

Acknowledgments

Nothing in life is accomplished in a vacuum. I want to thank the following people for helping me make this book possible:

Megan Elizabeth Bergman, the artist who created the art used to illustrate aspects of picture book design and development. Once I began to work with Megan, my project took on new life. Megan, you have a very bright future ahead of you.

Dr. Karla Wendelin and Professor Ned Hedges, both formerly of the University of Nebraska. Both nurtured my burgeoning interest in studying children's literature when I was an undergraduate. Without their guidance, I would not have been able to focus my studies on children's literature. How incredible to meet two other adults who loved children's books as much as I did!

The interlibrary loan staff at Lincoln City Libraries in Lincoln, Nebraska, for locating many of the articles and out-of-print books for I needed for my research. Every city needs a great library system, and Lincoln has one.

Barbara Ittner, my editor at Libraries Unlimited. Her patience with missed deadlines and meticulous editing helped me shape this book into the final product you now hold. It is a far cry from what I had initially envisioned, but in end it is the book it is supposed to be. Over the years I had amassed a great deal of picture book research culled from hundreds of articles and dozens of books. I had no idea how daunting it would be to actually form that mass of information into a book. I thank Barbara for helping me do that.

The staff at the Eric Carle Picture Book Museum in Amherst, Massachusetts. In March 2006 I had the opportunity to visit the museum. I was disappointed when I arrived to find out that in order to use the Barbara Elleman Research Library, I had to have an appointment. I did not; poor planning on my part. However, not only did the fabulous staff allow me to use the collection, but several staff members reorganized their schedules to allow me access and give me a personal tour of the facilities. The only thing that could have made that day better would have been if Mr. Carle had been in residence. Maybe next time . . . .

Joanne Ferguson Cavanaugh, for her unfailing faith in me. She consistently reminds me exactly what I am capable of—especially when I set my mind to it. Those who know Joanne know just how lucky I am to have her in my life.

And my family . . . .

Introduction

WHAT THIS BOOK IS

Many wonderful books have been published about the format of picture books, discussing narrative art, postmodern tensions, and publishing. There are books about using picture books in the classroom, bibliographies, and compilations of conversations with artists. What is lacking is a work that explores picture books in a very basic way—taking the format down to its basics and analyzing them a useful way. This book is meant to do just that.

The idea was to create a book that readers—educators, librarians, parents, and students—can easily digest, whether they are familiar with picture books or not. I wanted to help readers better understand what picture books are, how they have evolved over time, what elements they are composed of, how they are designed and made, and some of the issues involved in using picture books with readers. My is to help readers become better equipped to work with and talk about picture books. Most of all, I hope to engender a deeper appreciation of and encourage readers to further explore the fascinating world of picture books.

Approximately 500 picture books are discussed in *A Picture Book Primer*. With the sheer number of outstanding picture books available, I could have chosen dozens of titles for every one that I eventually chose to discuss. In most cases, the titles referred to should be available at the local library or bookstore.

Remember, this is a primer, so it is not meant to be exhaustive, but it does provide a thorough overview of picture books.

WHAT THIS BOOK IS NOT

This is not a book about how to get a picture book published. Although it covers the basics of picture book publishing, there are more appropriate sources for individuals interested in writing or illustrating picture books. Nor is this a guide on how to review picture books, although the review process is also discussed. It is not a bibliography or an attempt to identify "best picture books"; however, "what makes a picture book great" is addressed.

HOW THIS BOOK IS ORGANIZED

A Picture Book Primer is divided into eight chapters that explore picture books from various perspectives, including design, artistic media and style, multicultural issues, and literacy. One thing generally lacking in most resources that discuss picture books is a glossary of terms, principles, and facets of picture books.

Therefore, an exhaustive glossary of publishing, design, and artistic terms is included at the end of this book.

COMPANION WEB SITE

A companion Web site is available for readers interested in supporting materials: www.picturingbooks.com. The site features many interactive elements; in fact, most of the illustrations are presented in an interactive format many readers may find useful. In addition, there are downloadable supporting materials.

A NOTE ABOUT TERMINOLOGY

As you will see when you delve into the book, different terms can be used to describe the same thing. For example, design principles are sometimes called "principles of design" or "principles of art." Many art terms have different meaning and associations depending on the context. I do not claim to be an art authority, and have applied terms as I understand them.

A NOTE ABOUT CITATIONS

To keep the narrative from being bogged down with names, unless I am addressing an aspect of the author's or illustrator's style or technique, I use only titles and dates in the text. Full bibliographic information for all picture books discussed in *A Picture Book Primer* can be found in the bibliography at the end of the book.

Chapter 1

What Is a Picture Book?

A picturebook is text, illustrations, total design; an item of manufacture and a commercial product; a social, cultural, historic document; and foremost, an experience for a child.

As an art form it hinges on the interdependence of pictures and words, on the simultaneous display of two facing pages, and on the drama of the turning of the page.

On its own terms its possibilities are limitless.

—Barbara Bader,
American Picture Books from Noah's Ark *to the* Beast Within

In This Chapter
- A Picture Book Is . . .
- A Brief History of Picture Books
- Technological Evolution
- The Publishing Process
- Reviewing Picture Books
- Awards

The picture book is a format designed for children, but it can, and should, be enjoyed and appreciated by readers of all ages. Randolph Caldecott, a nineteenth-century English illustrator, is considered by many historians to be the "father of the picture book." He was the first to use illustration to complement and extend the text and created 16 picture books that changed children's publishing forever. What Caldecott seemed to know instinctively has been refined and reinvented many times during the past century by talented illustrators around the world. An appreciation of the art and story that make the format so special is often difficult to articulate. This guide take a closer look at the aspects that make picture books so special.

A PICTURE BOOK IS . . .

There is something special about picture books. The format that makes them distinct within children's book publishing also makes them unique among other visual media. A movie, television program, or Web site, no matter how stylish and flashy, somehow doesn't compare with the quiet sophistication of picture books.

Some adult readers,[1] unaware of the breadth and depth of the picture book format, generally consider picture books to be exclusively for children, particularly children under age eight. Describing the breadth and value of picture books to individuals unfamiliar with children's literature is challenging, especially if they hear "children" in children's literature and relegate the books and their creators to, as Maurice Sendak says, "Kiddiebookland."

The term *picture book* is somewhat lacking as a description of the vast body of titles it represents. A book with pictures? Pictures in a book? The continuum is broad, from wordless picture books, which tell the story exclusively thorough the illustrations, to books in which the illustrations are decorative.

Most authoritative sources on picture books cite the importance of the picture–text relationship, but it is still be difficult to pin down an adequate definition. Experts agree that picture books have illustration on every page. Aside from that, the lines of distinction begin to blur. Some critics offer straightforward definitions. Kathleen Horning states that picture books "have been especially developed as an art form with young children in mind. These thirty-two-page creations ingeniously combine words and pictures" (Horning 1997b).

Some definitions are complex. Lawrence Sipe (1998) says that picture books "are unified artistic wholes in which text and pictures, covers and endpages, and the details of design work together to provide an aesthetically satisfying experience for children." To complicate matters, some scholars spell picture book (two words) as picturebook (one word). Scholars Nikolajeva and Scott (2001, 2006) state that the compound spelling enables them to explore the image interaction, making the phenomenon picturebook distinct "from picture books, or books with pictures." Lawrence Sipe (1998) also employs the one-word spelling "in order to emphasize the unity of words and pictures that is the most important hallmark of this type of book."

Much has been written about picture books. For example, it is easy to find articles about how to use picture books in the classroom; bibliographies abound, as well as numerous theme-based lists for classroom use. The number of articles about postmodern picture books grows with each passing year. There are numerous articles deconstructing the picture books of David Wiesner, David Macaulay, and Anthony Browne.

Numerous metaphors have also been used to describe the relationship between the text and pictures. The marriage metaphor is the most frequently encountered. Some refer to the relationship as a dance, with two partners moving together in time and space to tell a story. Both of these metaphors describe a relationship that is less than complete without both halves present. However, while they explain the picture–text relationship as complementary, they fail to consider the degree to which that balance affects the picture as a whole (Nikolajeva and Scott 2001, 2006).

Rather than attempt to analyze the work of particular illustrators or authors, this guide analyzes the physical characteristics that drive the format. Narrative structures, design principles, and the creative process are also considered.

What makes a picture book a picture book? Is it a picture book if it has 32 pages?

The second question reflects a common perception about picture books. In 2007 two books were published that challenged that idea: *The Invention of Hugo Cabret* by Brian Selznick and *Gallop!* by Rufus Butler Seder. The first has 533 pages and the second 24 pages. Both titles have illustrations, but the manner in which the art supports and interacts with the text is vastly different than in commonly found 32-page picture books.

Sometime during the last 50 years, the number 32 became associated with picture books. According to editor Olga Litowinsky, this is because a large press sheet of printed pages, folded to size, can accommodate 32 pages (2001, 65–66). Although it is true that most picture books have at least that many pages, many have more. Examples of picture books that are longer than 32 pages are *Jackalope* (2003), illustrated by Janet Stevens, which has 56 pages; *The Three Pigs* (2001), illustrated by David Wisner, which has 40 pages; and *Snow White* (1974), illustrated by Trina Schart Hyman, which has 48 pages. In addition, the classic *Harold and the Purple Crayon* (1955), illustrated by Crockett Johnson, has 64 pages. Few would argue that these are not picture books, but obviously they do not meet the 32-page criterion.

Is something a picture book if it has both pictures and words? Can it be a picture book if has one element but not the other? Wordless picture books—that is, picture books without words—are becoming more popular. Furthermore, books that have a few words and phrases are often considered wordless, including David Wiesner's *Tuesday* (1991), which has twenty-three characters and no complete sentences. *Hug* (2000), illustrated by Jez Alborough, uses only one word ("hug") throughout the entire book, aside from when Bobo and his mommy are reunited and they say each other's names. Although these examples do indeed have words, they are considered wordless.

So . . . what exactly is a picture book?

Consider the criteria prescribed by the Association of Library Services to Children (ALSC), the American Library Association (ALA) division that oversees the Caldecott Medal, which is one of the most prestigious children's book awards. Awarded annually for distinguished contributions in illustration, the winner and honor titles are announced every January at the Mid-Winter Conference of the American Library Association. The criteria for the Caldecott Award define a picture book as

> *A picture book for children, as distinguished from other books with illustrations, is one that essentially provides the child with a visual experience. A picture book has a collective unity of story-line, theme, or concept, developed through the series of pictures of which the book is comprised.*—American Library Association

The criteria set forth by ALA do not specify length or page count. In fact, in 2008 the committee awarded the prize to *The Invention of Hugo Cabret* (2007), illustrated by Brian Selznick, which has 533 pages. The title is profusely illustrated, the illustrations propel the narrative, and although it has many of the picture book paratexts discussed in chapters 2 and 3, they work differently than in a traditional picture book. The author/illustrator himself does not call it a picture book; he calls it "a novel in words and pictures." With the exception of the back flap, Brian Selznick is never identified as an illustrator. On the other hand, *Gallop!*, a book of moving pictures, has the subtitle, "A Scranimation® Picture Book." *Gallop!* does not use a traditional medium, such as watercolors or collage. The illustrator Rufus Butler Seder currently is the patent holder for the technology used in *Gallop!*

> The Caldecott Medal was established in honor of nineteenth-century English illustrator Randolph Caldecott. Caldecott's *The Diverting History of John Gilpin* inspired the design by René Paul Chambellan that is emblazoned on the award. The first Caldecott award was given in 1938 to Dorothy P. Lathrop for her illustrations in *Animals of the Bible.*

For the purposes of this guide, a picture book is one in which text and pictures work together to tell a story. This guide takes no other position on exactly what a picture book is or is not, but rather offers a perspective from which to look at the picture book format. Later in this chapter the picture–text balance is discussed, and in chapter 5, "The Art of the Story," the picture–text relationship is further explored. However, as readers of this guide will discover, the gamut runs from picture books in which illustration dominates; to picture storybooks, which are titles with longer narratives; to illustrated books, in which art is decorative; to wordless picture books, which have few or no words.

Chapter 4, "Format or Genre?" discusses board books, beginning readers, and concept books. Although some sources do not consider these forms to be picture books, this guide broadly considers them a type of "picture book" or "illustrated book."

There are many books about picture books. *Illustrating Children's Books* (2004) by Martin Salisbury and *Writing with Pictures* (1997) by Uri Shulevitz are for potential illustrators. *How Picturebooks Work* (2001) by Maria Nikolajeva and Carole Scott and *Words About Pictures* (1988) by Perry Nodelman are scholarly explorations of the narrative aspects of picture books. The classic *American Picture Books from Noah's Ark to the Beast Within* (1976) by Barbara Bader is almost overwhelming in its historical coverage. What is lacking is a resource that thoroughly explores picture books on a basic level. Many of the titles mentioned above include glossaries but seem to omit some of the terms used to define picture books. Buried within the rich trove of information these books contain are the words and phrases needed to confidently discuss picture books. The glossary in this guide is rather exhaustive, and purposely so. It contains more than 200 terms from multiple disciplines—art, publishing, and design—that users of this guide can use to articulate an informed opinion about picture books.

In summary, the overall goal of this guide is to present the many facets of picture books in an accessible format that aficionados as well as experts can use to explore picture books in depth.

Figure 1.1 is a meme that attempts to create an overview of the terms often used when discussing picture books. The terms originate from several disciplines, including art and academia.

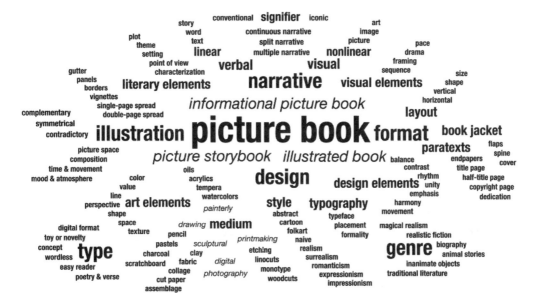

Figure 1.1. The picture book meme features hundreds of terms that are routinely applied to picture books. The meme is an attempt to organize the terms and create a relationship between narrative (text), art (picture), and design.

> For an interactive version of the picture book meme, visit www.picturingbooks.com. A downloadable PDF is also available.

Picture Book Classifications

One of the approaches frequently employed to break down the vast picture book canon is the picture–text balance. *Picture book*, *picture storybook*, and *illustrated book* are the three categories encountered most often. At one end of the spectrum are picture books, which tell the story primarily through pictures. The text is generally short. Illustrated books have larger blocks of text, sometimes entire pages, and the pictures are generally decorative. In between are picture storybooks, which have a more equal balance, with text being primary and pictures secondary. In both illustrated books and picture storybooks, the story is easy to follow and understand through the text alone, with the pictures playing a complementary role. In picture books, the illustrations fill in the gaps or work against the gaps in the text.

Some experts rigorously apply these definitions, while others use the term *picture book* to describe any children's book with illustrations, as long as the format is oversized and it is between 24 and 48 pages in length. As stated previously, some critics apply an alternate spelling, "picturebook" (one word), to describe their view of picture books.

In *A Picture Book Primer*, the following terms are used to categorize picture–text balance: *picture books*, *picture storybooks*, *illustrated books*, and *informational picture books* (including picture book biographies). These classifications are applied as a guide. They are not intended to provide a definition of what a picture book is. All the categories are similar in that illustrations play an integral role in each type; the difference between the categories becomes important in the picture–text relationship. (The dynamics of narrative structures that define, or draw a line, between categories, are addressed in chapter 5, "The Art of the Story.")

Picture Books

Picture books have illustrations on every page, with art almost dominating the text. The illustrations are pivotal to the story, with text playing an important but supporting role. Wordless picture books rely solely on illustrations and are designed to tell a story through a series of pictures carefully developed to carry the narrative. In figure 1.2 there is text on both pages, but the illustrations dominate the composition.

Figure 1.2. Picture books have illustrations on every page, with art almost dominating the text. The illustrations are pivotal to the story, with text playing an important but supporting role.

Uri Shulevitz, winner of the 1969 Caldecott Medal for *The Fool of the World and His Flying Ship*, sees a very distinct difference between picture books and picture storybooks. In his exploration *Writing with Pictures* (1997), Shulevitz states that picture storybooks are told with words, and the illustrations "amplify" the story.

"Pictures have an auxiliary role, because the words themselves contain the images," he says. In a "true" picture book, according to Shulevitz, the story is told primarily with pictures; when words are used, they assume an auxiliary role. Maurice Sendak's *Where the Wild Things Are* (1962) is often held up as a genuine picture book. Sendak uses white space to great effect to propel the narrative forward. His composition features pages with just text, three-quarter page spreads, and double-page spreads without words. In the beginning of the book, large amounts of white space surround the picture and text. Gradually the illustrations grow larger, eventually covering the entire page. After the wild rumpus, which is featured on three double-page spreads, Max returns to his home. The composition at the end of the book is similar to the beginning.

Picture Storybooks

In a picture storybook, the pictures complement the story, often mirroring the plot. Picture storybooks lean toward narrative prose as opposed to a rhyming text. A prime example of a picture storybook is the classic *The Story of Babar, the Little Elephant* (1933) by Jean de Brunhoff. In picture storybooks, as in the Babar story, the plot is established, with a discernible beginning and end, and text and pictures are equally balanced. In a well-designed picture storybook, the format reflects the meaning of the story; both the illustration and the text bear the burden of narration. While a good picture storybook ties the reader to the pictures and creates the drama of turning the page, text and pictures work together to propel the story forward. A good picture storybook establishes a context for the pictures that follow through the narrative text. Traditional literature is often categorized as picture storybook because illustrated folklore tends to have longer narratives that can be read and understood without pictures. However, anyone familiar with the art of Ruth Sanderson, Gennady Spirin, and K. Y. Craft has happily read their lushly illustrated versions of folk tales.

In figure 1.3 the pages have larger blocks of text. Instead of being spread over six or seven pages, the text is featured on two pages.

Figure 1.3. The text is condensed to two pages in a picture storybook. In a picture book, the same amount of text would be distributed over six or seven pages.

Illustrated Books

In an illustrated book, text takes center stage, with pictures playing a supporting role. Illustrations are for the most part decoration. The text also tends not to be driven by the pictures, so the drama that builds when the page is turned is missing. However, it can sometimes be the other way around. The stark black, white, and gray art in Tom Feelings's masterpiece *Middle Passage* (1995) is an example. As powerful as the story is, his illustrations capture the despair and utter terror of the situation.

Another example of an illustrated story is *Secret Lives of Walter Mitty and of James Thurber* (2006) by James Thurber, illustrated by Marc Simont. Walter Mitty was the first in the <u>WISP</u> (<u>Wonderfully Illustrated Short Pieces</u>) series from Harper Design, an imprint of HarperCollins. Although other adult stories have been illustrated, this was the first series of adult short fiction by a children's imprint. The series introduces a new generation of readers to classic editions of famous short stories illustrated by top children's artists. Other titles in the series include *Gift of the Magi/The Purple Dress* (2006) by O. Henry, illustrated by Chris Raschka, and *The Homecoming* (2006) by Ray Bradbury, illustrated by Dave McKean.

In figure 1.4 the large blocks of text are indicative of an illustrated book. The pages have art, but it is merely decorative.

Figure 1.4. The text dominates the pages in an illustrated book, with pictures playing a supporting role.

Beginning reader (or easy reader) books fit nicely in this category, because illustrations are used to emphasize or complement the story and are not the focus of the book. The role of beginning readers is to help children transition from picture books to fiction without illustration. Of course, adults can guide children toward independent reading while helping them retain an appreciation of pictures books. To abandon picture books as reading skills develop negates the sophistication and possibilities of the format.

Informational Picture Books

Informational picture books,[2] often just as bright and engaging as a standard picture book, are mostly used in an instructional capacity. Most concept books, including alphabet and counting books, are informational picture books. While most concept books feature a rhyming text, or sometimes just one or two words per page, their function is to introduce the alphabet or numbers. In figure 1.5 the left-hand page has a brief sentence asking the reader to use the illustrations to answer the question posed in the narrative.

Figure 1.5. Concept books are an example of an informational picture book. The text and the illustrations complement one another; neither overpowers the other.

Picture book biographies, a type of informational picture book, generally give readers a brief glimpse into a segment of the life of an individual. Limited by page count, they often focus on the highlights or major events in the lives of historical figures, often youth or early years. In a picture book biography the illustrations are essential to telling the story. Lavishly illustrated picture book biographies are becoming more popular. Authors Diane Stanley and Don Brown are noted for their picture book biographies. Libraries often catalog and shelve informational picture books in the nonfiction section. Picture book biographies can be longer than 32 pages but still feature illustrations on almost every page.

A BRIEF HISTORY OF PICTURE BOOKS

Social Implications and Precursors to the Picture Book

Before the seventeenth century, the concept of childhood didn't exist. Children's books published before 1865, when *Alice's Adventures in Wonderland* was published, were often didactic and used primarily for instruction. Children did not read for pleasure and amusement. In fact, the entertainment of children through reading was at best secondary and at worst completely overlooked or even frowned upon (Darton 1988).

Early children's books included primers, religious tracts, and alphabet books.[3] Supporting woodcuts and engravings served more as decoration than illustration. Much like stock art used in newspapers and magazines today, illustrations were not necessarily associated with a particular book. Rather, budget conscious publishers reused illustrations over and over in many books.

In the seventeenth century things began to change. John Locke (1632–1704) and Jean Jacques Rousseau (1712–1778) challenged the existing notions of childhood. Locke proposed the idea of the tabula rasa, or the child as a blank slate. He was the first Westerner to note that children had unique needs and abilities. LikewiseRousseau, believing in the innate goodness of children, promoted developing a child's imagination through play. He advocated gentle guidance and allowing children to grow through exploration and age-appropriate activities. For the first time in Western history childhood, with its innocence and inexperience, was identified as unique and distinct from adulthood.

Both Rousseau and Locke noted the dearth of quality literature for children, but it was a contemporary of Rousseau, John Newbery (1713–1767), a printer and bookseller, who ultimately identified the possibilities of a children's market. Although none of Newbery's books were specifically picture books, they did open the door for the next generation of publishers, allowing them to take children's publishing to the next level. He is credited with publishing the first true children's book, *A Little Pretty Pocket-Book*. Published in 1744, it was the first attempt to entertain and amuse children, and Newbery was not afraid to say so, using this as an avenue to market the book (Weinstein 2005).

Today, Newbery's name is not remembered for the classics he published. Even Newbery's most famous books—*Goody Two-Shoes* and *A Little Pretty Pocket-Book*—are virtually unknown outside the children's literature field. Rather, he is remembered for his intuitive sense of the market. During his lifetime he published small, well-designed, and inexpensive books for little hands—perfect for children to hold and call their own.

Children's publishing as we know it would be much different without the contributions of these three men. Today children's books are the only type of literature specifically categorized by age, a concept that Rousseau, Locke, and Newbery would undoubtedly embrace.

A timeline of the development of picture books is included in appendix B.

Early Illustrated Books: The First Picture Books

Picture books familiar to modern readers evolved from the early illustrated books for children. *Orbis Sensualium Pictus—The Visible World in Pictures* by Johannes Amos Comenius (1592–1670) is considered by many to be the first true picture book. It is a far cry from the picture books published in the last 100 years. Commonly known as *Orbis Pictus* and published in 1658, it was a picture dictionary illustrated with woodcuts, which was the only feasible means of illustration at that time. It was an unusual book for its time. What earns it the distinction of "the first picture book" is the creator's integration of illustration with text.

Comenius believed that children would learn Latin more quickly if they could make a visual association with the text. In many ways, Comenius was far ahead of his time. The combination of woodcuts with his Latin text satisfies the definition of a picture book because he acknowledged the use of illustration to expand and complement the text. His innovation also proved to be important; *Orbis Pictus* was used widely throughout the late eighteenth century.

Another early illustrated book, though not particularly a children's book, is *Kunst und Lehrbüchlein*, roughly translated as "art and teaching booklet." Published in Frankfurt Germany in 1580, it featured woodcut illustrations by Jost Amman (1539–1591). Two of these illustrations are of children. In one, a child is shown reading a hornbook, a primer made with a sheet of parchment that was mounted on wood, bone, or leather and protected by a thin sheet of transparent horn; in the other a child is shown playing. Rare indeed. Aside from primers and chapbooks, the two types of literature available to eighteenth-century children were fairy tales and nursery rhymes. (Ironically, many of the original fairy tales children read over 200 years ago have been altered today, with frightening words and images removed, to make them more palatable for modern children.)

The Nineteenth Century

The Industrial Revolution had a great impact on publishing and on children's books in particular, through improved printing presses and distribution. A growing literate middle class provided buyers for savvy publishers with a keen eye for the market. Hungry for knowledge and eager to buy books for their children, the evolving middle class began to view books as items of pleasure, not just as instruments of instruction. Book shops specializing in titles for children also began to appear.

Keep in mind that prior to the nineteenth century, illustration was used only as decoration. In fact, it was common practice to use the same illustrations in several books. It was many years before artists were identified by their unique style. It was not until almost 1800, when Thomas Bewick was commissioned to create art for *Pretty Book of Pictures for Little Masters and Misses; or, Tommy Trip's History of Beasts and Birds* (1799), that artists received credit for their illustrations in books.

Nineteenth-century illustrators found an audience eager for stories accompanied by illustrations. Childhood was now acknowledged as a time distinct from adulthood. For the first time illustrators had the technical means, such as improved printing presses, to produce books with children in mind. In addition, photography was emerging as a medium, and publishers were experimenting with ways to use it to improve print production.

During the nineteenth century children came to be clearly defined as an audience with literary needs distinct from those of adults. A mass of books designed for children flooded the publishing scene: picture books with nursery rhymes, poetry, limericks, fairy tales, fables, and adventure all appealed to the taste of children. Prominent illustrators who emerged at this time include Randolph Caldecott (1846–1886), Walter Crane (1845–1915), and Kate Greenaway (1846–1901).

In 1878 Randolph Caldecott illustrated *The Diverting History of John Gilpin*, which was written by William Cowper. The image of three jovial horsemen emblazoned on the Caldecott Medal comes from this picture book.

One of the most popular picture books in the nineteenth century was *Der Struwwelpeter* by Heinrich Hoffman (1809–1894), a Frankfurt physician. Hoffman, seeking a Christmas present for his son, was disappointed by the books he found on the store shelves, so he wrote his own. Published anonymously in 1845, the first English translation, *Slovenly Peter*, appeared in 1848. The book contained 10 illustrated and rhymed stories that parodied moral tales popular at the time. Heinrich's version featured exaggerated and often disastrous consequences of misbehavior.

Rebuses were another type of book popular in the nineteenth century, and they are still popular today. In a rebus illustrations replace rather than complement the text. A rebus is a puzzle in which words and letters are represented by pictures that either sound the same or represent the word. For example, a picture or drawing of a heart is often used to express the word "love" or even to replace the word "heart."

> *Caldecott's work heralds the beginning of the modern picture book. He devised an ingenious juxtaposition of picture and word, a counterpoint that had never happened before. Words are left out ñ but the picture says it. Pictures are left out—but the word says it. In short, it is the invention of the picture book.*
>
> ——Maurice Sendak, *Caldecott & Co.: Notes on Books & Pictures* (1988)

The Twentieth Century

1920s

The social and economic consequences of World War I included a reduction in book publishing, although this did not hinder the interest in developing quality literature for children. Children's publishing resumed after the war, particularly in the 1920s.

One apparent problem in 1920s publishing was a lack of new and original illustrators for children; most children's books in the first part of the decade were either reprints of Beatrix Potter titles or of nineteenth-century imitators of her. In the meantime, advancement in lithography technology made it easier for artists to create pictures that were easy to mass produce. The complicated techniques of etching and engraving were replaced by lithography. Ultimately, the 1920s produced a lot of new talent. Wanda Gag, a trained graphic designer, wrote and illustrated her own books. Gág's *Millions of Cats* (1928) is considered by many to be the first modern picture book for its innovative use of design, which complemented the text and extended the narrative. It won a Newbery Honor medal in 1930, one of the few picture books that did. C. B. Falls's *ABC Book*, with bold woodcut illustrations, was published in 1923. Margery Bianco Williams's *Velveteen Rabbit* (1922), with illustrations by William Nicholson, is now considered a classic. Nicholson is credited with experimenting with reproduction techniques and the introduction of offset color lithographs during the 1920s. *The Horn Book Magazine*, the first periodical devoted to children's books and reading, was established in 1924 by Bertha Mahony and Elinor Whitney.

1930s

The Great Depression of the 1930s was a productive time in terms of creativity, but artists felt the effects of a battered economy. The rise of the children's librarian and special efforts to call attention to the literary needs of children provided a boost that kept the market fresh despite limited publication. The 1930s saw the first serious publication of a thorough exploration of children's literature, F. J. Harvey Darton's *Children's Books in England*, and the periodical *Junior Bookshelf*, which devoted its pages to reviews of children's books. Allen Lane established the Penguin dynasty in England in 1935, which spawned Baby Puffin Books and Puffin Picture Books. The quality of these titles was bleak at best, yet the imprint kept children's book publishing alive and kicking. It was also the decade that heralded the first presentation of the Caldecott Award, with Dorothy Lathrop the first recipient for *Animals of the Bible*. In 1937, *And to Think That I Saw It on Mulberry Street* by Theodor Seuss Geisel, better known as Dr. Seuss, was published by Random House after being turned down by 28 publishing houses. Other prominent illustrators emerged at this time, including Maud Petersham and Miska Petersham, Jean de Brunhoff, Majorie Flack, and Kurt Wiese. Ludwig Bemelmans's first book about *Madeline* was published in 1939. The wordless picture book made its first appearance. *A Head for Happy* (1931) by Helen Sewell, thought not completely wordless, is a story about three girls trying to find a head for their stuffed doll. Although the book has text, it serves to "punctuate the story line and expel emotion" (Bader 1976). According to historian Barbara Bader, the first truly wordless picture book was *What Whiskers Did* (1932) by Ruth Carroll, a tale of the adventures of a Scottish terrier who breaks away from his owner.

1940s

World War II was even more devastating economically than World War I, and it resulted in a severe shortage of books. In an effort to combat the ravages of war on the book market, Simon & Schuster introduced the Little Golden Books, which, despite having sold more than two billion copies, were never considered "real" picture books by critics and librarians. Designed to be sturdy and hold up through multiple readings, each Little Golden Book had a standard format that was easily to identify. Titles had 44 pages, with 14 in color, and they were 8¼ by 6¾ inches, with a golden foil spine—perfect for small hands. At a time when children's books were only found in bookstores and libraries, the imprint broke with tradition and made sure its titles were stocked in department, drug, and variety, such as Woolworth's. Despite the paper shortage, several talents emerged: Robert

McCloskey, illustrator of *Make Way for Ducklings* (1941) and *Lentil* (1940); Robert Lawson; Roger Duvoisin of *White Snow, Bright Snow* (1947) and *Petunia* (1950); and Lois Lenski. Classic picture books published during the 1940s include *Curious George* (1940) by H. A. Rey and *The Little House* (1942), written and illustrated by Virginia Lee Burton. Two classics from Margaret Wise Brown and Clement Hurd, *The Runaway Bunny* (1942) and *Goodnight Moon* (1947), were also published during that decade. (*The Runaway Bunny* has the rare distinction of never having gone out of print.)

1950s

The 1950s heralded a new breed of artists, who looked to the past as well as to the future. The postwar years saw renewed interest in the children's library system, which stimulated the demand for quality as well as quantity. During the 1950s the career of Marcia Brown—three-time winner of the Caldecott Medal and six-time Honor recipient—began to blossom. Brown is noted for her experimentation with numerous illustration techniques. For example, her medium for *Once a Mouse* (1961) was woodcut illustrations, while the medium she used for *Shadow* (1982) was collage illustrations. Both titles won the Caldecott Medal. This is also the decade that introduced Maurice Sendak. During his early career, Sendak illustrated other authors' books. He won his first Caldecott Honor medal for his illustrations for Ruth Krauss's *A Very Special House* (1953). Other great talents that emerged in the 1950s include Ezra Jack Keats and Leo Lionni. Crockett Johnson's deceptively simple *Harold and the Purple Crayon* was published in 1955. In 1957 the world was introduced to *The Cat in the Hat*, the first of a type of book to become known as a beginning or easy reader. In Zurich, Switzerland, Jella Lepman founded the International Board on Books for Young People (IBBY). Today IBBY has more than 65 chapters, promoting children's books in every part of the world. Weston Woods Studio was founded by Morton Schindel in 1953. Since then, it has adapted more than 500 picture books into animated features. Weston Woods was an innovative force in the translation of picture books into audiovisual media.

1960s

The picture book format familiar to readers today blossomed in the 1960s. An influx of talented artists experimenting with an array of artistic media and reproduction techniques made the picture book a dominant format in children's literature. Leo Lionni and Eric Carle, both trained as graphic designers, were active in this period. Carle's *The Very Hungry Caterpillar* (1969) and Lionni's *Frederick* (1968) both became classics. Both artists worked in collage. Although Lionni was awarded four Caldecott Honor medals, Carle never won.

Artists were discovering the limitless possibilities of the picture book as an artistic outlet. This, and the recognition of the unity of words and pictures in the development of children, earned the picture book serious consideration. Sendak's *Where the Wild Things Are* (1963) is considered by many to be a "perfect" picture book. Other prominent picture books published in the 1960s include *The Snowy*

Day (1962), the first book to feature a child of color as the main protagonist, and *Stevie* (1969) by John Steptoe. In 1967, the Biennial Illustrations Bratislava (BIB) was established. Its conferences present the best in international children's illustration and gives artists from countries around the world an opportunity to present their work. In 1965 Nancy Larrick published a groundbreaking article, "The All-White World of Children's Books," in the *Saturday Review of Books*—the first published critique of the absence of children of color in children's literature.

1970s

Prior to the 1970s, the typical child depicted in a picture storybook was middle class and white. During that decade children of color were introduced into picture books, but the initial portrayals were rife with stereotypes and cultural inaccuracies. Children of different cultures were represented, but with white characteristics, without authenticity and substance. White children also received their fair share of misrepresentation; for years they had to bear the "Dick and Jane" stigma. A few writers, such as Ezra Jack Keats, made attempts to correct this in the 1960s and 1970s. The publication of *Stevie* (1969), the first book about a black child in a realistic setting, set the tone for what was to come. In 1974, the Coretta Scott King Medal was awarded to an illustrator for the first time. It was a major step toward rectifying the lack of authentic portrayals of Africa Americans. A flood of traditional literature inundated the market; mainly because it offered easy dissemination of cultural information outside white, mainstream America. Unfortunately, the bulk of this literature had inadequate, if any, source notes.[4]

1980s

The 1980s saw a rising consciousness of racial and sexual stereotypes in children's literature. In addition, writers began to tackle formerly taboo subjects such as AIDS, presenting poignant, touching messages about the devastating disease that touches the lives of many children. In the late 1980s and early 1990s multicultural literature for children blossomed—that is, literature created by authors and illustrators of color. Prior to 1990, less than 1 percent of all children's literature published was by authors of color. Children of color were now drawn by authors of color and thus could escape the bias of stereotyping that had plagued children's books since the publication of *The Story of Little Black Sambo* (1899) by Helen Bannerman. The importance of authentic, accurate depictions of race and the role it plays in child development was clearly recognized during the 1980s.

1990s

Imagine, just over 100 years ago, children had very few books they could call their own. Today, more than 4,000 children's titles are published annually, and the selection of picture books seems limitless. Modern techniques and production capabilities, such as improved lithographic processes, allow for easy reproduction of almost any artistic medium in print. During the 1990s, publishers recognized the potential of having children's divisions within publishing houses that hitherto did not cater to young audiences. The first picture book created with digital media, *Mr. Lunch Takes a Plane Ride* (1993), by J.otto Seibold was published. The fractured fairy tale craze was initiated by the publication of Jon Scieszka's and Lane Smith's *The True Story of the 3 Little Pigs* (1989). David Macaulay's *Black and White* (1990) introduced a new type of postmodern picture book. It won the Caldecott medal in 1991. A wealth of talented illustrators such as Lane Smith, Chris Raschka, Chris Van Allsburg, and David Wisner took the picture book from a format to an art form. However, many critics argue that too much emphasis is now placed on art, and that showmanship has created a format that is inaccessible to children.

The Twenty-first Century

Technology has changed the way books are created and produced. Authors were quick to adapt to computers when writing text for picture books. Now many illustrators use computers and software to create illustrations as well.

Digital art is fast becoming part of the illustration landscape. In the 1980s, technology allowed for the reproduction of full-color art that was accurate and less expensive. Media, such as oils, previously not practical for picture books, became commonplace. Now technology is the actual medium. With a computer, some software, and a scanner, innovative illustrators have braved the new frontier, with fabulous results.

At the same time that artists are creating art digitally, publishers are offering books in digital format. Electronic books and other digital formats have also pushed the boundaries, giving illustrators a whole new way to create and explore and giving readers new ways to experience stories. Consider digital libraries, such as the International Children's Digital Library (ICDL). Still early in its development, the ICDL collection has more than 1,900 titles in 39 languages.[5]

It is interesting that electronic versions of children's books have not received the same attention as adult publishing. The most substantial effort to build a functioning company specializing in e-picture books for children was launched by ipicturebooks.com in 2000, which in 2008 was defunct. Harold Underdown, formerly of ipicturebook.com, cites several reasons for this failure, the primary one being the challenge of marketing and selling e-picture books to consumers. He believes that e-books for children will eventually find a niche, and states that sales are steadily increasing; in five years there will be a rebirth of e-books for children. Perhaps he is right. A new company incorporated in 2008, Lookybook, is an online site that offers digital editions of hundreds of picture books. Read more about Lookybook in chapter 4.

TECHNOLOGICAL EVOLUTION

Printing Technology

The development of picture books is closely linked to the development of printing technology. Early printing was crude. Although the invention of moveable type in the mid-fifteenth century made it easier to reproduce text, it was several centuries before illustrations could be as easily reproduced on the page. In order to make multiple copies of an illustration efficiently, printing techniques were used. Prior to the twentieth century, most reproduction of illustrations was done by hand.

Early illustrators depended on engravers, working with primitive technology, to prepare their illustrations for the printing process. Book illustrations were limited to those that could be engraved in wood or metal and then transferred to paper by hand or by mounting them on plates in a moveable type press—a laborious and time-consuming process. Though not intentionally, engravers often removed an illustrator's distinguishing hallmarks, the details that made one illustrator's work distinct from another's.

Thomas Bewick (1753–1828) and George Cruikshank (1792–1878) contributed developments that helped advance engraving and printing techniques. Bewick, an engraver, circumvented the problems inherent in wood engraving by using the end grain of the wood instead of the plank, which was softer and reproduced poorly over time. Cruikshank, an illustrator, made allowances for the wood engraving process by matching his style to the capabilities of the medium, which resulted in higher-quality illustrations.

Over time, artists and printers gradually refined their craft. Through small advances, illustration moved from being merely decorative to being artistic. When photography and halftone engraving emerged at the end of the nineteenth century, artists finally began to see their illustrations reproduced faithfully, without an intermediary.

Technical developments in the nineteenth century greatly improved the availability and quality of illustration. At the beginning of the century, books were still produced by using techniques that dated back to the Renaissance. Until the end of the nineteenth century, illustrations were hand-colored, usually by someone other than the artist. However, at the end of the century, photomechanical techniques and improved printing presses heralded the golden age of illustration.

In the late nineteenth century, processes that were once done by hand became mechanized. Printing allows for the reproduction of one to multiple copies. Three principle means of transferring an artist's work to page are relief, intaglio, and lithographic (or planographic). Relief printing is above the surface, intaglio is below the surface, and lithographic is on the surface. Before the nineteenth century, relief printing was most common; during the nineteenth century intaglio or gravure was most common; and in the twentieth century lithographic and photogravure processes became popular.

Gravure involved engraving the image onto a metal or wood plate, applying ink to the engraving, then transferring the image to paper by impression. The engraving process was tedious and labor intensive. Lithography was much simpler to execute. In lithography, a drawing was applied onto a stone using a waxy substance. Water was applied to the stone, which repelled the oily ink mixture used for the drawing. When paper was pressed to the stone, it adhered to the wax and was repelled from the wet areas on the stone, transferring the image to paper.

To create an illustration with multiple colors, multiple stones were required, one for each color.

In the late nineteenth and early twentieth centuries, photomechanical processes superseded wood engraving and lithography, making a wide variety of painting and drawing techniques possible. The invention of the process now known as color separation made it possible to mass-produce color images. By 1905 publishers had improved the process to the point that the copies were very faithful to the original art. Many printers employed these new techniques for rapid mass production. In the twentieth century offset lithography was the economical way to mass produce high-quality picture books. The introduction of rotary presses, combined with offset lithography, made the process even more cost effective.

In the past 20 years, what is often called the digital revolution has made reproduction of art easier but has introduced other challenges. The same frustration that nineteenth-century illustrators felt at passing their art to an engraver is still experienced by artists today who deal with the challenges of modern technology and the havoc it can wreak on the finished artwork. Every picture book artist has probably experienced disappointment at the final printed product, simply because small but significant changes were introduced through technology—such as the color the artist painted becoming a shade darker in the final artwork.

A good relationship among the artist, the art director, and the production team helps the picture book look as the artist intended. Illustrators must not only master their technique, but also an understanding of the publishing process. Understanding what happens to their art at every stage of the process can help eliminate errors that occur after the art leaves the illustrator's hands.

The Golden Age of Illustration

The golden age of illustration spanned from 1905 through the end of World War II. It was a period of unprecedented excellence in book and magazine illustration, which many critics feel will never be reproduced (Dalby 1991, Meyer 1997).

The origins of the golden age lie in the innovations of George Cruikshank (1792–1878), who is credited with setting the standard in children's book illustration. Cruikshank influenced Edmund Evans, whose innovations in color printing contributed to the success of Walter Crane, Randolph Caldecott, and Kate Greenaway (Dalby 1991).

Advances in technology freed illustrators from dependence on engravers to transfer their artwork to the printing press. Artists were able to explore media hitherto expensive to reproduce. For the first time, accurate and inexpensive reproduction of art was possible.

Furthermore, the revival of folktales, inspired by the work of Andrew Lang and Joseph Jacobs, led to the popularity of lavish illustrated versions. The appreciation of old fairy tales and children's stories coincided with the threat posed by the advance of the industrial world to traditional values. People found solace in the art of the golden age illustrators.

In Europe, golden age artists were influenced by the Pre-Raphaelites and the arts and crafts movement. Artists who illustrated for children included Walter Crane, Edmund Dulac, Kay Nielsen, and Arthur Rackham. In America, the golden age was anchored by the Brandywine Valley tradition, begun by Howard Pyle and his students, Jessie Willcox Smith, N. C. Wyeth, and Maxfield Parrish.

The Digital Revolution

Computers are prevalent in almost every aspect of our modern lives—including the artist's studio. And though computers have made picture book reproduction easier, they have also introduced a host of other challenges (Robinson 2000).

Like any other technique, digital illustration has to be mastered. The opportunities are endless as software develops and technology advances. Software such as Adobe PhotoShop and Adobe Illustrator has created new and limitless opportunities for artists. Some illustrators use the computer to scan in images and experiment with color and texture. Some work exclusively in digital format. The tools of the digital artist include a graphic tablet and a stylus.

A graphic tablet (drawing tablet) is a computer device that allows illustrators to draw images and graphics with a stylus, an electronic tool that looks similar to a pen, and input them directly into the computer. The process is similar to drawing on paper with a pen or pencil. The drawing does not appear on the tablet, but rather is displayed on the computer monitor. The difference is that an illustrator can manipulate the image created with the stylus without redrawing.

Even artists who still create illustrations with traditional media depend on computers. For instance, preliminary sketches or finished artwork may be scanned and then burned to a CD-ROM or be e-mailed to the art director (Gralley 2006).

The software available to illustrators is sophisticated and capable of rendering illustrations in a printed book that readers may assume were created in the traditional way. Illustrations that look as if they were created with oils or pastels may have actually been created on a computer (Gralley 2006). In *Mr. Lunch Takes a Plane Ride* (1993), illustrated by J.otto Seibold, the first time the character touched paper was when the book was printed and bound.

THE PUBLISHING PROCESS

What happens to a picture book from initial idea to finished product, when it arrives at the library or bookstore? The process may vary by publishing company. In a nutshell, there are five stages from beginning to end: creation, acquisition, planning and design, production, and marketing. There are many people involved in the process: author, illustrator, editor, art director, designer, production staff, and marketing team.

Let's begin with the assumption that an author has written a story that has been accepted by a publisher. The "creation" step has been completed. (It is important to note that some publishers only accept manuscripts from authors and illustrators with agents. The author in this example has an editor who negotiates the contract for her.)

Acquisitions

After an author has written the story, it is submitted to a publisher. Depending on the market, there are several steps involved in submission. During the acquisitions process contracts are signed, and the editor works with the author to refine and develop the book.

There are several different types of editors:

- The acquisitions editor signs up a book, negotiates a contract with an agent or author, then passes it on to the developmental editor.

- The developmental editor actually edits the book's content and organization, working with the author and art director.

- The copy editor edits the manuscript for sense, style, punctuation, spelling, and grammar. Proofreaders often read the manuscript one final time.

As far as children's books are concerned, it is common for the acquisitions and developmental editor to be the same person. It is more economical to have the person who acquired the book see it through to publication. The editor, whose title may be acquisitions or developmental, works with the art director to find an illustrator.

Planning and Design

During the planning and design phase the art director, illustrator, and designer get to work, fleshing out the author's story with visual images.

The art director works with the illustrator, providing guidance as he or she works on a title. If the book author and illustrator are two different people, the art director chooses the illustrator, often giving very specific instructions about the type and style of illustration.

Once the illustrator has the manuscript, he or she begins creating the pictures. They begin with a storyboard, with thumbnail images of the illustrations, and the picture sequence is determined. The illustrator creates several versions, until both the art director and the illustrator are happy. Next comes the preliminary sketches, then the actual artwork. It can take up to a year to complete the illustrations for one picture book. Figure 1.6 is an example of a blank storyboard for a 32-page picture book.

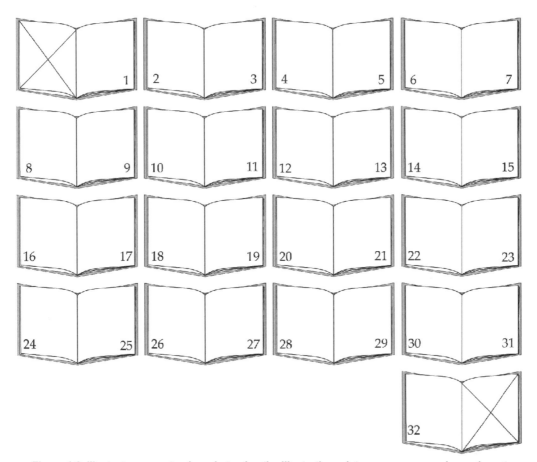

Figure 1.6. Illustrators use storyboards to plan the illustration, picture sequence, and page layout. From the initial idea until the book is finished, several storyboards are used.

At the same time that the illustrator is working on the picture, the designer is working on the supporting parts (paratexts), which include typeface, book jacket, and page layout. The designer plans the pages and designs the book jacket. He or she works closely with the art director and the illustrator to make sure the design and illustrations suit the story.

Production

The production manager oversees the actual production of the book. Some of the decisions a production manager makes include by whom and where a book is printed. Most books by American authors are printed outside the United States. The production manager is also responsible for finding special materials that may be needed, all the while keeping an eye on the budget. He or she works closely with the printer, who prepares the book for printing.

During the production phase, films are made of the illustrations, which in turn are made into plates that are used to make the printed pages. The first is a set of "blues" (or "bluelines"), so called because they have blue type on bluish-colored film. Errors that are not caught in the editing process have to be corrected on the negative, which is an added expense. If the book has full-color art, which most picture books do, then a second set of color proofs is made, so that the printer knows what the art should look like when it is printed. Most picture books are printed in large runs of over 10,000. The production manager who makes sure every detail is correct before final printing begins.

Once the sheets have been printed, the pages are folded, cut, and stitched, then the cover boards are glued on. The books are then packaged, boxed, and sent to the publisher's warehouse, from where they go to bookstores and libraries.

Marketing

The publisher's marketing department is responsible for creating promotional materials, such as posters, banners, catalogs, and display racks. The marketing department works closely with the sales department. At the same time the production team is printing the book, the marketing department is preparing press releases, advertisements, catalogs and flyers, and advanced reading copies or galleys for review journals.

When a character becomes very popular (think Curious George and Cat in the Hat), a multitude of spin-off products may be developed. Of course, this can be a dream come true for an author or illustrator. By licensing the use of the character, products ranging from stuffed animals to food products to games to clothing bring in additional fees above and beyond the royalties received from book sales. This practice of "merchandising" has become so prevalent today that some critics say popular children's books have become overly commercialized.

Why Do Picture Books Cost So Much?

One common complaint about picture books is that they are too expensive. At the time of this writing, the average price for a picture book is $16.95. It may seem hard to believe that a 32-page book should cost as much as a novel or work of nonfiction, but let's take a closer look at what goes into the cost of a typical picture book.

First of all, when it comes to profit, you can cut the retail price in half, to account for wholesale price. Typically, 50 percent of the price of the book goes to the wholesaler and bookseller to cover their overhead and profits.

On average, the publisher receives 50 percent, or perhaps a little more to cover its costs, from which it also receives its profit. The larger a print run, the cheaper the cost per unit, and the more a publisher can potentially save on costs. In the example below, assume the print run was 10,000 copies. that the publisher's 50 percent breaks down like this:

> 20 percent—overhead
>
> 10 percent—royalties (to author and illustrator)
>
> 11 percent—cost of paper, printing, binding
>
> 4 percent—plate preparation
>
> 5 percent—profit

So, as you can see, of the original 100 percent, only 5 percent is actual profit for the publisher. Of course, this assumes that the publisher is able to sell all of the first printing of 10,000 copies.[6]

REVIEWING PICTURE BOOKS

Picture books are reviewed in a number of print journals, as well as online sources. There are three types of reviews: descriptive, analytical, and sociological (Horning 1997b). Descriptive reviews are objective statements about the characters, illustrations, and story. Analytical reviews include statements about the literary and aesthetic elements in a book. The emphasis in an analytical review is on evaluation, comparison, and the title's contribution to the field. Sociological reviews include judgments based on nonliterary elements, such as controversial issues and predictions about popularity.

It is also important to note the difference between a review and literary criticism. A review appears close to the publication date and adheres to criteria established by the journal the review appears in. Reviewers are limited to a certain number of words and may also be restricted by other requirements, such as the fact that *School Library Journal* reviews are intended for librarians. Although parents and teachers may glean something from the review, they are not the target audience.

The major journals[7] that review picture books are *Bulletin of the Center for Children's Books*, *The Horn Book Magazine*, and *School Library Journal*. Not all titles reviewed are picture books. Some journals only review books, while others review all media published and developed for children and young adults. These three publications are discussed below. (For complete information regarding review submissions, please see each journal's Web site.)

Established in 1947, the *Bulletin of the Center for Children's Books* publishes 11 issues every year. It is a selective journal, annually reviewing approximately 900 trade books published for children and young adults (including picture books as well as other formats). Books reviewed include both recommended and not-recommended titles. The *Bulletin* only reviews trade and mass-market books. It does review titles by small and alternative publishers; however, vanity (self-published) titles are not considered. The *Bulletin* does not review reprints, but considers paperback originals. The Web site is bccb.lis.uiuc.edu.

The Horn Book Magazine is a selective review journal, reviewing about 350 children's titles per year. Established in 1924, the *Horn Book* is published six times a year. It only considers titles from publishers listed in *Literary Marketplace*. The staff selects titles that are outstanding in plot, theme, characterization, and style. Its sister publication, the *Horn Book Guide*, is published twice yearly and contains shorter appraisals of approximately 2,000 children's titles published in a given year. *The Horn Book* reviews the following formats: picture books, fiction, folklore, poetry, nonfiction, and audiobooks. Within each category are up to four broad age ranges that are dictated by grade level: primary, intermediate, middle school, and high school. The Web site is www.hbook.com.

School Library Journal (*SLJ*) reviews about 2,500 children's titles from established publishers per year. Established in 1954, it is published 12 times a year. It is intended for professional librarians. Reviews are both positive and negative, with recommendations both for and against purchase. Reissues and vanity (self-published) books are not considered. *SLJ* reviewers frequently compare new titles to previously published titles. Titles are evaluated for literary merit, quality of illustrations, and presentation. *SLJ* separates reviews into two broad categories, preschool to grade 4 and grade 5 and up, which are further subdivided at the discretion of the reviewer. The Web site is www.schoollibraryjournal.com.

AWARDS

There are numerous awards bestowed upon children's books by various organizations—local, regional, national, and international. Some of the most prestigious are discussed below.

> For contact information and a complete list of winners, please see www.picturingbooks.com.

United States

Boston Globe–Horn Book Award

The Boston Globe–Horn Book Award was first presented by the *Boston Globe* newspaper and *Horn Book Magazine* in 1967. It is one of the most prestigious honors in the United States in the field of children's and young adult literature. Awards are given in the categories of picture book, fiction and poetry, and nonfiction. A winner and honor books are awarded. The Web site is www.hbook.com/bghb.

Charlotte Zolotow Award

The Charlotte Zolotow Award is given annually to the author of the best picture book text published in the United States in the preceding year. Established in 1998, the award honors the work of Charlotte Zolotow, a distinguished children's book editor, who worked for Harper Junior Books. Zolotow is the author of more than 70 picture books, including the classic *William's Doll* (Harper, 1972).

The award is administered by the Cooperative Children's Book Center, a children's literature library of the School of Education, University of Wisconsin-Madison. Each year a committee of children's literature experts selects the winner from the books published in the preceding year. The winner is announced in January.

Any picture book for young children (birth through age seven) originally written in English, and published in the United States between January 1 and December 31, is eligible for consideration. The book may be fiction, nonfiction, or folklore, as long as it is presented in picture book form and aimed at children between birth and seven years old. Translated books, poetry, and easy readers are not eligible. The Web site is www.education.wisc.edu/ccbc/ books/zolotow.asp.

Coretta Scott King Award for Illustration

Awarded to African American illustrators for outstanding inspirational and educational contributions, the Coretta Scott King Book Award titles promote understanding and appreciation of the culture of all peoples and their contribution to the realization of the American dream. The award commemorates the life and works of Dr. Martin Luther King Jr. and honors Mrs. Coretta Scott King for her courage and determination to continue the work begun by her husband. The first winner was *Ray Charles* (1973) by Sharon Bell Mathis, illustrated by George Ford. The Web site is www.ala.org/ala/emiert/corettascottkingbookaward/ corettascott.cfm.

Golden Kite Award

The Golden Kite Award is awarded annually by the Society of Children's Book Writers and Illustrators (SCBWI) to recognize excellence in children's literature in four categories: fiction, nonfiction, picture book text, and picture book illustration. Awards are given to book creators, as well as editors and art directors, which sets the Golden Kite apart from other awards.

In addition to the award winners, four honor book recipients are also named by the panel of judges, which consists of children's book writers and illustrators. Established in 1973, the Golden Kite is the only children's book award judged by a jury of peers. Eligible books must be written or illustrated by SCBWI members and submitted by publishers, authors, or illustrators. The Web site is www.scbwi.org/awards/gk_main.

Randolph Caldecott Medal

Named for nineteenth-century English illustrator Randolph Caldecott, the Caldecott Medal celebrates distinction and distinguished contribution to American picture book illustration. It is awarded annually by the Association for Library Service to Children (ALSC), a division of the American Library Association (ALA), to the artist of an American picture book for children. A panel of experts diligently examines thousands of books published in the previous year. After months of deliberation, the panel selects one winner and a varying number of honor titles.

The illustration on the Caldecott Medal, as mentioned previously, is a reproduction of an illustration from Randolph Caldecott's picture book *The Diverting Story of John Gilpin*. The Web site is www.ala.org/alsc/ caldecott.html.

International

Amelia Frances Howard-Gibbon Illustrator's Award (Canada)

Founded in 1971, the Amelia Frances Howard-Gibbon Illustrator's Medal is awarded to an outstanding illustrator of a children's book published in Canada during the previous year. An illustrator must be a Canadian citizen or a permanent resident of Canada to be eligible. Winners include *The Dragon's Pearl* (1991), illustrated by Paul Morin, and *The Party* (1997), illustrated by Barbara Reid. The Web site is www.cla.ca.

Australian Children's Book of the Year Award

Founded in 1952, the Children's Book of the Year award is given to an author and illustrator for outstanding contributions. Titles published in the previous year are considered. Among the winners and honorable mentions are *Sunshine* (1981), illustrated by Jan Omerod; *Possum Magic* (1983), illustrated by Julie Vivas; and *Animalia* (1986) by Graeme Base.

Biennial Illustrations Bratislava (BIB)

Established in 1967, BIB hosts an international competition of children's book illustrators. Generous support from UNESCO (United Nations Educational, Scientific and Cultural Organization) and IBBY (International Board on Books for Young People) makes the biennial event possible. It is the only large, noncommercial event of its kind in the world. During the 40 years of its existence, BIB has presented over 40,000 illustrations by nearly 5,000 illustrators from 90 countries around the world. From its beginning, the BIB has sought to present the best in international children's illustration for children, as well as to give illustrators from other countries a chance to present their works.

BIB awards include the Grand Prix BIB, 5 Golden Apples, and 5 plaques. The Web site is http://www.bibiana.sk/uvod_e.htm.

Hans Christian Andersen Award

Every other year, the International Board on Books for Young People (IBBY) presents the Hans Christian Andersen Award to an author and an illustrator whose complete works have made an important and lasting contribution to children's literature. Winners must be living at the time of the nomination, and the entire body of author's/illustrator's work is considered. Often referred to as the "Little Nobel Prize," the HCA is the highest international recognition given to creators of children's books. Each national section of IBBY is eligible to nominate authors and illustrators from that country. The IBBY Executive Committee elects the international jury of 10 members from a pool of candidates nominated by the national sections of IBBY. The award for writing has been given since 1956, and the illustrator's award since 1966. The award consists of a gold medal and a diploma, presented at a festive ceremony during the biennial IBBY Congress. A special Andersen Awards issue of IBBY's journal *Bookbird* lists all the nominees and documents the selection process. Among the many winners are Maurice Sendak from the United States (1970), Anthony Browne from the United Kingdom (2000), and Kveta Pacovská from the Czech Republic (1992). The Web site is www.ibby.org.

Kate Greenaway Medal for Illustrators (United Kingdom)

The Kate Greenaway Medal for Illustrators was established in 1956 by the Youth Libraries Group, a division of the British Library Association. The medal honors an illustrator of children's books. It is awarded annually for the most distinguished work published in the United Kingdom. It is considered the top British children's book illustration award. Winners include *Each Peach Pear Plum* (1977), illustrated by Janet Ahlberg; *Zoo* (1991), illustrated by Anthony Browne; and *I Will Not Ever Never Eat a Tomato* (1999), illustrated by Lauren Child. The Web site is www.carnegiegreenaway.org.uk.

Russell Clark Award (New Zealand)

Founded in 1975, the Library and Information Association of New Zealand Aotearoa (LIANZA) awards the Russell Clark Award annually to the artist who has produced the most distinguished picture book or illustrations for a children's book. The award was named for Russell Clark (1905–1966), a well-known New Zealand illustrator popular in the 1940s and 1950s. Winners include *Kiwi Moon* (2005), illustrated by Gavin Bishop, and *Mr. McGee and the Big Bag of Bread* (2004), illustrated by Pamela Allen. The Web site is www.bookcouncil.org.nz.

> For a complete list of award winners, please see www.picturingbooks.com.

CONCLUSION

In this chapter, picture book basics were introduced. A brief overview of the history of picture books and a short description of the publishing and review processes offer a framework from which to move through the rest of the book. Picture/text balance and some commonly used terms applied to picture books were also introduced. This is just part of what make picture books such a dynamic format. The next two chapters explore picture book paratexts (supporting parts), illustration, design, artistic media, and artistic style.

ENDNOTES

1. To avoid awkwardness, the term *reader(s)* is used throughout the book to indicate all picture book audiences. At times users may that find that the terms *viewer(s)* or *listener(s)* may be used in the place of *reader*.

2. I do not consider children's nonfiction from series such as True Book from Children's Press or Eyewitness Books from DK in my definition of "informational picture book."

3. In the introductory survey to *Children's Books in England*, Harvey Darton (1988) defines children's books as those "printed works produced ostensibly to give children spontaneous pleasure, and not primarily to teach them, nor solely to make them good, nor to keep them profitably quiet." He precludes alphabet books, primers, spelling books, didactic tracts, and studies of childhood.

4. Betsy Hearne, "Cite the Source: Reducing Cultural Chaos in Picture Books, Part One," *School Library Journal* (July 1993): 23–27.

5. International Children's Digital Library (ICDL), http://www.icdlbooks.org/about/fastfacts.shtml.

6. Adapted from Harold Underdown, "Why Does a Hardcover Picture Book Cost $16?," http://www.underdown.org/bookcost.htm.

7. Age designations are culled from examining the printed versions of the journals, as well as using each journal's Web site. The *Horn Book* staff did not respond to a request for verification. At various points in the journal's history, different age designations have been applied. *School Library Journal's* book review section is divided into preschool to grade 4 and grade 5 and Up, with the reviewer assigning the appropriate grade level for each individual book (e-mail correspondence with Trev Jones, *School Library Journal's* book review editor).

Chapter 2

Anatomy of a Picture Book: Supporting Parts (Paratexts)

Design exists as a supportive bit of stagecraft. Sometimes an elaborate set is most effective and sometimes a bare stage and a few lighting cues provide all that's needed.

—David Saylor, "Look Again:
An Art Director Offers Some Pointers on Learning to See," *School Library Journal*

In This Chapter
- Book Jackets
- Shape and Size
- Supporting Parts (Paratexts)
- Illustrations
- Typography

When readers open a picture book, their focus is often on the art and story. They respond spontaneously to the story and pictures, based on preference and emotion. From his experience reading reviews and attending conferences as a designer, David Saylor (2000) states that readers are usually daunted by design, finding it difficult to discuss it. According to Saylor, "responding emotionally to what we see is easy, but going beyond that takes more effort." Design gives the pictures and text a framework upon which to build. In this chapter and the next, the aspects of picture book design are examined, and the "anatomy" of picture books is explored. Equipped with adequate terminology, librarians, teachers, parents, and students can confidently analyze and think more critically about picture books—and the design decisions that often make a book successful.

BOOK JACKETS

The anticipation of opening a book can be one of the most satisfying parts of reading. The first few moments readers spend with a book involve a process of discovery, an exploration of the possibilities within. Reader response is directly tied to a book's physical aspects (i.e., format). The way the book feels, its shape, and its size inform the reader's experience.

Hardcover picture books come with book jackets[1] made from heavy, almost waxy feeling paper. They have flaps that wrap around the front and back part of the book. Book jackets feature artwork that complements the book's content and often include an illustration from the book, although not always. See figures 2.1 and 2.2.

Figure 2.1. An example of the outside of a book jacket that has been removed from a picture book.

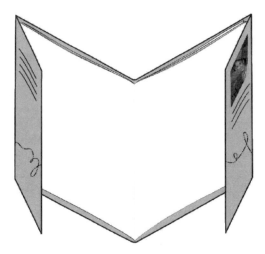

Figure 2.2. An example of the inside of a book jacket that has been removed from a picture book.

Book jackets had an inauspicious beginning. Appearing in the 1830s, book jackets, usually plain brown wrappers, were designed to protect books during transport from publisher to reader. They were usually discarded after purchase. In the late nineteenth century publishers began to see the potential of book jackets as marketing devices. During the 1920s book collecting became popular, and the book jacket became a valuable part of the package. Savvy collectors recognized the value of the book jacket. Insisting that only a protected first edition would do, these early collectors elevated the humble book jacket from disposable ephemera to an integral part of book design.

Although a dazzling cover does not guarantee the quality of the content, book jackets are an important part of the overall design of picture books. Thousands of picture books are published every year. Even the most well read librarian or educator is unlikely to be familiar with all the publishers, imprints, authors, and illustrators. Librarians rely on professional journals to keep them informed about forthcoming titles. They also use reviews to help them make the best use of limited budgets. Reviewers rarely see the book jacket (Horning 1997a) and often don't even mention it in the review. In a way, a book jacket, although not an impartial source, provides readers with information in the same way review journals help librarians make informed collection development decisions.

Book jackets give readers, especially children and parents, a tool that allows them to make informed decisions. In a *Publishers Weekly* survey reported in 1999, 75 percent of the 300 booksellers who responded stated that the book jacket was the most important physical element of a book (Rawlinson 2000). Although the booksellers were concerned with the visual appeal of the book jacket, an earlier study by *PW* revealed that book buyers appreciate blurbs and plot summaries as well (Rawlinson 2000).

Some libraries remove the book's jacket during processing. The principal argument for this practice is that the image on the jacket is already on the support boards of the book. In some cases it is dictated by budget constraints; removing the jacket saves time and money. It is also easier and quicker to get a book to the shelf when the jacket is discarded. However, to relegate the book jacket to the role of a mere marketing tool or protective device negates the design advances in children's books in the last half century.

The time spent exploring the book jacket enhances the reading experience. A good deal of expense and effort go into the construction of the book jacket. A book jacket transcends practical use as a marketing device to offer readers a glimpse of wonders to come.

A picture may be worth a thousand words, and the same can be said of book jackets. Consider the work of Molly Leach, dynamic designer of the picture books by the outlandish duo author Jon Scieszka and illustrator Lane Smith, and you will be convinced of the power of a book jacket to extend the meaning of a picture book. Valuable information on the jacket includes author and illustrator bios, publisher information, price, intended audience, a brief plot summary, and reviews of previous work by the author/illustrator.

The Parts of the Book Jacket

Flaps

Book jackets have two flaps. The front flap generally contains a brief summary of the story, price, and age designations. The back flap has a brief biography of the author and illustrator, reviews of previous titles, and publisher information. This information is sometimes called flap copy (Horning 1997a). Illustrators can be very creative with art adorning the flaps. In *The Red Book* (2004), Barbara Lehman added a picture of herself hard at work illustrating. In *Math Curse* (1995), the flaps have been cleverly incorporated into the design. Instead of listing a dollar amount, the price of the book was presented as a math problem: [($3.25 + $1.75)] x 3 + $1.99 = $16.99. In *You Forgot Your Skirt, Amelia Bloomer* (2000) illustrator Chelsea McLaren cleverly incorporates a sewing pattern in to the design. Figure 2.3 shows a typical front flap with a brief summary, sometimes called a blurb, and a vignette, or spot art, that complements the illustrations. Figure 2.4 includes a picture of the illustrator and a brief bio.

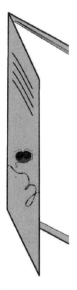

Figure 2.3. The front flap contains a summary of the book, often referred to as a blurb, and a vignette that hints at the story within the pages.

Figure 2.4. The back flap contains a brief bio and a photo of the author/illustrator.

Spine

This is generally the only part of the book readers see when it is on the shelf. The typography and color scheme of the spine usually blend with the jacket design. Information included on the spine includes the title, author, and publisher. In addition, a publisher's logo, sometimes called the colophon, is also visible on the spine. In a wraparound cover, the spine is carefully incorporated into the jacket design, as on *Chicka Chicka Boom Boom* (1989). The coconut tree wraps from the front to the back. Had the designer not incorporated the tree into the spine, it would have broken up the image.

Covers

The covers are the front and back of the book jacket. In the last decade or so, publishers have printed the front and back boards of picture books with the same art that graces the book jacket, minus the flaps. That is, a book looks the same with or without the book jacket, at first glance. However, as already discussed, the book jacket extends beyond the practical and acts as an important part of the design of picture books. There are several types of covers: wraparound, single image, and dual image.

Wraparound

Art on this type of cover begins on the front and wraps around to the back. When removed, the jacket can be laid flat and examined for details about the story and clues to the characters. For example, in *Harold and the Purple Crayon* (1955), Harold's squiggles begin in the front and continue on the back cover, creating a unifying image. In *Rosie's Walk* (1968), readers see the front half of the fox lurking in the lower left-hand corner of the front cover. The cover of *Dog and Bear: Two Friends, Three Stories* (2007) is similar. To see the entire image of the dog, readers have to lay the book face down. *Dog and Bear* also has reviews of the illustrator's previous books on the back On the back is the back half of the fox and continuation of the countryside. Hutchins's choice to show only half of the fox heightens the tension and drama. Figure 2.5 is an example of a wraparound cover that has to laid flat to see where the fly's trail ends.

Figure 2.5. After readers lay the cover flat, they can see that the fly trail that seems to end on the front cover actually starts on the back cover.

Single Image

One image appears on the front of this type of cover. The back of the book may contain another small illustration or a solid color that blends with the cover. In Ian Falconer's *Olivia* (2000), the heroine is demurely portrayed on a stark white backdrop. On the back cover, Olivia's back is turned away from the reader, and she is reading advanced praise for Falconer's first book. The designer's decision to use the book's character to draw attention to the reviews is very playful and allows readers a glimpse of Olivia's personality. On the front cover of Caldecott-winning *Kitten's First Full Moon* (2005), Kitten sits among the flowers and grass, coyly licking her paw, the full moon in the background. The back cover features just the moon with the phrase, "What a night!" Before readers open the book, they know they are in store for an adventure. In most of Kevin Henkes's picture books, the back covers are coordinating solid colors with lists of his previous picture books. In figure 2.6 a simple solid background without any art or text draws attention to the front cover.

Figure 2.6. A simple solid color on the back cover can be just as effective as a cover with art.

Dual Image

On a dual image cover, images from the story appear on the front and back of the book. Often by studying these illustrations, readers can find clues to the story. On the front of Barbara Lehman's wordless *The Red Book* (2004), readers see the first boy running with his book. On the back, tucked into the lower right-hand corner is another boy, a character readers later discover is an integral part of the story. In *Silent Night* (2001) the front cover features Santa Claus, finger to his lips. The back cover shows a barking dog against a solid yellow background. In figure 2.7 a review of the picture book is incorporated into the back cover along with art that complements the front cover.

Figure 2.7. A small vignette that complements the front cover and a review of the book grace the back cover.

SHAPE AND SIZE

The shape and size of a picture book make an impression on the reader, often before the pictures or the story. The designer and illustrator work together to decide a trim size, which is the actual size of the pages. The actual book is slightly larger to cover and protect the pages. Together shape and size can make a statement. It is not an accident that Beatrix Potter's *The Tale of Peter Rabbit* is small, measuring roughly 6 by 4 inches. The diminutive size is perfect for the small hands of a child, Potter's intended audience. Picture books have two shapes, rectangular or square.

Shape

The rectangular shape of a picture book can be vertical or horizontal. A book with vertical orientation leads the eye from top to bottom, whereas a book with horizontal orientation leads the eye from left to right. Each direction has a direct effect on the mood and tone of the book. For instance, in *The Snowy Day* (1962) by Ezra Jack Keats, the jacket shows Peter walking in the snow. Beginning on the back cover and leading to the front is a trail of Peter's footprints in the snow. The oblong shape of the book works well with the line of footprints and gives the reader a sense of Peter's journey.

The illustrator's decision to use one or the other orientation is purposeful and makes a statement. In *Tops & Bottoms* (1995) author Janet Stevens opted to have the book open vertically rather than horizontally. Stevens's decision to have the pages flip from top to bottom as opposed to the traditional right to left directly affected the feel and experience readers have with this trickster tale about the harvest season.

A book with a square shape often suggests circular motion, suggesting movement. For example, in *The Color Zoo* (1989) Lois Ehlert's square format builds into a variety of shapes that spring from the implicit circle within the square. The reader's eye is led through the bold graphic design, seeking the images Ehlert hides within.

Size

The size of a book is usually determined by the horizontal or vertical orientation. If a book is 8 by 11 inches, it usually has a horizontal orientation. If a book is 12 by 9 inches, it generally has a vertical orientation. These measurements are called the trim size, or the actual dimensions of the pages in the picture book. The actual book may be slightly larger because the cover boards extend beyond the trim size of the pages.

There are a few standard trim sizes in picture book publishing, with 8 by 11 and 12 by 9 being the most common. Some design decisions call for a specialty size, such as *Color Zoo* (1989), which is 9 by 9 inches.

SUPPORTING PARTS (PARATEXTS)

As stated previously, readers often respond spontaneously to a picture book, overlooking the design aspects that are the framework for picture books. Perhaps a reader is uncomfortable discussing design or simply does not have the background to consider the design and how it works with pictures and text. Design is about communication; it is the tool that helps communicate a message to the reader. It should present picture books in the best light possible. Great design speaks to hearts and minds, enriching the reading experience (Saylor 2000). According to scholar Lawrence Sipe (2001), the supporting parts of picture books function as signs in semiotic terms. Each part has the potential to contribute to the overall meaning of the title.

The supporting parts of picture books, often referred to as paratexts, enhance and extend the picture book experience. These elements have been conceived and designed to support the overall design of the book.

Supporting parts are divided into front matter and back matter. Often several elements are gathered on one page. For instance, the dedication and copyright may appear together on one page. Illustrators and designers sometimes create small vignettes, also called spot art, that hint at the story within or use other elements from the story to tie the book together.

All or some of these may be included in a picture book. In informational and traditional literature titles, authors and illustrators often include a glossary, pronunciation guide, and introduction. Though rare in picture books, a table of contents is sometimes included. In *Babushka's Mother Goose* (1995), illustrated Patricia Polacco, the table of contents lists the rhymes included in the collection. *The Stinky Cheese Man* (1993) has one as well, which designer Molly Bang used to deconstruct the parts of a picture book.

It was once easy to separate the individual elements discussed below into front and back matter. Traditionally, front matter includes the half-title page, title page, foreword, and preface, in that order. However, designers of picture books often play with these elements to create a unique feeling for a book. For example, in "*Let's Get a Pup!" Said Kate* (2001),[2] by illustrator Bob Graham, the traditional title page is not the first page, but rather several pages into the book, so that the designer could incorporate Kate's narrative into the title page. It is quite ingenious.

Children are most familiar with the hilarious, often deadpan, fractured tales in Jon Scieszka's and Lane Smith's *The Stinky Cheese Man and Other Fairly Stupid Tales* (1993). Librarians and booksellers are also familiar with this book, which has been one of the most successful in picture book history. What many people don't know is that these Scieszka and Smith have a third collaborator, designer Molly Leach. *Stinky Cheese* was the second Scieszka/Smith book that Leach designed. In *Stinky Cheese,* she deconstructs the picture book format, calling readers' attention to the different aspects of book design. The narrator, Jack, makes a mockery of the title page, which appears after the first story, and features the phrase, "title page." On the back cover Little Red Hen draws our attention to the ISBN, asking "What is this doing here? This is ugly. Who is this ISBN guy anyway?" Leach uses varying styles and sizes of type, adding to the chaos created by the characters' tendency to wander into each other's stories.

Front Matter

Front matter introduces a picture book; it comprises a series of pages that appear before the body of book. It is the invitation to continue. It allows the designer an opportunity to reveal aspects of the story, and a good designer takes full advantage of the opportunity—although, especially in picture books, this order may be altered and certain elements may be combined or not used. In picture books, the front matter includes end papers, the half-title page, the title page, the copyright page, and a dedication or acknowledgments. Some informational picture books also have a foreword.

Endpapers

Endpapers are considered a decorative or ornamental part of the book packaging, but they often tie in with a theme or story. Pasted onto the inside of the front and back boards, endpapers are often decorated with a design or motif that complements the story or with one color that is dominant in the illustrations. In *Scranimals* (2002) illustrator Peter Sís decorated the endpapers with a map of Scranimal Island. Sís, noted for his fine line and cross-hatching technique, incorporated the assorted denizens into the delicate illustrations. Sometimes endpapers are solid colors that complement the story. In the Caldecott-winning *Hey, Al* (1986), the front endpaper is light brown, the color of Al's room at the beginning of the book. The endpapers at the back are vivid yellow, the color Al paints his room. The dual colors signify Al's growth and development. In figure 2.8 (p. 38), dual endpapers have been used to signify that the toad and fly have not yet made one another's acquaintance.

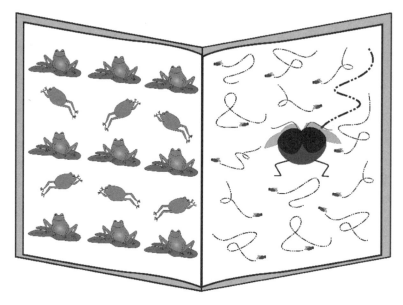

Figure 2.8. On the left endpaper, the toad is alone. The fly is alone on the right endpaper. This was a deliberate design decision to indicate that the toad and fly have not met.

Half-Title Page

The half-title is usually the first page of the book and features just the title, no author or publisher information (see figure 2.9). Half-titles are a carryover from an earlier publishing practice, when books were sold without covers. The half-title pages protected a book that was stacked in piles in bookstores (Horning 1997a).

Figure 2.9. The only elements on this half-title page are the title and a small vignette, or spot art, that hints at the story within.

Title Page

This is the page at the beginning of the book that contains the full title of the book, including any subtitles. Traditionally on the right-hand (or *recto*) page, it usually (but not always) has the name(s) of the author, illustrator, and publisher. If it has been translated from another language, the name of the translator may also appear. See figure 2.10.

Figure 2.10. The title page has the name of the author and illustrator, as well as the publisher.

Copyright Page

The copyright page is usually found near the beginning of the book, on the back of the title page. It contains information about the book, including the ISBN, a brief summary of the story, Library of Congress subject designations, the publisher, the copyright date, and author and/or illustrator notes. For design purposes, it is sometimes included in the back matter in picture books. In *Madlenka* (2000), the copyright page is the last page in the book and features an illustration of the earth, with the countries that Madlenka's neighbors hail from highlighted. Figure 2.11 (p. 40) shows two examples of copyright pages. The first is a copyright page in the traditional location in the front matter. The second is a copyright page that has been incorporated into the back matter, in this case, the last page with illustrations.

Dedication/Acknowledgments

In the dedication and acknowledgments, the author and illustrator thank people who helped with the creation of the book. Dedications are sometimes incorporated into the copyright page.

Author's or Artist's Notes

These notes are brief explanations written by the author or illustrator about the creation of the book or its features. Notes often function as additional information, as opposed to directly affecting the art or the story. For instance, if an illustrator used a special process to create the illustrations, he or she may include an explanatory note. Likewise, authors may include source notes, especially if it is a work of traditional literature. . For example, in *My Name Is Georgia* (1996), author/illustrator Jeannette Winter included a brief bibliography of references in her author's note.

Figure 2.11. Sometimes the dedication, author's notes, and copyright are together on one page. The first example is a copyright page in the front of the book. The second is a copyright page in the back matter.

Foreword

The foreword is written by someone who is a well-known expert on the topic of the book. This person often gets a special credit on the front cover, title page, and back flap. In Michael McCurdy's *The Gettysburg Address*, the foreword was written by Gary Willis, an adjunct professor of history at Northwestern University and the Pulitzer Prize–winning author of *Lincoln at Gettysburg: The Words That Remade America* (1992), a logical choice to write the foreword for McCurdy's book.

Back Matter

Back matter is the portion of the book that comes after the body of the book. Just like front matter, its order may be altered and certain elements may be combined or left out. Back matter is more common in informational picture books and picture book biographies.

Glossary

The glossary is an alphabetically arranged list of the vocabulary specific to the subject, with brief definitions. In picture books this is often a pronunciation guide as well, and it is common in bilingual picture books. *Possum Magic* (1990) includes a glossary of Australian words and a map marking the cities visited by Hush and Grandma Possum. Another title with a glossary is *At Gleason's Gym* (2007), which includes words specific to boxing.

Index

The index is an alphabetical list of topics and key words found in a book, with the page numbers where they are located. Indexes are common in informational or picture book biographies, but not in rhyming stories or concept books.

Colophon

The colophon is usually the last page in a picture book. It is an old tradition that has recently begun to reappear, increasingly, in picture books. The colophon includes information about the typeface and production of the book, including the names of the designer and typesetter. It may contain information about where the title was printed and who did the color separations. This information is sometimes included on the copyright page; when it is not it is usually on one of the last pages in the book. *Stellaluna* (1993) has a copyright page in the front, but a colophon in the back identifies what media the illustrator used, who did the hand-lettered display type, and the names of the designer and production supervisors.

Afterword

The afterword is usually written by the author or illustrator, although it can be by another individual associated with the book, or by someone who is a well-known expert on the topic of the book. In the tenth anniversary edition of *Aunt Flossie's Hats (and Crab Cakes Later)* (2001), author Elizabeth Fitzgerald Howard included an eight-page afterword that featured family photographs. In the afterword Howard shared her family history and additional information about the real Aunt Flossie.

ILLUSTRATIONS

What makes illustration so important in picture books?

More than just adorning the text or complementing the story, illustrations in picture books extend the story's meaning, and often tell another story altogether. Children's illustration has many unique characteristics. It takes more than artistic ability to create a successful picture book. The most successful picture book creators have an inherent understanding of the world of children. To fully address that uniqueness is beyond the scope of this book, but the following discussion analyzes some of the finer points to see how they come together to create a picture book.

Not always, but with increasing frequency, the author and illustrator of a picture book are the same person. When the author and illustrator are different people, it may surprise many to know that the two usually never meet. In rare cases, picture book teams have formed, but this is usually after many years in the business.

If the author is not the illustrator, planning is required to ensure that story and art flow and complement each other. The editor and designer are the mediators in this process. The editor usually chooses both the designer and the illustrator for the text. The author almost never has input in the selection process.

Chapter 1 explored various types of illustrated children's books—picture books, picture storybooks, and illustrated books. This chapter looks at elements that distinguish these three types of picture books. Many elements come together to create a successful illustration.

Elements in Illustration

Vignettes

Sometimes called spot art, vignettes are small illustrations integrated into double-page illustrations or isolated and balanced against text. Vignettes provide balance and variety and can offer an aside or comment to the reader. Sometimes a series of vignettes are used to make up a double-page spread. For example, in *Olivia* (2000) are the words "Of course Olivia's not tired at all." The illustrations show four small images of Olivia leaping across the double-page spread with a white background. (Illustrator Ian Falconer makes great use of white space in *Olivia*.) In figure 2.12 four vignettes of the two main characters are used across a double-page spread in lieu of an illustration.

Figure 2.12. Four vignettes are used to create a double-page spread.

Borders

Borders function as frames and are used to enclose text or illustrations. Borders can be simple lines or elaborate and detailed artwork that provides additional information about the story. Borders provide balance and variety in picture books, as well as emphasizing story themes or elements. In the picture book biography *Joan of Arc* (1998), illustrator Diane Stanley uses elaborate borders indicative of the Middle Ages to frame both the illustrations and text. Illustrator Jan Brett's detailed borders, which frame her illustrations, are a hallmark of her work. In *The Mitten* (1989), a traditional Ukrainian tale, birch bark panels are filled with intricate details from Brett's meticulous research into the culture, adding richness and substance to the art. In figure 2.13 the fly's trail is used as a decorative border, making deliberate use of an element found in the rest of the art in *Butler and the Fly*.

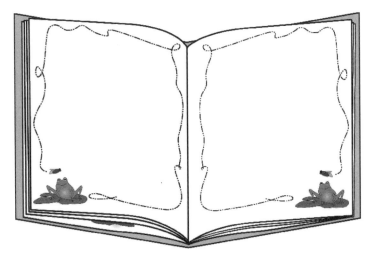

Figure 2.13. The deliberate use of the fly's trail in the border mimics an element found throughout the book.

Gutters

Gutters are the open space between the pages where the pages form the spine. When laid flat, the gutter becomes apparent. If a designer or illustrator does not plan for the gutter, it can mean that illustrations "disappear" into the gutter. In figure 2.14 the gutter interferes with the illustration because the illustrator did not plan for the gutter.

Figure 2.14. The toad is off center and appears awkward because he "falls" into the gutter.

Panels

Panels are illustrations that are broken apart for effect. They add visual pacing or rhythm to the story and allow the illustrator to achieve artistic statements not possible in a single- or double-page spread. In *Beautiful Warrior* (1998), designer David Saylor was inspired by an exhibit of Chinese art he saw at the National Gallery in Washington, D.C. He used panels, which are a feature in traditional Chinese art, to create visual interest. He wanted to create a dynamic yet formal setting that honored the theme and complemented McCully's illustrations. In *Lon Po Po: A Red-Riding Tale from China* (1989), illustrator Ed Young applied the same principle. Illustrations are frequently grouped in panels, which allows Young to offer two distinct perspectives simultaneously on the three sisters, who try their best to outwit the wolf, and the wolf, in his glorious yet frightening splendor. In figure 2.15 the panels are used to show two perspectives. In the left-hand panel, the fly looks down at something green in the pond. Even though the fly is not visible, we know that the perspective is not the toad's. In the right panel, the toad looks out at the reader, oblivious that he is being watched.

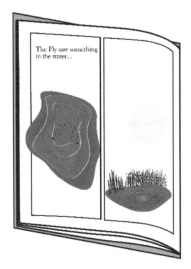

Figure 2.15. A two-panel spread allows two different perspectives: in the first the fly is watching the toad, and in the second the toad is looking out at the reader.

Page Layout

Double-Page Spread

Double-page illustrations spread across both pages of an open book. They are ideal for landscape views or scenes involving a large number of characters. Text may be absent or included on both pages. When interspersed with single-space illustrations, double-page spreads also allow readers a point to pause, or bestow a moment of drama or reflection to the story. An example is *Why Mosquitoes Buzz in People's Ears* (1975). Almost all of the illustrations are double-page spreads, but the text is sometimes on both pages of the spread and at other times just on one side of the spread. In figure 2.16 the text is spread across the double-page spread. The organization leads the eye from the left-hand side to the right-hand side.

Figure 2.16. In a double-page spread the illustration spans both pages of an open book. Text may or may not be present on both pages.

Single-Page Illustration

Single-page illustration is confined to one page. Large blocks of text are often placed opposite a single-page illustration. These illustrations are common in picture storybooks, which have a lot of text. Folktales tend to have layouts in which single-page spreads dominate because they often have longer narratives. The text may have borders or other decorative elements, which helps balance the text page with the illustration page. For example, the illustrations in Paul O. Zelinsky's *Rapunzel* (1997) are single-page illustrations. This type of layout is more formal. In figure 2.17 the text is isolated on the right-hand side of the page; the left-hand side has a close-up of the fly looking down at the toad in the pond.

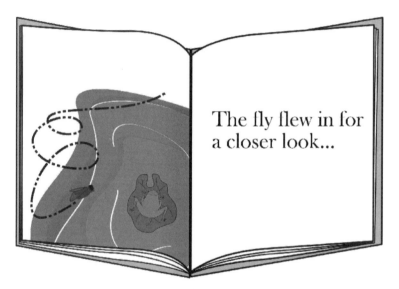

Figure 2.17. The emphasis is placed on the illustration because the text is isolated on the right-hand side of the book.

TYPOGRAPHY

Typography involves the art of choosing a font style (or typeface) and arranging print on the page. Like any other aspect of design, typography should be fluid and seamless in the final product. Often unnoticed, thoughtful typography decisions enhance the text. In the hands of a capable designer, typography becomes a tool—a way to extend or subvert meaning. There is more involved than matching a typeface to the story; the designer must consider both the aesthetic and practical demands of the text. Decisions that are fun and quirky may fight design or be impractical. Typography helps designers capture the essence of the story; when the right combination of typeface, size, and arrangement is achieved, typography becomes art. Typography includes text formality and placement, typeface, type size, and color.

Formality and Placement

Text layout is vital to the design of a picture book. The positioning of the text is an integral part of the design of the book. Where and how the text is placed on a page affects the mood and tone of the story.

Text placement can be formal or informal. The arrangement of words on the page of a book should directly relate to the illustrations, so it is common for a designer to see the text before the illustrator does. The placement or arrangement of text affects the story, and designers must be judicious when making decisions. With just 32 pages to work with, book designers must make several decisions: line length, number of words per page, and size of type. Designers strive to balance the text with the illustrations to propel the story forward. There are degrees of formality: very formal, formal, informal, very informal, and absent. Formal implies regularity, while informal placement is guided by whimsy or story line rather than structure. Absent refers to picture books in which there is no typography at all.

Very Formal

Text placed opposite illustrations or on adjacent pages is very formal. Books by Allen Say, who is noted for his biographical accounts of his family, typically have a very formal layout. In *Tea with Milk* (1999), a story that continues the story of the Caldecott-winning *Grandfather's Journey* (1993), a young Japanese woman returns with her parents to Japan. Masaka, or May as she prefers to be called, acquiesces in her parents' wishes, but she feels foreign and out of place in Japan. Formal text placement is well suited to Say's eloquent prose. Borders and frames create an even more formal appearance.

Diane Stanley's picture book biographies and Margaret Early's literary retellings feature text opposite lush paintings, with text made exquisite by being bounded with graceful borders. In figure 2.18 a very formal arrangement is used, with text below the illustrations.

Figure 2.18. Very formal arrangements feature text either above or below, but in either case it is the same on both pages.

Formal

Text placed beneath or above illustrations is formal. The placement of text above and beneath illustrations can alternate in high or low positions and from page to page and within the same book. Text can also be above and beneath an illustration on the same page. In Allen Say's *Grandfather's Journey* (1993), the formality of the text reflects the loving images of Say's poignant tribute to his grandfather. In addition to suiting the story, the text placement also reflects the graceful formality of Japan, its traditions, and its culture. A large typeface or hand-lettered text would fight with Say's delicate watercolor paintings. Likewise, had the designer placed the text erratically, it would have worked against the formality of the design as a whole. In figure 2.19 a formal arrangement is used, with text both above and below the illustrations.

Figure 2.19. Formal arrangements feature text both above and below illustrations.

Very Informal

Two or more arrangements used on the same page (e.g., above and shaped) are called "combined" and are considered very informal. Several illustrators and designers experiment with text in this way, including designer Molly Leach of *Stinky Cheese* fame. Another exceptional talent is Maira Kalman. A professional designer, Kalman is noted for her groundbreaking approach to children's book design. One feature that shines in Kalman's books is her approach to typography. Her eclectic style of naïve art, hand-lettered text, and quirky text arrangements makes each book a visual experience. Kalman, the author and illustrator of the Max Stravinsky picture books, is an innovative and daring artist. In the first book in the series, *Hey Willie, See the Pyramids* (1988), her illustrations mix the bizarre with the mundane. The dialogue of the children in the story is featured on black pages with stark white type. On the back cover of the sequel, *Max Makes a Million,* reviews of Kalman's other books form the flower's buds that burst from Max's hat. In figure 2.20 a very informal arrangement is used. The text is irregular and allowed to conform to the fly's trail on the left-hand page, but is placed beneath the illustration on the right-hand page

Figure 2.20. Very informal arrangements feature irregular arrangements as well as text placed either above or below illustrations.

Informal

When text is shaped or is irregular to fit inside, outside, or between illustrations, it is informal. Many designers shape or manipulate text around images in the illustrations to convey meaning. Children today are growing up in a visually stimulating world, and they find delight in unexpected treatments of type. Arched text in vibrant colors may not be suited for reading instruction, but it makes for a delightful reading experience. In *Zin! Zin! Zin! A Violin* (1995), the designer used the text to complement the musical elements in the book. Straight, angled text runs along the flute; curved text mimics the coattails of a musician and the movement of the cat. In figure 2.21 (p. 50) an informal arrangement is used. The text is irregular and allowed to conform to the fly's trail and the curves in the grass.

Figure 2.21. Informal arrangements feature irregular arrangements that fit inside, outside, or between illustrations on one or both pages.

Absent

The last text arrangement is absent. Having no text, as in a wordless book, is considered the most informal approach. Wordless picture books, sometimes called "stories without words," convey meaning only through the illustrations. The challenge for the illustrator of a wordless picture book is twofold, because in addition to illustrating a story, he or she is charged with telling a story without using words. Even though text is absent, a series of interconnected pictures offer story as rich as, perhaps richer than, one with words. In *The Red Book* (2004) illustrator Barbara Lehman uses a wordless format and a cyclical tale of two children meeting to show the power of story, leaving the reader wondering just where the book begins and ends. Illustrator David Wiesner, noted for his wordless picture books, has won the Caldecott Award for two wordless titles, *Tuesday* (1992) and *Flotsam* (2006). Figure 2.22 is an example of absent text arrangement.

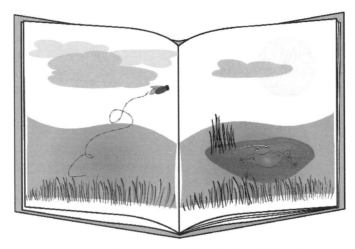

Figure 2.22. Absent, or wordless, texts are informal.

Typeface

The typeface is the type or lettering used for the text. The terms *typeface* and *font* are often used interchangeably. However, there is a difference: A typeface is the design of a character, whereas a font is a complete set of characters in any one design or style of type.

Typeface is an integral part of the design of the picture book, and designers are faced with many considerations when choosing typefaces. The choice of typeface may reflect the setting of a book (such as an old-fashioned typeface for a story set in historical times) or simply the need for legibility.

Before choosing a typeface, designers read the text and get a feel for the story. From there they decide on the typeface. Typefaces are often chosen for the sole purpose of creating a design statement, which may or may not be successful. Designers look to express the spirit and distinction of the illustrations or story. Although some typefaces may be fun, funky, or otherwise, they should not obscure the characters, which should be easy to recognize.

Before computers became commonplace in the printing world, designers had limited typefaces to choose from. With the expanded use of computers in the publishing industry, the selection of typefaces is now almost endless. Typical decisions a designer must make involve size, color, and style.

Hand-lettered text is becoming more commonplace in picture books, often used as a design element. Simms Taback, illustrator of *Joseph Had a Little Overcoat* (1997); Sara Fanelli, illustrator of *First Flight* (2002); and Maira Kalman, illustrator of *Max Makes a Million* (1990) intersperse hand lettering with regular typefaces and collage. Occasionally hand lettering is chosen to complement a book. In David Shannon's *No, David!* (1998), the hand-lettered text lends credibility to the story of a little boy learning to control his impulses. Page after page features an impish childlike writing, alluding to the fact that David himself is responsible for the markings.

Different typefaces can be used to unify a story. In Carolivia Herron's *Nappy Hair* (1997) several typefaces are used to reflect the African American call-and-response tradition, one for Herron's narrative, and others for various character responses. Likewise typeface can be used to take a story to new levels. In *Voices in the Park* (1998) by Anthony Browne, the story is told through four voices with different viewpoints. The designer used a variety of typefaces, one for each voice, to set them apart from one another. The type in *I Stink* (2002) is thick, chunky, and full of personality, a perfect complement to the smudgy, smoke-filled grunts and groans of the garbage truck.

Type Size

Designers may increase or decrease the size of the text to emphasize certain portions of the story. In *Wemberly Worried* (2000) the typeface is large to reflect the character's anxiety. The more Wemberly worries, the larger the text becomes. The juxtaposition of the small image of Wemberly against the increasingly larger typeface illustrates Wemberly's growing anxiety.

Following is an example of several common typefaces, all set in 12-point type. Notice the difference in spacing and length of the line.

Humpty Dumpty (Century Gothic)

Humpty Dumpty (Trade Gothic)

Humpty Dumpty (Verdana)

Humpty Dumpty (Goudy)

Humpty Dumpty (Helvetica)

Humpty Dumpty (Times New Roman)

The size of the text in a picture book involves other considerations as well. Picture books can have over 2,000 words, and the designer may have to use a smaller type size to accommodate the standard 32-page format. However, when print is too small, it can be difficult for a child to read independently. To show the effect of font size on text, the words Humpty Dumpty, shown in Times New Roman, are displayed below in six common sizes found in picture books. Note how the type appears heavier and darker as the font size increases.

14 point Humpty Dumpty

16 point Humpty Dumpty

18 point Humpty Dumpty

20 point Humpty Dumpty

22 point Humpty Dumpty

24 point Humpty Dumpty

Color

The color of text is also important in picture books. Books without pictures almost always have dark type on a white or light-colored page. However, when a dark-colored typeface is placed over a dark background, it is difficult to read—for children as well as adults. The situation is similar for light-colored text on light backgrounds. For books in which art occupies a full page, designers are faced with challenging design decisions. In *Uptown* (2000) by Bryan Collier, text is placed on a busy background and placed high on the page. Designer Martha Rago opted to use bright pink, yellow, and white to make it stand out against the dark artwork. Although this works for *Uptown*, this can be a risky design decision.

Text as Illustration

Many picture books incorporate text into the illustrations. Concrete poems, which take the shape of the object they describe, are one example. In *A Poke in the I* (2001), a book of concrete poems, each poem is a work of art, which illustrator Chris Raschka embellishes with collage. The poems are printed in different typefaces on the white background; Raschka uses the white space generously, allowing the poems the prominence they demand. Text as art is often seen in front and back matter.

The playful use of text on copyright pages, jacket flaps, and back covers has also become common. In *Zat Cat! A Haute Couture Tail* (2001), illustrator Chelsea McLaren, the book designer, put the copyright information in the shape of the Eiffel Tower. The extra attention to detail adds to the overall mood of the book, which is set in Paris, France. *Bembo's Zoo* (2000) is an alphabet book with illustrations done in the typeface Bembo, which was created by Francesco Griffo in the fifteenth century. Illustrator Roberto de Vicq de Cumptich's creations are composed of both lowercase and uppercase letters, laid side-by-side or end-to-end; often one letter is repeated to create a particular aspect of the animal's body. For instance, the lowercase "i" is used to create the scaly back of the iguana. *Bembo's Zoo* has an interactive Web site that features an animated version of the book: www.bemboszoo.com.

CONCLUSION

As noted in the quote by David Saylor at the beginning of this chapter, design exists to support the pictures and text. Designers strive to find the perfect balance; sometimes using a light touch is the best approach. Some books require more dramatic design. Design gives the pictures and text a framework upon which to build. In this chapter we examined layout and paratexts, or supporting parts—elements of the design process. This chapter and the next are designed to provide a framework upon which to build knowledge of picture book design. Although it can be daunting, understanding the process enables you to confidently explore picture book design. In chapter 3 art elements, design principles, artistic media, and artistic style are explored.

ENDNOTES

1. *Dust jacket* is often used interchangeably with *book jacket*. I choose not to use this term because I think "dust" implies protection, negating the role and contribution the book jacket plays in the overall aesthetic of picture books.

2. This refers to the American edition of *Let's Get a Pup, Said Kate*. The U.K. edition was published with the dialogue tag.

Chapter 3

Anatomy of a Picture Book: Picture Space, Design, Medium, and Style

Design is an essential part of any picture book. It is the first aspect of a book that a reader judges. It is the frame-work for the text and illustration. It is the subtle weave of words and pictures that allows both to tell one seamless tale.

—Jon Scieszka, "Design Matters," *The Horn Book*

In This Chapter

- Picture Space and Composition
- Design Elements
- Art Elements
- Artistic Media
- Artistic Style

A finished picture book may look effortless to the reader. However, the time and planning involved in creating just one book is mind-boggling. Chapter 2 explored the different parts of a picture book, including book jackets, paratexts (supporting parts), and typography. Although these elements often include art and design and are very important in picture books as a whole, they are external. This chapter examines the internal aspects of picture books: the art elements and design principles artist use when creating illustrations, as well as artistic media and style. Illustrations help clarify many of the principles and concepts discussed.

PICTURE SPACE AND COMPOSITION

Composition structures what viewers see, when they see it, and how they see it. The composition of a picture functions like the skeleton does in the human body. According to illustrator Uri Shulevitz (1997), the composition of a book is "felt." He calls the picture space and composition "the hidden aspects" of pictures. Picture space is the depth of space, which includes the objects and the space around them. Composition is the way the elements are organized within that space.

Picture Space

Picture space is initially flat because the surface upon which it is created is usually flat. A figure drawn on a piece of paper generally appears flat. The edges of the paper create a frame that surrounds the illustrations. Through the use of perspective and deep or flat space, an illustrator creates the illusion of depth. In flat space the lines and contours are used to depict two dimensions; in deep space they convey volume and three dimensions. Objects and figures appear to recede backward into depth from the picture plane.

The first square in figure 3.1 is a frame for the illustration, which is really just a box. In the second square, diagonal lines and another box—smaller and centered inside the larger one—add the illusion of depth.

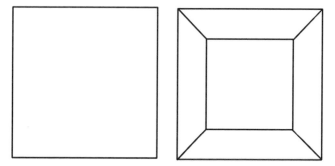

Figure 3.1. Adding a smaller inset box and diagonal lines connecting the corners creates an illusion of depth.

In figure 3.2 an object is added. It appears flat, even though it has curves. It floats on the page, disparate and out of place. An object that a viewer expects to recede into the background hangs awkwardly in the picture space.

Figure 3.2. The toad seems out of place. An object that should have depth lacks dimension and substance.

In figure 3.3 the object is set back in the picture space. The edges of the paper (represented by the larger square) frame the object, adding depth. The same frame now bounds the picture space, and the object no longer looks out of place. In a finished illustration, other artistic elements, such as shading and perspective, replace the lines, which appear obvious in the figure.

Figure 3.3. The toad sits back in the frame and no longer feels awkward or out of place because the illusion of dimension adds depth.

Composition

A picture is made up of many elements, including size, shape, and texture. When viewers look at a picture, they are aware of the subject, and details often immediately draw their attention. What may not be as obvious is the composition (Shulevitz 1997). Good composition allows the various elements to reside in the picture space.

The picture surface can be composed in a variety of ways. Two commonly encountered types of picture surface arrangement are *symmetrical* and *asymmetrical*. In symmetrical picture surfaces (see figure 3.4, p. 58), the division of objects and their "weight" are evenly balanced. This gives a sense of stability and order. In asymmetrical picture surfaces (see figure 3.5, p. 58), the division of these elements is unevenly balanced, creating variety and movement. Asymmetrical picture surfaces can be said to be dynamic, rather than static (see figure 3.6, p. 58).

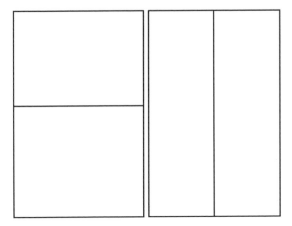

Figure 3.4. In a symmetrical composition, the division of space is equally balanced. It is stable but static.

Figure 3.5. In an asymmetrical composition, the division of space is unequal, giving it a dynamic quality.

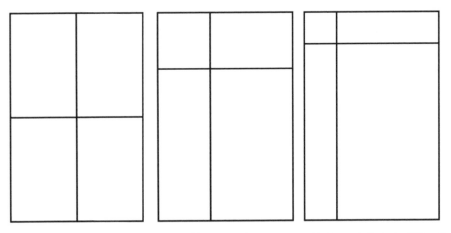

Figure 3.6. The first arrangement is static. The second arrangement is less static but still hesitant, making it appear to be a mistake. The third arrangement is dynamic because it is clear the unequal balance was intentional.

DESIGN ELEMENTS

Design is the overall organization or composition of a work, the arrangement of its parts. The picture book designer orchestrates all the elements of a picture book—illustrations, typography, and layout—creating a picture book. In a successful picture book, these aspects of design work together, creating a sense of unity. Design is presentation; it matters.

Early in the production process of a book, a designer meets with the illustrator to discuss trim size, layout, and text placement.

Artists use art elements and design principles to create an illustration. Inspired by the illustration, designers use layout and typography to enhance and complement art and create a product. In *The Spider and the Fly* (2002), illustrator Tony DiTerlizzi chose to create a backdrop reminiscent of an old silent film. The illustrations, a play of tones of black, white, and gray, bring new life to Mary Howitt's 1829 poem. Gothic elements are interwoven throughout the book via the use of spider webs that are mimicked in the typography.

In effective design, the visual elements and principles of design mesh, achieving an overall sense of unity. In a picture book, design is the visual effect the illustrations and text have as an integrated presentation. The factors illustrators must consider in the design of a picture book include composition, text placement, typeface, shape, and size.

Design is the arrangement of the elements of art in a composition. In design there are seven principles (also called principles of art or principles of design):[1] balance, contrast, emphasis, harmony, movement, rhythm, and unity. Artists apply these principles in varying degrees to control and order the elements of art. The applications can cause the principles to overlap, oppose, or take precedence over each other.

> Explore interactive design elements at www.picturingbooks.com.

Balance

Balance refers to the overall visual weight of a composition. Without it, the composition looks awkward and unstable. When objects in an illustration are the same or similar on both sides of the composition, it has formal balance. Informal balance is the arrangement of divergent forms.

There are three different types of balance: symmetrical (or regular), asymmetrical, and radial. The human figure has symmetrical balance; that is, it is the same on the right and left sides of a central axis. When something is asymmetrically balanced, parts of the object are not distributed equally on each side, but their total weight is balanced. Think of a plant in a pot. The plant looks balanced, even though the number of leaves on each side may be unequal. Radial balance originates from the center, like a daisy. All of the petals may not be exactly the same, but they extend from one point in the center.

In figure 3.7 (p. 60) three objects represent balance. Imagine a line down the center of the toad and the fly. The two halves of the fly are equal; the two halves of the toad are unequal. However, both still feel balanced. The pond feels stable because the balance radiates from the center.

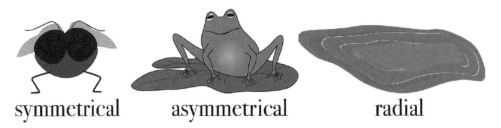

Figure 3.7. The fly has symmetrical balance, the toad has asymmetrical balance, and the pond has radial balance.

Contrast

Contrast is an abrupt, unexpected change in a visual element. It creates definition of objects and encourages eye movement. Artists can create contrast through value, color, texture, and shape. Color contrast can be achieved through hue, saturation, and value. Complementary colors (red/green, yellow/purple, blue/orange) seem to vibrate when they are placed together in a composition. By juxtaposing colors of different values (light/dark), an artist can create a sense of depth. By varying the thickness and thinness of lines or combining horizontal and vertical lines, an artist creates contrast. Contrast can also be created through shape: curved shapes are calming and jagged shapes create edginess. In figure 3.8, placing round objects that offer a calming effect with jagged, pointed tips of the grass creates contrast.

Figure 3.8. The smooth edges of the pond offset the vertical, pointed wildflowers, creating contrast.

Emphasis

Emphasis occurs when an artist stresses certain elements of the design over others to create a focal point. The eye of the viewer focuses on the area of emphasis or center of interest first, then moves across the rest of the composition. An artist uses emphasis to direct and focus the attention of the viewer on the most important parts of a composition (and usually the story). An artist creates emphasis through size, color, texture, and shape. A design lacking emphasis is monotonous and uninspired. Figure 3.9 uses a large toad in the center of the illustration for emphasis.

Figure 3.9. The eye is immediately drawn to the large toad in the center. Eventually the eye moves to the arrangement of the smaller toads surrounding the large one.

Harmony and Variety

These two characteristics are closely related, because both combine the elements of art (color, line, shape, texture, and value) to create visual interest and to guide the eye through the composition. Both convey meaning through repetition, proximity, and simplicity. It is the degree to which each is used that creates the contrast between the two. Harmony is a subtle way of combining elements of art to accentuate their similarities and bind the picture parts into a whole (see figure 3.10, p. 62). Variety gives a composition interest and vitality by abruptly changing an element (see figure 3.11, p. 62). Whereas harmony is subtle, variety is more obvious. Variety, contrast, and harmony give unity to a composition.

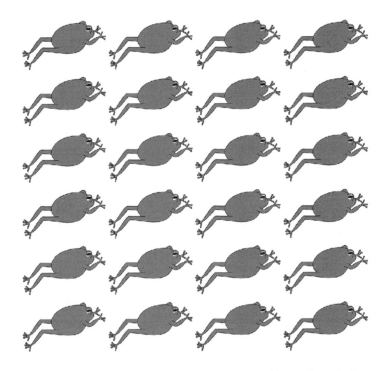

Figure 3.10. The toads are all facing the same direction. The repetition and proximity create harmony.

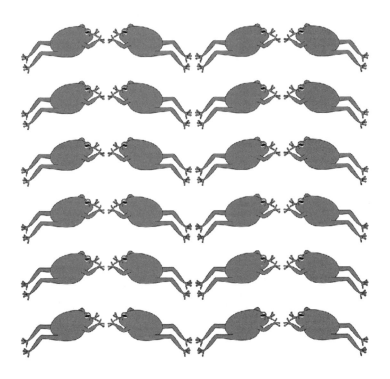

Figure 3.11. The rows of toads alternate in two directions. There is still repetition and proximity, but there is also variety.

Movement

Movement guides a viewer's eye through the work, usually to a focal point. The artist arranges parts of an image to create a sense of motion by using lines, shapes, forms, and textures, or by combining elements of art to produce the look of action. For example, by incorporating a series of diagonals lines, a sense of movement is created. Consider a staircase. The diagonal line in a staircase causes the eye to move upward or downward, depending on its orientation. Through shape and scale (the size of shapes), and by creating a series of different focal points, an artist creates movement. In figure 3.12 the fly is small in the background and grows larger as it nears the foreground of the illustration. The trail that fills in the gaps between the different versions of the fly guides the viewer's eyes.

Figure 3.12. The fly trail leads the eye from the background to the foreground of the illustration. In addition. the size of the fly increases and it changes direction, which creates a sense of movement.

Rhythm

Rhythm is the regular repetition of elements of art to produce the look and feel of movement. An artist creates movement in illustration by repeating colors, shapes, lines, or textures. The repetition of the elements invites the eye to jump rapidly or glide smoothly from one image to the next. Rhythm allows artists to create a feeling of organized movement. Elements placed at regular intervals create a calming rhythm. Sudden changes in position and size create a lively rhythm. Variety keeps rhythm exciting and active, moving the eye around the artwork. In figure 3.13 rhythm is achieved by bunching blades of grass closely together and spacing them at regular intervals.

Figure 3.13. The grass is spaced at regular intervals and closely bunched together, creating a sense of rhythm.

Unity

Unity is the quality of completeness a composition has. In a unified work of art, all parts come together to form a whole; each part of a composition feels as though it belongs with the rest. Like bricks in a wall, a composition needs all of its components or it might fall apart. An artist achieves unity by balancing all the aspects of the composition and employing art elements and design principles. One way to achieve unity is through repetition of color, shape, and texture. In addition, by grouping objects closely together, an artist creates proximity, which unifies a composition. In figure 3.14 different elements combine to create a finished illustration that has unity. Using contrasting shapes and varying the size of objects in the picture space creates a balance.

Figure 3.14. The finished illustration has unity achieved through the application of art elements and design principles.

ART ELEMENTS

Explore interactive art elements at www.picturingbooks.com.

Art elements (sometimes called visual elements or elements of art) are the tools artists use to create a piece of art:[2] color, value, lines, perspective, shape, space, and texture. Artists manipulate these elements to achieve a desired effect. An element may dominate a composition or not be used at all. The elements are the "language" an artist uses to convey meaning.

Color

Color (or hue) includes the six basic colors: red, orange, yellow, green, blue, and violet. Red, yellow, and blue are the *primary* colors. These three colors are mixed to create *secondary* colors: green, orange, and purple. Complementary colors are opposing hues, positioned across from each other on the color wheel: red/green, yellow/purple, and blue/orange. Primary colors are also used to create *tertiary* colors: red/orange, yellow/orange, yellow/green, blue/green, blue/violet, and red/violet. (*Intermediate* is another word for tertiary.)

Intensity refers to the strength or saturation of a color. The intensity of a hue is decreased when it is mixed with the color opposite it on the color wheel. Illustrators use intensity of color to convey mood. A dull or pastel color seems soft and sensitive; a bright color seems brash and lively. Colors are referred to as warm (red/yellow/orange) or cool (blue/green/purple).

Color conveys setting, theme, or mood. An illustrator's use of color is important and often a defining characteristic of style. For instance, most of Lois Ehlert's books are filled with strong, bold colors. The term *palette* refers to the array or range of color an artist uses in a particular work or on a consistent basis.

Over the last century psychologists have discovered what artists have known for centuries: color affects mood and emotion. Humans respond physically to color. They often associate feelings with color. For example, a sad person is said to feel blue, and a jealous person is said to be green with envy.

Value

Value is the lightness or darkness of a color. A color to which black has been added is called a shade and has a darker value. A color to which white has been added is called a tint and has a lighter value. Pink is a tint of red. Burgundy is a shade of red. Value is used to suggest depth, volume, and mood. Paintings that use only one color and the tints and shades of that color are called monochromatic (one = mono/color = chromatic). For example, a book created with black, white, and shades of gray is considered monochromatic. In figure 3.15 (p. 66), each square is 20 percent lighter than the square that precedes it. The gradation is apparent; however, if each square was 1 percent lighter, the change would be subtler and not visible to the eye.

Figure 3.15. Each square is 20 percent lighter than the square that precedes it.

Lines

Lines may be thick or thin, whole or broken. They can also be straight, curved, or jagged. Jagged lines convey enthusiasm, anger, and energy. Curved lines are sensuous, organic, and rhythmic. There are three basic types of line: horizontal, vertical, and diagonal. Horizontal lines are peaceful and calming. They also provide order and move the eye from left to right. Vertical lines suggest stability and strength, giving the effect of a photograph. Diagonal lines express spontaneity and stimulate the eye, providing action and movement on the page. Look for diagonal lines in staircases and hills.

Illustrators use lines to convey meaning and guide the viewer's eye across the page. Different types of lines are used for different purposes. Contour lines not only show the edges of the shapes being drawn but also go onto the surface of the object to generate the three-dimensional qualities of the form. Gesture lines indicate action and physical movement. (See figure 3.16.) They are done quickly in the form of a rough sketch as the model moves and lack detail. Hatching and cross-hatching refer to lines drawn closely together. They create value in the drawing, adding depth, form, and texture.

Figure 3.16. The gesture lines surrounding the fly indicate that he is mad or perhaps upset. Contour lines make the outline of the toad.

Perspective

Perspective is the position or angle from which a picture is viewed. It gives the illusion of depth on a two-dimensional surface by organizing items from a certain point of view. It also gives readers a glimpse of a world they might otherwise miss. The artist can use views from above or below, as well as from various angles to the side, to create a unique visual experience.

There are two major types of perspective: *atmospheric* and *linear*. Altering objects' size and placing them in conjunction with parallel lines that seem to converge (unite) in the distance at a vanishing point(s) creates a linear perspective. In linear perspective, objects appear to get smaller and closer together the farther away they are. Through the use of the vanishing point, illustrators can create distance and depth.

Atmospheric perspective, sometimes called aerial perspective, creates a faraway effect through pale or diffused colors. Illustrators can add an illusion of depth in the picture space on a flat surface by blurring objects and adding tones of blue or gray to them. Duller and faded hues achieve the same effect. Blurred lines, decreased sizes, and diminished details also contribute to the overall effect. In figure 3.17 a line of trees is shown using the vanishing point and lines that were used to create the appearance of distance. In figure 3.18 the same line of trees is shown without the lines.

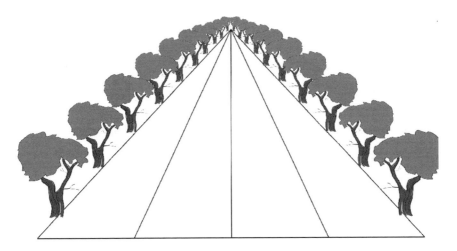

Figure 3.17. The lines and vanishing point help create a sense of perspective. The trees are evenly spaced and get smaller the nearer they are to the vanishing point.

Figure 3.18. The lines have been removed and the stream makes the images appear less rigid.

Shape

Shapes, both simple and complex, can suggest character and setting. They can be concrete and easily recognizable, or distorted and abstract. There are two types of shape: organic and geometric. Organic shapes are irregular and curvy. They symbolize natural objects, such as trees and humans (see figure 3.19). Artists use organic shapes to convey spontaneity, sincerity, and unpredictability—like life itself.

Geometric shapes include triangles, circles, rectangles, and squares. They are most often used for non-natural (or human-made) objects, such as buildings, houses, and cars (see figure 3.20). Geometric shapes are precise, exact, and orderly. They can be complex, stable, or sometimes even rigid. They are often used to convey order and design.

Figure 3.19. Organic shapes are irregular and curvy. These shapes symbolize nature and humans.

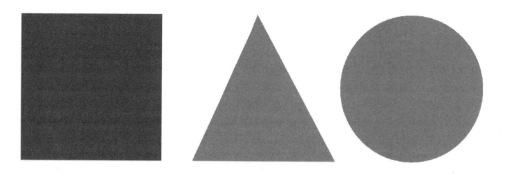

Figure 3.20. Geometric shapes are precise, exact, and orderly. Objects such as buildings, houses, and cars are geometric.

Space

Space is the visual illusion of dimension that invites the viewer into a picture. It may be deep, shallow, or flat. To create a three-dimensional effect or sense of depth on a flat, two-dimensional surface, artists use various devices, including overlapping objects, relative size, and position of images. The empty areas in an illustration are referred to as "negative (ground) space" (or sometimes "white space"). "Positive (figure) space" is the enclosed area surrounded or defined by negative space.

In the figure–ground relationship, the eye interprets figure or ground objects as opposing elements. If the figure–ground relationship is ambiguous, as is the case with flat pictures, then viewers will have a hard time focusing on either object. If objects meant to be close recede and objects that are intended to recede appear close, a picture may lack contrast. When there is not enough contrast between the figure and ground, pictures are difficult to read (Shulevitz 1997). (See figure 3.21.)

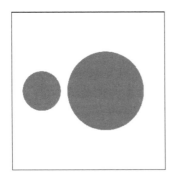 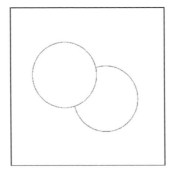 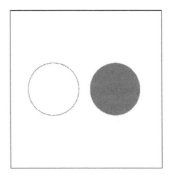

Figure 3.21. In the first frame the larger circle seems closer; in the second frame the circles are the same size, but overlapping makes the top one seem larger; in the third frame the circles are the same size, but the solid circle seems to recede while the hollow circle comes forward.

Texture

Texture refers to the surface characteristics of the art. In the case of picture book illustration, texture adds a tangible feel to the object—an urge to reach out and touch the picture. Texture can be visual. Artists can create the illusion of texture through the choice of medium (such as types of paint) and the surface receiving the medium (the types of paper). The possibilities are endless: smooth, bumpy, soft, hard, shiny, furry, and gritty. Many illustrators use illustration/graphic software, such as Adobe PhotoShop and Adobe Illustrator, to create texture in their artwork. Illustrator Lane Smith used to spray acrylic varnish onto his oil paintings, which bubbled up and created texture. Smith now uses a computer to incorporate and layer his textures. Texture can also be tactile, that is physically felt, such as the rough paper used in many of Chris Van Allsburg's books. In many board books, tactile elements are deliberately added, such as the sandpaper that represents the father's unshaven face in *Pat the Bunny* (1940).

ARTISTIC MEDIA

The artistic medium (plural media) is both the tool and the surface an illustrator uses. Technique is the manner in which an artist applies one medium to another medium. Many artists have a preferred medium, often being renowned for their work with it. For instance, Lois Ehlert is known for her graphic cut-paper art, and Brian Pinkney for his scratchboard illustrations. Denise Fleming, a paper artist, makes her own paper. To make her paper, Fleming pours cotton rag fiber that has been soaked in water through hand-cut stencils onto a screen, where the pulp is allowed to dry. The result is an image in handmade paper. Fleming says, "The paper is the picture. The picture is the paper" ("Fleming" 2007).

Chris Van Allsburg is an artist who works in many types of media. Known for the charcoal pencil illustrations that earned him a Caldecott Honor for *The Garden of Abdul Gasazi* (1979) and a Caldecott Medal for *Jumanji* (1981), he became more interested in other media as his career progressed. In *The Wreck of the Zephyr* (1983), a story-within-a-story, his first full-color book, Van Allsburg used pastel over paint. According to the illustrator, "as time went by, I became more interested in picture making, and taught myself to use different materials, such as dry and oil pastels, craypas, crayons, colored pencils, and paint. Now I decide if a book should be black and white or color as a result of how I imagine the story while I am thinking about it" ("Van Allsburg" 2005).

Information about what media an illustrator used in a particular book can often be found on the copyright page. In addition, illustrators often provide artist's notes for titles that required elaborate preparations or special techniques. There are several techniques[3] for applying media: painting, drawing, sculptural, printmaking, and photography/digital art. When an artist employs two or more techniques, that is using mixed media. For example, Stephen T. Johnson used drawing technique (pastels and charcoal) with painterly technique (watercolors and gouache) to create the illustrations for *Alphabet City* (1995), his tribute to the hustle and bustle of city life. In *There Was an Old Lady Who Swallowed a Fly* (1997) Simms Taback used sculptural (collage), painterly (watercolor), and drawing (pen and ink) techniques in his version of the traditional rhyme. In *Hard Hat Area* (2004) Susan L. Roth used photography (photomontage used as background) and sculptural (collage) techniques in her homage to construction workers.

Painterly

With the technique of painting, forms are created by manipulating color and tone. Painting is characterized by open forms, in which shapes are defined by the paintbrush rather than by outline or contour. Often referred to as the painterly technique, painting includes the following media: acrylic, gouache, oil, tempera, and watercolor.

Acrylic

Acrylic paint has a synthetic base that dissolves in water. Developed in the 1950s, it was the first major development in paint technology for hundreds of years

(Salisbury 2004). Colored pigments are added for an opaque, flat finish. Acrylic paint dries faster than oil paint and has a different consistency. Extremely versatile, acrylic paint dries very quickly and can be applied in thick layers for an opaque effect. If the paint is applied in thin layers, the artist can achieve a transparent effect. Acrylic paint can also be applied thickly, which adds texture to the painting. For examples of acrylic medium, see *Working Cotton* (1992), illustrated by Carole Byard; *Miss Rumphius* (1982), illustrated by Barbara Cooney; *George Shrinks* (1985), illustrated by William Joyce; *The Paperboy* (1996), illustrated by Dav Pilkey; *The Rough-Face Girl* (1992), illustrated by David Shannon; *My Name Is Georgia* (1996), illustrated by Jeanette Winter; and *Stellaluna* (1991), illustrated by Janell Cannon.

Gouache

Gouache (pronounced *gwash*) is a French term used to describe a type of watercolor paint. The word is derived from the Italian word *guazzo*, which means a watering place. Pigments used are ground in water and mixed with white pigment (chalk) in a gum mixture. Whereas watercolors are transparent and allow the white of the paper to show through the paint, gouache is opaque and can be applied in solid colors. When dry, gouache has a matte finish, which makes it easy to scan or reproduce electronically. For examples of gouache medium, see *The Wonderful Tower of Watts* (1994), illustrated by Frané Lessac; *The Trouble with Baby* (2003), illustrated by Marisabina Russo; *The Hare And the Tortoise* (2006), illustrated by Giselle Potter; and *Good Queen Bess: The Story of Elizabeth I of England* (2003), illustrated by Diane Stanley.

Oil

Oil paint, created by mixing colored pigments with an oil base, gives a rich look to an illustration. The thickness of oil paint can vary. It dries slowly and must be added to the painting in layers. Benefits of working with oil paint are that it allows previous layers to show through as more paint is applied, and it creates rich colors and texture. For examples of oil paint medium, see *Time Flies* (1994), illustrated by Eric Rohmann; *The True Story of the 3 Little Pigs* (1989), illustrated by Lane Smith; *King Bidgood's in the Bathtub* (1985), illustrated by Don Wood; *Aunt Flossie's Hats (and Crab Cakes Later)* (1991), illustrated by James Ransome; *Bintou's Braids* (2004), illustrated by Shane W. Evans; and *Swamp Angel* (1994), illustrated by Paul O. Zelinsky.

Tempera

Tempera is similar to watercolor, except that colored pigments are mixed with a sticky base, such as egg yolk. Tempera is a tricky medium to use because it dries quickly, but it produces vibrant, solid colors. In *Magic in the Margins: A Medieval Tale of Bookmaking* (2007), illustrator Bonnie Christensen used egg tempera with ink in the paintings reminiscent of illuminated manuscripts. It is an apt choice, as it was the medium used by medieval monks. Illustrator Ashley Bryan works with a combination of tempera and gouache in *The Night Has Ears: African Proverbs* (1999). For other examples of tempera paint, see *Fancy That* (2003), illustrated by Megan Lloyd; *Engelbert Joins the Circus* (1997), illustrated by Roberta Jones; *Perceval: King Arthur's Knight of the Holy Grail* (2007), illustrated by Gennady Spirin; and *The Waterfall's Gift* (2001), illustrated by Richard Jesse Watson.

Watercolor

Watercolors are finely ground-up pigments that come dry (in cans or pans) or wet (in tubes or bottles) and are added to water. The ratio of water to pigment affects the lightness or darkness of the color. The more water, the lighter the color. The various stages of dilution are called washes. Watercolors are transparent, which allows the paper to show through, creating highlights. Watercolor paint is subtle and expressive, yet very flexible. Before *Mirette on the Highwire* (1992), Emily Arnold McCully had illustrated dozens of books. At the suggestion of her art director, she abandoned the media and techniques she had used for years and approached the illustrations for *Mirette* in a completely different fashion. Compare the simplicity of *Picnic* (1984) with the rich color and impressionistic style of *Mirette*, which was a dramatic departure for the illustrator. The gamble paid off: McCully won the Caldecott Medal for *Mirette* in 1993. Jerry Pinkney is another illustrator who works in watercolors. Pencil lines are allowed to peek through the transparent watercolors, which gives Pinkney's illustrations a distinctive quality. For other examples of watercolor medium, see *The Stray Dog* (2001), illustrated by Marc Simont; *The Library* (1995), illustrated by David Small; and *Tuesday* (1992), illustrated by David Wiesner.

Drawing

Drawing is the depiction of shapes and forms on a surface by means of lines. The approach is known as linear. There are many types of drawing techniques, which vary depending on the effect an artist is trying to achieve. Pencil is often combined with other types of media. Drawing includes the following media: pastels, pencils, and scratchboard.

Pastels

Pastels consist of pigments that are formed into manageable sticks. Pastels can be either soft or hard, which affects the final images. Similar to crayon but not as greasy, and similar to chalk but not as powdery, pastels can be rubbed and altered to create just the right effect. For examples of pastels, see *Hoops* (1997) or *Goal* (2001), illustrated by Stephen T. Johnson; *An Ant's Day Off* (2003), illustrated by Nina Laden; and *The Grandad Tree* (2001), illustrated by Sharon Wilson.

Pencils

Pencils are rods, encased in wood or mechanical holders, with cores containing graphite, colored wax, or charcoal, which can be sharpened to a fine point. Artists can use the point for fine lines or the side for broad strokes. Pencils allow illustrators to incorporate fine detail into an illustration. Graphite drawing pencils are available in more than 20 degrees of hardness. Soft pencils create soft lines; the finer the pencil, the harder and more precise the line. Illustrator Chris Van Allsburg's meticulous charcoal pencil illustrations in *Jumanji* (1981) earned him a Caldecott Medal. Known for soft pencil illustrations reminiscent of days gone by, illustrator Peter McCarty earned a Caldecott Honor for *Hondo and Fabian* (2002). The soft palette is used again in the sequel *Fabian Escapes* (2007). For other examples of pencil technique, see *Song and Dance Man* (1988), illustrated by Stephen Gammell; and *Full Moon* (2001), illustrated by Brian Wilcox.

Scratchboard

The scratchboard technique involves scratching an illustration into the black painted surface of a white or multicolored board with a sharp instrument. Several layers may be used if an illustrator is working with watercolors or acrylics. Techniques such as hatching or stippling allow for greater detail and texture. If an illustrator is working with color, layers are scratched off one by one to create different shades of color. Illustrator Brian Pinkney discovered the scratchboard technique while attending the School of Visual Arts in New York City. Scratchboard, which is his signature medium, allows Pinkney to sculpt an image. As he explains, "When I etch the drawing out of the board, I get a rhythm going with my lines which feels like sculpture to me" ("Pinkney, [Jerry] Brian" 2004, 189). For examples of scratchboard technique, see *The Faithful Friend* (1995), illustrated by Brian Pinkney; *The Gettysburg Address* (1995), illustrated by Michael McCurdy; and *Butterfly Eyes and Other Secrets of the Meadow* (2006) illustrated by Beth Krommes.

Sculptural

Traditionally, assemblage, collage, cut paper, fabric and thread, and modeling clay are not considered sculptural. However, in this guide I group them with sculptural techniques because they are neither painterly or drawn, but rather cut, molded, glued, sewn, and manipulated, and in the case of Joan Steiner, painstakingly constructed. Artists who work with three-dimensional art photograph the result to create the illustration.

Assemblage

An assemblage is a three-dimensional composition made of found objects and commonplace items, such as buttons, cloth, and string. Materials are arranged and then photographed. The I Spy series by Jean Marzolla and Walter Wick contains perhaps the most famous example of books that feature this type of medium. Joan Steiner's first *Look-Alikes* (1998) and her more recent *Look-Alikes Around the World* (2007) are astonishing compositions of everyday objects that have been gathered and arranged to represent everyday scenes. Readers enjoy searching for the hundreds of ordinary objects Steiner incorporates into her arrangements. Saxton Freymann and Joost Elffers created original constructions from fresh fruits and vegetables in *Dog Food* (2002) and *Baby Food* (2003) and then photographed the results. The duo captures a dizzying array of expressions in their fruit and vegetable sculptures. In *Dog Food*, phrases related to dogs, such as "hot dog," are interpreted with hilarious results. In *Baby Food*, the theme is baby animals. A baby mouse is made from radishes, as well as a puppy from bananas and a chick from pears. The illustrations in Jeannie Baker's wordless picture book *Home* (2003) were created as constructions that were photographed for the final art. Compare this technique with collage, which tends to comprise more two-dimensional objects.

Collage

A collage is a three-dimensional design created by gluing flat elements such as newspaper, wallpaper, fabric, wood, photographs, cloth, and string to a flat surface. The word *collage* is derived from the French word *coller*, meaning "to paste." Artists have very specific reasons for choosing the bits and pieces they use for each illustration. Close examination of collage art can yield some interesting conclusions about the story. In the Caldecott-winning *Smoky Night* (1994), illustrator David Diaz layered bold acrylic illustrations on startling photographs punctuated with scraps of paper, cardboard, matchsticks, glass, and plastic bags to create the illustrations. In *Beaks* (2002) Robin Brickman paints on handmade watercolor paper, cutting, shaping and gluing the differently painted pieces of paper for a three-dimensional effect, which is photographed for the final illustration. Compare this technique with assemblage, which tends to comprise more three-dimensional objects. For other examples of collage technique, see *The Very Hungry Caterpillar* (1969), illustrated by Eric Carle; *Martin's Big Words* (2001), illustrated by Bryan Collier; *Little Blue and Little Yellow* (1959), illustrated by Leo Lionni; and *Hard Hat Area* (2004), illustrated by Susan L. Roth.

Cut Paper

Cut-paper illustrations consist of two-dimensional images that are strategically cut and arranged. Illustrations can be simple, as in Lois Ehlert's *Color Zoo* (1989), or very complex, as in David Wisniewski's *Golem* (1996). Robert Sabuda has a knack for matching cut paper to setting. He used marbleized, hand-painted paper to create a mosaic effect in *Saint Valentine* (1992). The choice of mosaic is particularly suitable to the classical Roman setting of the book. For *Arthur and the Sword* (1995), Sabuda created cut-paper illustrations with a stained-glass window effect that is indicative of medieval art. For other examples of cut-paper technique, see *Seven Blind Mice* (1992), illustrated by Ed Young; *In Daddy's Arms I Am Tall* (1997), illustrated by Javaka Steptoe; *Horace and Morris But Mostly Dolores* (1999), illustrated by Amy Walrod; *There Was an Old Lady Who Swallowed a Fly* (1997), illustrated by Simms Taback; *Mouse Paint* (1989), illustrated by Ellen Stoll Walsh; and *Color Zoo* (1989), illustrated by Lois Ehlert.

Fabric and Thread

Fabric and thread crafted illustrations are unique and take many painstaking hours to create. *Dia's Story Cloth* (1992), stitched by Nhia Thao Cha and Chue Cha, is an example of needlepoint that is an important part of cultural heritage. In *A to Zen: A Book of Japanese Culture* (1992), illustrator Yoshi created the batik illustrations that capture the beauty and simplicity of Japanese art and culture. In *The Farmer and the Poor God* (1996), Yoshi used colored dyes on raw silk. For other examples of fabric and needlework techniques, see *Hannah and the Seven Dresses* (1999), illustrated by Marthe Jocelyn; and *Mary Had a Little Lamb* (1995), illustrated by Salley Mavor.

Modeling Clay

Modeling clay is an oil-based product that does not dry out and can be melted and cooled repeatedly. Plasticine® is one of the most popular brands. It does not harden beyond its original state, which makes it easy to manipulate and mold with fingertips. Popularized by Nick Park, creator of the Wallace and Gromit cartoons, Plasticine® is used by several illustrators. For examples, see *The Subway Mouse* (2005), by Barbara Reid; and *Big Week for Little Mouse* (2004), illustrated by Kim Fernandes.

Printmaking

Printmaking involves engraving, etching, or carving an image onto a block, plate, or other object and creating a negative. The block or plate is covered with ink and pressed onto a flat surface, such as paper or fabric, creating a positive image. There are many types of printmaking techniques, including etching, linoleum cuts, monotype, and woodcuts.

Etching

Etching is a process in which a needle is used to draw onto a wax ground applied over a metal plate. The plate is submerged in a series of acid baths. The acid bites into the metal surface unprotected by the wax ground. When the wax ground is removed, ink is forced into the etched depressions. After the un-etched surfaces are wiped clean, an impression remains. Etching is often confused with engraving. Both methods are intaglio printmaking techniques (below the surface). However, in etching, acid is used to cut into the surface. In engraving, a sharp tool is used. For examples of etching technique, see *Pigs from A to Z* (1986), illustrated by Arthur Geisert; and *Joan of Arc: The Lily Maid* (1999), illustrated by Robert Rayevsky.

Linocuts or Linoleum Cuts

Linocuts are similar to woodcut illustrations, except that wood, which is a natural medium, has natural grains that show through the carvings, whereas linoleum, which is made by humans and has a flat surface, allows artists greater freedom to create their own patterns. Linoleum is also softer and more pliable than wood, making it easier to carve. Linoleum cuts are examples of relief printing. Caldecott Award–winning artist Margaret Chodos-Irvine is noted for her linocuts. Her method involves cutting the image into sheets of battleship linoleum, a thick, pliable material, onto which she rolls ink. She then prints the image onto paper using an etching press. For images with more than one color, she uses multiple blocks. *Sarah Ella Gets Dressed* (1996) is a fine example of Chodos-Irvine's method. For other examples of linocut technique, see *Winter: An Alphabet Acrostic* (2002), by Leslie Evans; *I Once Was a Monkey: Stories Buddha Told* (1999), by Jeanne M. Lee; *The New Alphabet of Animals* (2004), by Christopher Wormell; and *Blueberry Shoes* (1999), illustrated by Evon Zerbetz.

Monotype

Monotype is a form of printmaking in which no element of the print is repeatable. Paint or ink is applied to the surface of a plate and then printed, but the plate itself is not etched or engraved. Monotypes are unique, like paintings, but the process allows artists to incorporate resists, layers, and embossments into the illustrations. Carla Golembe used this type of printmaking technique in *Why the Sky Is Far Away* (1995). The approach allowed her to create stylized figures that stand out from the background despite the fact that the picture space is flat and lacks depth. Golembe also used this technique in *How the Night Came from the Sea* (1994). The black figures slink across the pages, popping against the bright colors that make up the background.

Woodcuts

Woodcuts are illustrations carved into wood with chisels and knives. An artist draws an image onto a block of wood and carves away the area around the image. A raised portion remains on the block, which is then covered with paint or ink and pressed to another surface, usually paper. The natural grain of the wood is allowed to enhance and contribute to the illustration. Woodcuts are an example of relief printing. Caldecott Award–winning artist Mary Azarian used woodcuts to illustrate *Snowflake Bentley* (1998), to great effect. The rough grain that is the hallmark of this technique allowed Azarian to evoke the late nineteenth century, filled with lanterns and stovepipe ovens, which is the setting of this biographical picture book. For other examples of woodcut technique, see *Antler, Bear, Canoe: A Northwoods Alphabet* (2002), illustrated by Betsy Bowen; *Mr. Ferlinghetti's Poem* (2006), illustrated by David Frampton; *A Story, a Story* (1970), illustrated by Gail E. Haley; and *Uncle Sam & Old Glory: Symbols of America* (2000), illustrated by Christopher Manson.

Photography and Digital Art

Many artists today use photography to illustrate picture books in lieu of traditional media. In 1971 Greenwillow published *Look Again*, conceived and photographed by Tana Hoban. It was one of the first picture books to feature photographs as the medium. Prior to *Look Again,* photographs were primarily used in informational titles. Some artists combine photographs with collage, creating an interesting effect. Ann Grifalconi did this very successfully in *Flyaway Girl* (1992). Photographs are still most commonly found in information books for children.

Digital artists use computers, scanners, and software as media.

Digital Art

Digital art can be the medium. *Mr. Lunch Takes a Plane Ride* (1993), illustrated by J.otto Seibold, is the first picture book created entirely on a computer, in this case a Macintosh. Some illustrators incorporate elements digitally and use software to manipulate or enhance the images. In *Michelangelo* (2000), illustrator Diane Stanley scanned images from Michelangelo's art and incorporated them into her picture book biography about the master. Whereas Seibold created his entire book digitally, other artists use technology to scan in line drawings or sketches and then use the software to add color and texture. Illustrator Bee Willey began to experiment with digital techniques after an injury, when her previous method of laying down large amounts of color with crayon became difficult. Over a period of time she began to incorporate more digital techniques into her work, often achieving unexpected results. Today, many artists use technology to replace tasks once done by hand. Illustrator Lane Smith used to spray acrylic varnish onto his oil paintings, which bubbled up and created texture. Smith can duplicate the same effect on the computer without using messy chemicals. One of the advantages of adding color digitally is that artists can explore a variety of colors without having to mix paint. More and more artists are exploring the possibilities of working digitally, and it is becoming increasingly commonplace. Early examples of picture books enhanced digitally include *Cook-a-Doodle-Doo* (1999), by Janet Stevens; *Henny Penny* (2000), by Jane Wattenberg; and *Bright and Early Thursday Evening* (1999), by Don Wood and Audrey Wood.

Photography

Photography is most common in informational books for children; however, many artists also use it to illustrate picture books in lieu of traditional media. *Going Fishing* (2005) is the sixth of a series of picture books by Bruce McMillan set in Iceland. Unlike other media, photography allowed McMillan to access the immediacy of living in a frigid landscape in a series of breathtaking panoramas. The day-to-day aspects of a fishing family in Iceland are captured in startling close-ups that reveal both the joy and hardships of living in a northern climate. Some artists combine photographs with collage, creating an interesting effect. In *Hard Hat Area* (2004), illustrator Susan L. Roth took photographs from two high locations in New York City to create a photomontage that she used as a background for her collage art. Ann Grifalconi did this very successfully in *Flyaway Girl* (1992). For other examples of photography, see *Harvest* (2001), photographed by George Ancona; *Look Again* (1971), photographed by Tana Hoban; and *Chidi Only Likes Blue: An African Book of Colors* (1997), photographed by Ifeoma Onyefulu.

ARTISTIC STYLE

Artistic style refers to artistic expression that has been developed over time, sometimes centuries, with many identifiable characteristics. For instance, consider the attention given to light and quick brush strokes in impressionism. Style can also refer to the distinguishable features that set one artist's work apart from another's. There are endless examples, but consider the fine lines and cross-hatching technique of Peter Sís or the bold colors and graphic quality of Lois Ehlert. Some illustrators' work is more distinctive than others. Stephen Gammell's work is instantly recognizable by swift pencil marks and paint splatters that appear to be cast off, on closer inspection giving his work a distinctive quality. Some picture book illustrators work in many different styles. David Shannon's artistic style in *No, David!* (1998) is naïve, while most of his other work is expressionistic, such as *The Rough-Face Girl* (1992), an Algonquin retelling of "Cinderella." In *How I Became a Pirate* (2003), Shannon's style merges elements of the cartoon style with expressionism for a comic effect that suits the hilarious tale. Rachel Isadora is another illustrator who explores many styles, ranging from realistic in *Luke Goes to Bat* (2005), to pop art reminiscent of Andy Warhol in *ABC Pop!* (1999), to stylized illustrations with a folk art appeal in *The Princess and the Pea* (2007). Learning to identify and understand a particular style can heighten the reading experience. Though Shannon works in many styles, with experience, readers are usually able to identify what aspects of each style make an illustration a David Shannon book.

Although there are distinctive hallmarks of each artistic style, personal interpretation can lead to using different terms or making different identifications altogether. For instance, in this guide we consider the illustrations in *Ox-Cart Man* (1981) to be an example of folk art style, whereas librarian Kathleen T. Horning identifies the art as an example of naïve style. *Abstract* and *expressionistic* are often used to describe the same picture book. For example, in this guide Frank Morrison's illustrations in *Jazzy Miz Mozetta* (2004) are categorized as abstract, but another reader may think that they are indicative of the expressionistic style. Nine styles are discussed in this guide: abstract, cartoon art, expressionism, impressionism, folk art, naïve art, realism, romanticism, and surrealism.

Abstract Art

Abstract art is nonrepresentational, departing from a literal representation of reality and truth. It depicts concepts, ideas, or emotions in an attempt to get at their essence. Abstract art focuses on intrinsic form and surface quality. Artists exaggerate or simplify objects and forms, placing emphasis on mood and feeling without regard for direct representation. In *Abstract Alphabet: A Book of Animals* (2000), illustrator Paul Cox substitutes abstract shapes for the letters of the alphabet. Astute readers must decipher the disconnected blobs and flattened geometric forms that ultimately spell out the names of the animals referred to in the subtitle. In *Penguin Dreams* (1999), illustrated by J.otto Seibold, the asymmetrical images, created on a computer, complement the distorted landscape in which they reside. For other examples of abstract style, see *Tippintown: A Guided Tour* (2003), illustrated by Calef Brown; *Jazzy Miz Mozetta* (2004), illustrated by Frank Morrison; *Max Makes a Million* (1990) illustrated by Maira Kalman; *Enemy Pie* (2000), illustrated by Tara Calahan King; *You Forgot Your Skirt, Amelia Bloomer* (2000), illustrated by Chesley McLaren; *Norma No Friends* (1999), illustrated by Paula Metcalf; *That New Animal* (2005), illustrated by Pierre Pratt; *The Maestro Plays* (1994), illustrated by Vladimir Radunsky; *Only Passing Through: The Story of Sojourner Truth* (2000), illustrated by R. Gregory Christie; and *The Little Giant* (2004), illustrated by Sergio Ruzzier.

Cartoon Art

Cartoon art is reminiscent of Saturday morning cartoons. Pictures are silly and goofy, and the artist makes no attempt to make the art appear realistic. Many artists have very distinctive styles and are easily recognizable, for example Tomie de Paola's use of small black dots for eyes and short, squat bodies for characters. Kevin Henkes's use of panels and vignettes in his illustrations make his picture books distinctive. James Marshall (1942–1992) was one of the most prolific picture book illustrators. The illustrations for his first book, *Plink, Plink, Plink* (1971), written by Byrd Baylor, were largely overlooked. His second book for children, *George and Martha* (1972), launched a long and successful career that included six more titles featuring the adventures of the lovable hippopotami. His parody retellings of fairy tales were particularly popular. *Goldilocks and the Three Bears* (1988) was a 1989 Caldecott Honor Book. He also illustrated the series The Stupids and Miss Nelson, written by Harry Allard. Known for his ability to add depth and substance to seemingly simple stories, Marshall created or co-created more than 40 books for children. For other examples of cartoon-style art; see *Parts* (1997), illustrated by Tedd Arnold; *Strega Nona* (1975), illustrated by Tomie de Paola; *Comic Adventures of Boots* (2002), illustrated by Satoshi Kitamura; *Lilly's Purple Plastic Purse* (1996), illustrated by Kevin Henkes; *The Day Jimmy's Boa Ate the Wash* (1980), illustrated by Steven Kellogg; *Martha Speaks* (1992), illustrated by Susan Meddaugh; and *The Adventures of Robin Hood* (1995), illustrated by Marcia Williams.

Expressionism

Expressionism is a style that conveys the emotion experienced by the subject. Developed by twentieth-century artists, expressionistic art has the appearance of reality, but facial expressions or structural lines may be exaggerated or distorted for effect. It is a style commonly used in picture book illustration, but there are many illustrators whose works stand out. For examples of expressionistic style, see *The Rough-Face Girl* (1992), illustrated by David Shannon; *Zathura* (2002), illustrated by Chris Van Allsburg; *When Harriet Met Sojourner* (2007), illustrated by Shane W. Evans; and *Rapunzel* (1997), illustrated by Paul O. Zelinsky.

Impressionism

Impressionism is a style developed by nineteenth-century French painters that focuses on light. Artists use paint to create a broken or reflected sense of light, which captures a sensory impression of life rather than a detailed portrayal of reality. Bright colors and swift brush strokes often mark impressionist art. In *Lon Po Po: A Red-Riding Tale from China* (1989), illustrator Ed Young allowed the play of light and shadow to the balance illustrations. Young, who dedicated the book to the wolves of the world who allow their name to be used as a symbol of humans' fear of darkness, often places the wolf in dark shadows, yet his eyes shine brightly with light. For other examples of impressionistic style, see *Swift* (2007), illustrated by Robert J. Blake; *Arlene Sardine* (1998), illustrated by Chris Raschka; *Freedom's Gifts: A Juneteenth Story* (1997), illustrated by Sharon Wilson; and *Lord of the Cranes* (2000), illustrated by Jian Jiang Chen.

Folk Art

Folk art expresses traditions passed from generation to generation and reflects commonly held beliefs, values, and customs. Although similar to naïve art, what makes folk art distinct is the sense of place often inherent in the illustrations. The artist spends a lot of time researching costumes, mood, and spirit. The finished illustration has a homemade or handcrafted look. For examples of folk art style, see *Ox-Cart Man* (1971), illustrated by Barbara Cooney; *Romeo and Juliet* (1998), illustrated by Margaret Early; *The Girl Who Loved Wild Horses* (1979), illustrated by Paul Goble; and *The Folks in the Valley* (1992), illustrated by Stefano Vitale.

Naïve Art

Naïve art is very childlike and is identifiable by its flat, two-dimensional quality. There is little detail and no regard for anatomy. Artists who employ the naïve style often do not have formal artistic training. For examples of naïve style, see *Dinosaurs; Dinosaurs* (1989), illustrated by Byron Barton; *One of Those Days* (2006), illustrated by Rebecca Doughty; *Tippy-Tippy-Tippy Hide* (2007), illustrated by G. Brian Karas; *New York; New York!: The Big Apple from A to Z* (2005), illustrated by Frané Lessac; *Neeny Coming; Neeny Going* (1996), illustrated by Synthia Saint James; and *A Chair for My Mother* (1983), illustrated by Vera B. Williams.

Realism

Realism is representational of everyday life. Subjects and objects are portrayed with detailed accuracy, shown as they appear in real life. Realistic paintings feature recognizable objects and are filled with detail, appearing almost like a photograph. For examples of realistic style, see *Amazing Grace* (1991), illustrated by Caroline Binch; *Luke Goes to Bat* (2005), illustrated by Rachel Isadora; and *Kamishibai Man* (2005), illustrated by Allen Say.

Romanticism

Romanticism is not a style commonly associated with picture books; however, it is sometimes employed in picture books. This style emphasizes the opulent atmosphere around the subject in a bold, dramatic manner. In *Cinderella* (2000), illustrator K. Y. Craft uses a rich color palette that is dark and haunting to create a sumptuous atmosphere, bringing the transformation of Cinderella full circle with minute detail evocative of the past, painstakingly applied. The romantic style is most powerful when applied to folklore and fairy tales. For other examples of romantic style, see *Sleeping Beauty* (2002), illustrated by K. Y. Craft; *Cinderella* (2002), illustrated by Ruth Sanderson; *The Magic Nesting Doll* (2002), illustrated by Jacqueline K. Ogburn; and *The Tale of the Firebird* (2002), illustrated by Gennady Spirin.

Surrealism

Surrealism is characterized by imaginative details and provocative and bizarre images. Images may be distorted or have dreamlike qualities that are marked by startling shifts in objects and people. For example, in *Dinner at Magritte's* (1995) illustrator Michael Garland conceived a boy's imaginary visit with noted surrealist Rene Magritte. The picture book is a tribute to both Magritte and Salvador Dali, with imagery from both artists' paintings, including Magritte's bowler hats and Dali's melted clocks. In *Something's Not Quite Right* (2002), illustrator Guy Billout created startling imagery that alters perception and challenges viewers. Illustrations are independent scenes with phrases in which Billout juxtaposes the extraordinary with the ordinary. For example, in "Ice Age" a ship navigates a street of ice, splitting the frozen ground with its prow. Anthony Browne, Chris Van Allsburg, and David Wiesner are known for the surrealistic imagery in their books. For other examples of surrealistic style, see *Five Fingers and the Moon* (1994), illustrated by Aljoscha Blau; *Voices in the Park* (1998), illustrated by Anthony Browne; *Freedom Child of the Sea* (1995), illustrated by Julia Gukova; and *The Three Pigs* (2001), illustrated by David Wiesner.

CONCLUSION

Picture space and composition are essential to the structure of an illustration. This chapter explored materials, techniques, and styles that artists use when creating illustrations for picture books. Illustrators use design principles and art elements to create picture space and a pleasing composition. The choice of medium and an illustrator's style are integral to the overall feeling a picture has. Through the application of these principles, an illustrator is able to create a picture book that extends and often alters the text.

ENDNOTES

1. Many art terms have different meaning and associations, depending on context. The seven design principles used in this guide were selected because they appeared most frequently in the reading done for this topic. Some critics cite fewer or even combine some that are discussed separately here. Not all critics agree on these or refer to them using the same terminology.

2. The seven elements are based on my understanding of the art elements.

3. I chose to break down the types of media used in picture books into five categories—painting, drawing, sculptural, printmaking, and photography/digital—because I think each medium included in each technique has similar characteristics.

Chapter 4

Format or Genre?

When it is very well done, it is an artistic achievement worthy of respectful examination and honor. Even failures, and especially near misses, deserve the kind of attention and understanding given to serious creative endeavors.
—Karla Kuskin, "To Get a Little More of the Picture:
Reviewing Picture Books," *The Horn Book* (1998)

In This Chapter
- Format
- Genres

Critics, scholars, educators, and librarians often refer to the picture book canon as a genre. This chapter attempts to challenge that assumption by exploring the various types of picture books, from the standpoint that picture books have both format and genre. Both are two important aspects to consider when examining picture books. In this chapter "picture book" is used very broadly when looking at the various types readers encounter. Analyzing books for both their physical aspects (format) and content (genre) is important.

Does it matter if picture books are called a format or a genre? This guide takes the position that it does. Picture books are a format. In other words, within the field of children's literature, picture books are defined by their physical characteristics (as are picture storybooks, illustrated books, and informational picture books). This does not begin to address design, illustration, and narrative issues. What it does do is draw attention to the components of picture books.

The term *genre*[1] is often used to define the field of picture books. This is problematic and often confusing because there is a clear distinction between format and genre: format dictates the physical aspects—presentation or arrangement. For instance, the lack of words in a wordless book is a physical characteristic, as are the vertical positioning and larger typefaces in a beginning reader.

Genre emphasizes content, which is the type of story, its style, subject matter, or other shared characteristics. Although many people use the term *genre* to describe picture books as a whole, it is actually the physical characteristics that set them apart from other types of children's literature.

Within the format of picture book are types, categories, and genres. *The Cat and the Hat* (1957) is an easy reader (type) *and* an animal story (genre). David Weisner's *Tuesday* (1991) is a wordless book (type) *and* magical realism (genre). (See figure 4.1.)

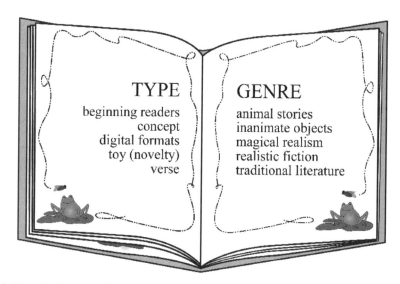

TYPE

beginning readers
concept
digital formats
toy (novelty)
verse

GENRE

animal stories
inanimate objects
magical realism
realistic fiction
traditional literature

Figure 4.1. "Type" addresses the physical characteristics that these types of books have in common. "Genre" addresses the content, which is the type of story, its style, or its subject matter.

On the other hand, the very distinct format of picture books dictates that these stories share other characteristics that may make them *seem* like a genre. Though this guide asserts that picture books are a format first, it concedes that readers may refer to the picture book canon as a genre. For example, narratives, both visual and verbal, may dictate a certain rhythm to the story—where the reader is looking at an image and then reading text, and perhaps both simultaneously. In this case, picture books could easily be perceived as a genre. Also, picture books tend to have stories that have happy endings. They appeal to a specific set of readers. In fact, most readers probably consider beginning (or easy) readers a form of fiction. This guide takes the position that there are types of picture book—again, used broadly. For example, *Horn Book* places reviews of beginning readers in its "fiction" section.

This differentiation among formats, types, and genres may seem like nitpicking, but when readers are exploring many books and attempting to make an informed judgment, distinguishing between type and genre becomes important. Readers must consider the format and content separately, and then again, together. Similar to the relationship between the narrative and illustrations, format (outside) and content (inside) are components that make up a book.

FORMAT

In addition to the broad categories of picture book, picture storybook, illustrated book, and informational picture book, there are subcategories, defined by particular characteristics that make them distinct: beginning readers, concept books, digital formats, toy (novelty) books, and verse.

Beginning Readers

Beginning readers are transitional books for children moving from picture books that are read to them to chapter books that they read on their own. They are also called easy readers, first readers, new readers, and early readers. These books are designed to be read with minimal or no assistance from an adult. They provide early readers with important tools as they develop and hone their reading skills. The principal difference between a picture book and a picture storybook is the amount of text; titles with longer text are often referred to as picture storybooks. Like picture storybooks, beginning readers depend on illustration to help tell the story, but the pictures, although important, are secondary. People commonly assume that picture books are ideal for children who are learning to read because they generally have short text and pictures. Although many picture books are easy for children to read independently, the majority contain vocabulary above the level of a beginning reader (Horning 1997a).

The Cat and the Hat (1957), the story that introduced Dr. Seuss's most famous character, began in a bet between the author and his publisher at Random House. Seuss, challenged to write a book with fewer than 250 words, wrote *The Cat in the Hat* in only 236 words.[2] It became the first of a type of book for children known as "beginning" or "easy" readers. Not long after Random House introduced the Beginner Books line, Harper launched its I Can Read series with *Little Bear* (1957) by Elsa Holmelund Minarik, the first of five Little Bear books. Another outstanding beginning reader is *Frog and Toad Are Friends* (1970). A Caldecott Honor book, it is the first of four titles in Arnold Lobel's Frog and Toad series. Another in the series, *Frog and Toad Together* (1972), was a Newbery Honor book. Award committees rarely acknowledged beginning readers before 2004, when the American Library Association created the Geisel Award (see box). This honor attests to the quality of Lobel's Frog and Toad series (Horning 1997a).

Some beginning readers are more story based, such as those by Dr. Seuss and the Henry and Mudge series by Cynthia Rylant. When reading these books, children don't feel that they are "learning to read" or improving reading skills." Other books, such as those in Random House's Step into Reading series, are specifically developed to help children improve their reading skills through a series of levels. Readers with stepped levels can have anywhere from a few words to several paragraphs per page. The use and number of sight words, repetition, and predictability also varies (Horning 1997a). However, both share the same physical makeup. Beginning readers always have a vertical orientation, usually measure 6 by 9 inches, and have 48 to 64 pages. Illustrations are usually placed in the upper portion of the page, and the number of lines per page is more or less consistent.

Beginning readers share other characteristics that make them ideal for children learning to read. Typefaces are usually 18 point or larger. They also have short sentences and fewer lines per pages, as opposed to a picture book. The white space in beginning readers is used purposefully. There is extra space between words and lines, and text tends to be placed on the bottom half of the page or at least placed consistently from page to page.

To honor outstanding beginning reader titles, the Association of Library Service to Children (ALSC), a division of the American Library Association, established the Theodor Seuss Geisel Award in 2004. The award is given annually to a title published in the United States the previous calendar year. Unlike awards that honor just text or just illustration, the Geisel Award is presented to both the author and illustrator of the winning title. Presented for the first time in 2006, the award recognizes authors and illustrators who demonstrate literary and artistic achievement in the creation of beginning, or easy, readers. The first winners were author Cynthia Rylant and illustrator Suçie Stevenson for *Henry and Mudge and the Great Grandpas* (2005). The pair has been working together on the series since 1987, when *Henry and Mudge*, the first book in the series, was published. In addition to a winner, a varying number of honor books are also awarded.

Concept Picture Books

It is generally accepted that concept books introduce letters, numbers, size, shapes, and colors. However, it is an overstatement to claim that children learn concepts from books (Carlson 1996). In actuality, children learn through direct experience with objects, actions, and events. Later in their development, children learn additional concepts by viewing pictures of objects, actions, and events. Concept books are not a replacement for firsthand experience; however, they can be powerful tools for early childhood learning. By pairing books with firsthand experience, adults can help children expand their understanding of concepts (Carlson 1996).

Understanding types of concepts helps educators, librarians, and parents identify concept books. Cognitive skills that children learn can be divided into classification, seriation, number, temporal, and spatial.

Classification is the ability to sort and group. Children note similarities and differences by sorting and grouping objects. Picture books that cover classification include *Spots, Feathers, and Curly Tails* (1988), illustrated by Nancy Tafuri; *Caps for Sale* (1940), illustrated by Slobodkina Esphyr; and *How Many Snails?* (1988), illustrated by Donald Crews.

Seriation is the relationship between objects and the ability to place them in order or sequence. Children learn to count cardinal numbers (one, two, three) and ordinal numbers (first, second, third). This skill includes counting by multiples, such as twos, fives, tens, etc. Examples of picture books that cover seriation concepts are *First the Egg* (2007), illustrated by Laura Vaccaro Seeger; and *A Remainder of One* (1995), illustrated by Bonnie MacKain.

Number is an understanding of quantity, such as more/less. One-to-one correspondence is the matching of items, such as shoes and socks. In the beginning a child engages in rote counting without attaching meaning. Later a child engages in rational counting, that is, attaches meaning, such as the name of the number to the numeral representation, or seeing 10 objects and associating them with the numeral 10. Examples of picture books that cover number concepts aree *Ten Black Dots* (1986), illustrated by Donald Crews; *The Doorbell Rang* (1986), illustrated by Pat Hutchins; and *The Orange Had 8 Slices* (1992), illustrated by Donald Crews.

The *temporal* concept is the gradual understanding of time as a continuum, such as before and after. It also includes the order of events and the relationship between cause and effect. Picture books that cover temporal concepts include *Today Is Monday* (1993), illustrated by Eric Carle; and *Time Flies* (1994), illustrated by Eric Rohmann.

The *spatial* concept is an understanding of the way objects and people occupy and move through space. This also includes spatial relationships, such as on top of the table, behind the wall, etc. Picture books that cover spatial concepts include *Over Under* (2005), illustrated by Tom Slaughter; *Apollo* (2002), illustrated by Caroline Grégoire; *Pezzettino* (1975, 2006), illustrated by Leo Lionni; and *Shrinking Mouse* (1997), illustrated by Pat Hutchins.

Concept books are intended to clarify and help children learn their letters, numbers, and other concepts—they should never frustrate or confuse children. Clarity is very important, so that children do not become confused. Objects and numbers should be easily identifiable; there should be a close relationship between text and pictures. In the case of counting books, the numbers of objects to be counted should be clear and accurate. Illustrations should be uncluttered, with plenty of space to set off the distinction between the numbers and objects. In figure 4.2 (p. 88), the image complements the text. A child learning to count can easily identify that the image of one fly is representative of the text. In figure 4.3 (p. 88), the distinction is less clear. The illustration features three flies and the text reads, "One angry fly." If a child cannot identify which fly is angry, he or she may be confused or even frustrated.

There are many exemplary concept books in picture book format. Some authors specialize in concept titles. Tana Hoban's photographic concept books have charmed generations. When her *Look Again!* (1971) was initially published, photography as a medium in picture books was rare. Hoban's picture books are filled with stylized photographs of everyday objects that challenged the notion that photography was not appropriate as a medium in picture books. In *Look Again!* the reader finds die-cut shapes on a black page with a hint of a photograph showing through. When the page is turned, the actual photograph appears—sometimes revealing what the reader least expects. The success of *Look Again!* inspired Hoban to create other books in a similar style. *Take Another Look* (1981), *Look Look Look* (1988), and *Look Book* (1996) follow the same wordless format.

Figure 4.2. A child reading this book can clearly make a distinction between the image and the text.

Figure 4.3. The ambiguity between the illustration and the text here may be confusing for a child.

Concept books are commonly used in a learning environment. The best concept books feature objects for children to identify that are spaced on the page. They also have consistent themes, with a typeface that makes letters and numbers identifiable. For example, in a Halloween-themed title, although it might look visually pleasing, a spidery script or Gothic-style lettering to embody a sense of horror or fear may be difficult for young children to read. Instead, there should be a close text/picture relationship, with the illustrations matching the key word.

Through my photographs and through open eyes I try to say, "Look! There are shapes here and everywhere, things to count, colors to see and always, surprises."
—Tana Hoban, autobiographical essay in the *Washington Post*

Alphabet Books

Alphabet books fall in three categories: theme, potpourri, and sequential. Theme alphabet books follow a thematic or topical focus. Cathi Hepworth's *Antics!* (1992) is a theme alphabet book because it follows the theme of ants. Hepworth cleverly conceived a sophisticated alphabet book in which all the entries from A to Z have the root "ant" somewhere in the word. For instance, for "B" there is Brilli**ant** with an accompanying illustration of an ant scientist. The letter "O" for Observ**ant** features an ant dressed as Sherlock Holmes viewing something through a magnifying glass. Although the title is intriguing and fun, many of the words used (e.g., xanthophile, quarantine) will be beyond the vocabulary of most children.

Potpourri alphabet books offer the author the greatest freedom, tying alphabet letters to any number of specific objects; they are the reason for so many "A is for. . . " titles. The objects depicted in these titles have no apparent connection to each other—they simply begin with the appropriate letter of the alphabet. Wanda Gág's *The ABC Bunny* (1933) is an example. Although the bunny is the constant, the objects selected to represent letters have no obvious connection.

The sequential story alphabet book relies on a continuous story line to introduce the alphabet to children. *The Story of Z* (1992) is a sequential story alphabet book with a continuous storyline. In *The Story of Z* the letter "Z," tired of being last all the time, secedes from the alphabet. However, things don't turn out as she planned. "Z" quickly realizes how many words depend on her, and she makes amends by being the last letter of the alphabet and thus always last in line. In *Bad Kitty* (2005) illustrator Nick Bruel incorporates four alphabet stories into one feline tale about a kitty who reacts badly when her owners run out of her favorite foods. Bruel's engaging cartoon illustrations capture the antics of Kitty, who ultimately atones for her bad behavior—alphabetically.

There is a lot of diversity within this seemingly simple category of picture books. In addition, some titles are more appropriate for younger readers, while others appeal to all ages. In *The Turn-Around, Upside-Down Alphabet Book* (2004), illustrator Lisa Campbell Ernst presents an optical journey in which letters are represented by the bold graphics. Other titles appropriate for younger children include *Alphabatics* (1986) and *Chicka Chicka Boom Boom* (1991).

Other alphabet books will appeal to older children. In *Abstract Alphabet: A Book of Animals* (2000), illustrator Paul Cox substitutes abstract shapes for the letters of the alphabet. Readers are challenged to decipher the disconnected blobs and flattened geometric forms that ultimately spell out the names of the animals referred to in the subtitle. Other titles for older readers include Graeme Base's *Animalia* (1986) and Lucy Micklethwait's *I Spy: The Alphabet in Art* (1992), which require careful examination. Titles that introduce other cultures, such as *Ashanti to Zulu* (1976) and *A to Zen: A Book of Japanese Culture* (1992), or aspects of history, such as *The Folks in the Valley: A Pennsylvania Dutch ABC* (1992), will also appeal to older readers.

Number Books

Number books range from simple to complex. Donald Crews's *Ten Black Dots* (1986) and Eric Carle's *1, 2, 3 to the Zoo* (1974) are intended for preschoolers, whereas Lloyd Moss's *Zin Zin Zin a Violin* (1995) is designed for older children. Moss uses a rollicking rhyme with a singsong narrative to complement Priceman's delightfully detailed paintings. Some number books have a narrative built in, such as *Just a Minute: A Trickster Tale and Counting Book* (2003). Others use themes that allow the illustrator to freely incorporate an idea or design, such as Ellen Stoll Walsh's *Mouse Count* (1991) and *One Leaf Rides the Wind* (2002), which features haiku. *Quilt Counting* (2002) by Lesa Cline-Ransome builds on the theme of the tools needed to make a quilt; James Ransome's paintings have a folksy feel that complements Cline-Ransome's stitched narrative.

Other Types of Concept Books

Other types of concept books deal with themes of color, shape, size, and opposites. Like alphabet and number titles, they can be simple or complex.

Color books introduce basic concepts, such as how secondary colors are made from primary colors. In *Mouse Paint* (1989) by Ellen Stoll Walsh, three mice begin an adventure in color when they discover three jars of paint—red, blue, and yellow. Walsh slowly introduces the secondary colors through various mishaps and the curious mice, which are continually amazed by the new colors they create when two are mixed together.

Innovative shape books do more than show the basic shapes of circle, square, and triangle; they introduce basic spatial and geometric concepts. Imaginative authors and illustrators use shape books to introduce other subjects as well. In *A Triangle for Adaora: An African book of Shapes* (2000), Ifeoma Onyefulu explores the Africa landscape, using vivid photographs. What is so appealing about this book is that it doubles as a cultural introduction.

The Wing on a Flea (2001) was originally published in 1961. Ed Emberly's rhyming text is paired with basic shapes found all around. "A Triangle could be the wing on a flea or a beak on a bird, if you'll just look and see." Lucy Micklethwait has created an intriguing series of concept books based on great works of art. *I Spy Shapes in Art* (2004) features paintings by David Hockney, Henri Matisse, Georgia O'Keeffe, and Andy Warhol. In addition to introducing concepts, it also opens the doors to the world of fine art to children. Other titles by Micklethwait include *I Spy: An Alphabet in Art* (1992) and *I Spy Two Eyes: Numbers in Art* (1993). The narrative in the series is built on the timeless refrain, "I spy with my little eye . . . ."

Concept books that introduce opposites can feature anything from size to emotions. A new edition of a 1938 classic, *Bumble Bugs and Elephants: A Big and Little Book* (2006) by Margaret Wise Brown, pairs opposites of size against each other in classic paintings by Clement Hurd. "Once upon a time/there was a great big bumble bug/and a tiny little bumble bug" and so forth. The font changes from large to small to complement the illustrations. In *Where Is the Green Sheep?* (2004), first-time illustrator Judy Horacek introduces opposites in a series of lighthearted illustrations that complement Mem Fox's lyrical prose. The refrain "But where is the green sheep?" repeated throughout the book is introduced on the front flap.

Books That Combine Concepts

Many concept books combine several concepts—shapes and colors, number and letters, and so forth. For example, in *Color Zoo* (1989) Lois Ehlert masterfully introduces both shape and color, including the basic shapes (circle, square, oval, triangle) and the primary and secondary colors. The boldly designed book is presented in a series of cutouts layered in such a way that the illustration changes with each turn of the page. Each configuration is an animal: a tiger's face (a circle shape) and two ears disappear with a page turn to leave viewers with a square within which is a mouse. The mouse's square frame, removed, reveals a fox. There are three such series, and each ends with a brief round up of the shapes used so far.

In *26 Letters and 99 Cents* (1987) Tana Hoban combines letters and numbers in an innovative way. The book is both a letter and number identification book, with the added bonus of introducing small monetary sums. Letters are presented in both upper- and lowercase and then paired with objects representing each letter. When the reader flips the book over, Hoban shows and describes numbers and coins. Hoban pairs photos of numbers with pennies, nickels, dimes, and quarters in a variety of combinations.

In *Food for Thought* (2005) Saxton Freymann and Joost Elffers explore colors, shapes, number, letters, and opposites with their signature fruit and vegetable creations. Bright backgrounds with uncluttered design place the focus on the concepts.

Digital Formats

Children's book publishers have been slow to explore digital formats. Picture books in particular are challenging to publish in digital format. Like printed picture books, reproducing illustration digitally can be expensive. In addition, the number of images associated with picture books means that an electronic picture book has a larger file size than an e-book that is just text.[3] The interdependence of pictures and text and the complexity of the target customers are two major issues that challenge publishers of children's e-books. However, digital picture books have recently begun to appear, and whether the reading public will embrace or shun them is yet to be determined.

An e-book is an electronic or digital version of a printed book. Some digital picture books offer readers opportunities to interact with the text by incorporating animation, sound, music, and narration. The final product is allows readers to participate in the story. Digital books are read on computers or other electronic devices. Some companies allow their software to be downloaded so that a reader is unnecessary. There are picture books that begin as print, and there are digitized picture books that may never be printed.

Two primary entities offer digital picture books at the time this guide was written: the International Children's Digital Library (ICDL), a nonprofit organization, and a company called Lookybook, founded in 2008.

The ICDL's slogan is "a library for the world's children." The collection boasts over 2,400 picture books in 41 languages. Readers can view picture books on the ICDL Web site. ICDL also offers a reading device that can be downloaded, which allows users to read picture books offline. The promise of the International Children's Digital Library is free access to a multitude of picture books from cultures children might not otherwise be exposed to. With the cost of bringing international picture books across borders, the ICDL holds great promise for the future. The Web site is www.icdlbooks.org.

Lookybook, founded in 2008, is an online site that offers digital editions of hundreds of picture books. As of early 2008, the site had over 200 titles, with a goal of having more than 1,000 titles digitized by summer 2008. Readers flip through pages as if they were actually reading a book. They can also add books to a personalized bookshelf and write recommendations. The service is free for now, but may charge fees in the future. The Web site is www.lookybook.com.

In a provocative *Horn Book* article, "Liftoff: When Books Leave the Page," illustrator Jean Gralley explores a world with "Books Unbound." Gralley created an accompanying online presentation, which she gave at the opening exhibition for Children Should Be Seen: The Image of the Child in American Picture-Book Art, which was organized by The Eric Carle Museum of Picture Book Art in Amherst, Massachusetts, and the Katonah Museum of Art in Katonah, New York. In "Books Unbound," Gralley explores the possibilities of digital picture books. Gralley (2006) states that print picture books are "flat, uni-directional and static." She goes on to state that digital picture books are "dimensional, multi-directional, and in-motion." Readers can view Gralley's "Books Unbound" presentation at www.jeangralley.com/books_unbound.

There is a difference in what Gralley proposes, which can often look like nothing more than an Adobe Flash presentation, and what Lookybook and ICDL offer. The latter have digitized versions of print picture books. Gralley proposes creating digital picture books that begin on a computer and are viewed onscreen, perhaps never existing in print format.

Although the technology is exciting, the thrill of the digital versions of picture books may eventually wane. In "Accessing the International Children's Digital Library," scholar June Cummins (2004) discusses how her son's initial excitement with the ICDL ultimately faded. After several successive nights of snuggling on her lap to read a book from the ICDL collection on the computer, he asked his mother to "read a book in bed." The Lookybook Web site even features a disclaimer, "nothing will replace the magic of reading a book with your child at bedtime, but we aim to replace the overwhelming and frustrating process of finding the right books for parents and their kids."

Toy (Novelty)

Toy Books

Sometimes called novelty books, toy books include board books, pop-up books, flap books, and cut-out books. They can be simple, with flaps and tabs, or very complex, requiring upward of 300 pieces per book, and they demand interaction, which may be why children love them so much. They provide a wonderful doorway to children's literature and are quite fun to incorporate into storytime.

Board Books

Board books are made of laminated cardboard pages, with sturdy, rounded edges. A baby or toddler views a board books simply as a toy, and adults can expect children to handle them roughly, chew on them, and throw them around rather than "read" them. There are several categories of board books. High contrast board books have a striking balance between the object and the background. Touch and feel books have textured surfaces, ranging from fuzzy to smooth. Songs and rhyming books feature popular chants and rhymes paired with colorful photos and simple illustrations. Concept board books, like concept picture books, feature simple concepts in an accessible format. Unlike picture books, concept board books have few, if any words. The focus is on very basic concepts: colors, shapes, animals, letters, and numbers.

Pop-Up Books

These books feature three-dimensional illustrations that "pop" up as the page is opened. More than just an illustrator, the creator of a pop-up book is a master of detail and manipulation. Often called a paper engineer, the pop-up artist blends imagination and design into intricate, three-dimensional art dazzling to behold. Months of careful planning are required from first draft to finished product. Robert Sabuda, the most successful paper engineer working today, admits to constantly cutting his fingers as he designs a new book. Pop-up books are constructed by hand; that's right—even with all of the technology we have today, machines are still not able to mass produce pop-up books.

Flap Books

These books feature flaps that hide certain parts of the picture or introduce an alternate idea into the illustration. Lift-the-flap books have cardboard flaps that readers can open and close throughout the story, making the reading experience hands-on and interactive. They can be simple, like Eric Hill's *Where's Spot?* (1980), a title that targets toddlers, or complex, such as Robert Sabuda's *Christmas Alphabet* (1994, 2004), which is a pop-up book with flaps that appeals to children as well as adults.

Cut-Out Books

Like flap books, cut-outs rely heavily on die-cut to enhance the story by hiding and then revealing aspects of the story. In Simms Taback's *Joseph Had a Little Overcoat* (1999), Joseph's coat is getting old and tattered, so he makes a jacket. When the jacket begins to wear out, he makes a vest, and so on down to a small button. What is so captivating about Taback's illustrations is how the die-cuts move the story forward. As the page is turned, readers discover what Joseph fashions from the piece of clothing that has worn out.

In *Go Away Big Green Monster* (1993), Ed Emberly begins his tale with a black page and two big yellow eyes floating above the bold white text. "Big Green Monster has two big yellow eyes." Each successive page adds a new feature until the monster is complete. The story continues, and as the pages are turned, the monster slowly disappears. The final page is once again black, with the words "And don't come back! Until I say so."

Verse

Verse includes poetry, lullabies, nursery rhymes, and other rhyming texts. What makes something a "verse" is its format, whether written in formal lines (usually short) or stanzas, using techniques of meter, rhyme, metaphor, or simile—or combinations thereof.

Children love rhythm and rhyme. The bouncing lyrics and pace invite participation, and they are fun for group reading. From lullabies to songs to jump rope rhymes, children love the singsong aspect of verse.

Although infants and toddlers delight in verse, studies show that when asked, most children claim they dislike poetry. Is it poetry they dislike, or the idea of poetry? Poetry is fun; learning about poetry too often isn't. But learning about the different forms of poetry and poetic devices can be fun. Picture books can significantly change the way children feel about poetry. The visual complement of the illustrations and design invite children to engage, despite initial resistance or feelings of dislike.

A good selection of single poem picture books is available. These are pictures books with just one poem, such as *Uptown* (2000) by Bryan Collier. There are also titles that build on a theme, such as *Laughing Tomatoes and Other Spring Poems = Jitomates risuenos y otros poemas de primavera* (1997) by Francisco X. Alarcon (which also happens to be a bilingual collection in English and Spanish).

Verse includes all forms of poetry (acrostic, concrete, free verse, haiku, and limericks and nursery rhymes.

Poetry

Poetry takes many forms and affects readers and listeners differently. A wide range of topics and feelings can be found in children's poetry, from serious to silly and playful.

When introduced in early childhood, poetry helps a child build literacy skills and encourages the love of reading. Poetry gives children an outlet to express their creativity by allowing them to share their feelings and experiences. Children also enjoy listening to poetry, even if they don't know what all the words mean. The rhythm and rhyme, as well as the play on words, capture their attention, stimulating imagination. The repeated words and refrains and rhyme schemes remind children of people they know, places they have been, and experiences they have had.

Acrostic Poetry

In acrostics, the first letters of the lines, when read together vertically, spell out a word. The imagery and word are usually built upon the subject of the poem. Steven Schnur's *Autumn: An Alphabet Acrostic* (1997) is an example of the acrostic form in a picture book. Schnur paired up with illustrator Leslie Evans on three other titles: *Spring:* (1999), *Summer* (2001), and *Winter* (2002). Together the four books complete a series about the four seasons, with Evans's hand-colored linoleum cuts nicely complementing the theme.

Concrete Poems

These are shape poems. The letters and words (typography) are used to convey or extend the meaning of the poem. A famous example is "Mouse's Tale" from *Alice's Adventures in Wonderland* (1865) by Lewis Carroll, in which the words of the poem form the tail of a mouse. In *Meow Ruff* (2006) Joyce Sidman used concrete poetry as the vehicle to tell a story about a small dog who escapes and a little cat who is abandoned at curbside. The illustrator, Michelle Berg, who is also the designer, used flat colors and a variety of typefaces to showcase the power of the concrete poem form.

Free Verse

Free verse gives children the freedom to rhyme at any time, in any way, as much as they want . . . or not at all. Explaining free verse is difficult, because it doesn't follow any rules. Free verse encompasses various styles of poetry, including those that adhere to strict meter or rhyme. When free verse poems contain rhyme, it is usually applied freely. *Honey, I Love* (2003) by Eloise Greenfield, and Tom Feelings's *Soul Looks Back in Wonder* (1993) are examples of free verse picture books

Haiku

Haiku traditionally includes a reference to the seasons, known in Japanese as *kigo*, which translates as "season word." Haiku poems have 17 syllables in all. The first line has 5 syllables, the second line has 7 syllables, and the third line has 5 syllables. Imagery is the essence of haiku form, nature being a central theme. *If Not for the Cat: Haiku* (2004) by Jack Prelutsky is a haiku book built on the theme of animals.

Limericks

Limericks are funny poems with five lines that rhyme. The limerick rhyme scheme is A-A-B-B-A; in other words, lines 1, 2, and 5 rhyme and lines 3 and 4 rhyme. *Limerick!* (2004) is a collection of limericks by Edward Lear (1812–1888). Another example is *Uncle Switch: Loony Limericks* (1997) by X. J. Kennedy.

Nursery Rhymes

Nursery rhymes are rooted in the oral tradition, and they generally tell a story. The soothing, rhythmic sounds have been staples of childhood for centuries. In the eighteenth century, illustrated collections began appearing, and they still do with regularity.

Some of the most popular types of nursery rhymes are Mother Goose rhymes. Originating from many sources, passed down in folklore fashion, some were penned by famous authors and disseminated by publishers, generally without author attribution. Over time they have become collectively known as Mother Goose rhymes.

In 1697 Charles Perrault published *Histoires ou contes du temps passé* (*Histories and Tales of Long Ago, with Morals*). The frontispiece features an old woman circled by children, with the caption *Contes de ma mère l'oye* ("tales of my mother goose") underneath. This was the first appearance of the Mother Goose character, though the book contains none of the rhymes associated with Mother Goose. John Newbery attached the name Mother Goose to a collection published under the title *Mother Goose's Melody*, which includes the childhood staples "Jack Be Nimble," "Little Miss Muffett," and "Little Boy Blue," establishing the association with the wizened woman generations of children have come to know and love.

One of the most familiar versions of Mother Goose is Blanche Fisher Wright's *The Real Mother Goose*, published in 1916. The familiar black-and white checkerboard cover graces the shelves of many children.

Today Mother Goose rhymes have become a childhood staple. Among the favorite rhymes are "Jack Be Nimble" and "Little Jack Horner." Mother Goose has received numerous makeovers throughout the years. Illustrators who have honored her include Tomie de Paola, Rosemary Wells, and James Marshall.

In 1969 Eve Merriam retold the tales in *Inner City Mother Goose*. Reprinted in 1982 and again in 1996 with illustrations by David Diaz, Merriam's biting social commentary, though not suitable for children, is interesting to share with young adults. Other picture book versions include *William Joyce's Mother Goose* (1998) and *Babushka's Mother Goose* (1995) by Patricia Polacco.

GENRES

Genre is a literary term used to designate a type of story with shared characteristics—for example, mystery, adventure, romance, science fiction, history, traditional literature, and anthropomorphic (animal) stories. Genre theory is a field of study that is beyond the scope of this book. Depending on how readers approach the concept of genre, different genres cross over or blend, creating new or distinct ones. The standard genres accepted for most picture books are animal stories, magical realism, realistic fiction, historical, and traditional literature (sometimes called folklore).

Animal and Toy Stories

Animal and toy stories are realistic stories that have animal or inanimate objects as the main characters. Animals and objects talk, walk, dress, and otherwise behave like humans. There is usually little or no magic other than the animals or objects having human characteristics, which renders them capable of otherwise extraordinary feats. Settings can be imaginary or contemporary. An example is Lilly in *Lilly's Purple Plastic Purse* (1996).

Some animal stories feature animals in their natural setting, but with human characteristics. For example, in Beatrix Potter's *The Tale of Peter Rabbit* (1900), Peter lives in a burrow with other rabbits but wears a little jacket. In others, the animal is simply an animal, such as Marc Simont's *Stray Dog* (2001)—the dog is a dog. In fact, *Stray Dog* is based on a true story about a family who found and befriended a stray dog during a family picnic. Peter McCarty's *Hondo and Fabian* (2002) is a sweet, simple story about one day in the lives of two pets. Hondo, the dog, goes to the beach, while Fabian, the cat, stays home, eluding the family toddler and getting into trouble. It was a Caldecott Honor book, and the popularity of the pair of pests spawned a sequel, *Fabian Escapes* (2007).

Although animal and toy stories may seem simplistic or even "childish," to diminish their importance is a mistake. It is the simplicity and childlike perspective that make these stories powerful, because creatures in animal stories represent children. Anthropomorphic animal characters in picture books—and the list is endless— represent the child. Consider Kevin Henkes's heroine Lilly, in *Lilly's Purple Plastic Purse* (1996). Any five-year-old girl could easily experience all of Lilly's adventures.

Magical Realism

Magical realism is a fusion of reality and imagination, with dreamlike imagery that heightens the experience. Ordinary activities are infused with a sense of wonder and promise. Anything is possible: a boy can take a purple crayon and create a fabulous dream world, a board game can come to life, or a boat can transport a frustrated child to a land where Wild Things rule. These tales can have a contemporary or an imaginary setting.

Some critics use the term *fantasy* to describe books in which magic and imagination drive the story. For instance, *Jumanji* (1981) by Chris Van Allsburg has elements of fantasy but is rooted firmly in our world. What is most striking about the book is that it has an ordinary setting, in which the fantastic transports the reader to another dimension where magic occurs.

Realistic Fiction

Realistic stories feature sympathetic characters with whom children easily identify and empathize. For the last two decades or so authors have explored timely, somber topics in picture books, such as divorce, cancer, death, homosexuality, adoption, and AIDS. Realistic books can have a contemporary or historical setting. Historical fiction can be considered a separate genre (see below). Powerful in their execution, realistic books allow children to see themselves in literature.

Of course, not all realistic books are about serious subjects. In *I Love My Hair* (1998) a child celebrates her ethnic heritage; in Allen Say's *Grandfather's Journey* (1993) the author lovingly recounts his family's past. *When Sophie Gets Angry—Really, Really Angry . . .* (1999) may have naïve paintings with a bright palette, but the narrative is dead serious: a child dealing with her emotions.

Realistic fiction shares many characteristics. It is a form of fiction, based on real ideas or events, that accurately reflects life as it is or could be. The events, though fictional, could actually happen. The characters do not have special skills or powers.

Historical

Historical picture books feature stories set some time in the past, which can be from as few as 50 years ago to as many as hundreds of years ago. Subjects from the American Civil War to World War II to biblical times are covered in dozens of titles from various perspectives. For instance, there are picture books about World War II from the Jewish, American, and Japanese perspectives. *Baseball Saved Us* (1993) and *The Bracelet* (1993) are about life in a Japanese concentration camp; *Let the Celebrations Begin!* (1991), *Star of Fear, Star of Hope*, and *Rose Blanche* (1985) are stories about the treatment of Jews; *But No Candy* (1992) and *Don't You Know There's a War On?* (1992) tell readers about the American experience; and *The Little Ships: The Heroic Rescue at Dunkirk in World War II* (1997) focuses on one rather unique event in England during the war. There are many picture books that offer a unique perspective on the American Civil War and slavery.

Picture book biographies offer readers a brief overview of the life of an individual, not always but usually famous or known for some heroic endeavor. Limited in page count, picture book biographies often focus on the highlights or major events in the lives of historical figures, often youth or the early years. Examples are *Shake Rag: From the Life of Elvis Presley* (1998), illustrated by Floyd Cooper; and *If I Only Had a Horn: Young Louis Armstrong* (1997), illustrated by Leonard Jenkins.

Historical picture books are richly illustrated and thoroughly researched, featuring extensive background notes. They often include maps, timelines, and bibliographies.

Traditional Literature

Traditional literature (sometimes called folklore, folk literature, or fairy tales) features the accumulated stories passed down through oral storytelling, from generation to generation. Each tale type has characteristics that set it apart from other types. For example, although magic may be present in a folktale, it is a requirement for a fairy tale. Although both beast tales and fables feature animal characters, there is no obvious moral in a beast tale. Traditional literature gradually altered and transformed through various oral tellings before it was recorded in written form.

It is also one of the most popular genres in picture books. Before emphasis was placed on multicultural literature, most schools and libraries were dependent on folktales to introduce other cultures to children (Horning 1997a). Unfortunately, early picture book versions of folklore lacked source or background notes, which made it difficult to assess the authenticity of the title (Hearne 1993a). Good source notes help readers make informed decisions about the authenticity of the book. In a two-part groundbreaking article that changed the way we think about traditional literature in picture book format, scholar Betsy Hearne (1993a, 1993b) asked, "How do you tell if a folktale in picture-book format is authentic, or true to its cultural background? What picture books have met the challenge of presenting authentic folklore for children?" She defined what makes a good source notes and gave examples of good and bad source notes. According to Hearne readers should look for the following:

- cites specific source(s)

- adds a description for cultural context

- describes what changes were made to the tale

- explains why the changes were made

Early picture books generally lacked these features, but now that Hearne has brought attention to how important authority and authenticity are, most traditional literature picture books now include source notes.

Origins

There are two competing theories in traditional literature about the origin of stories: monogenesis and polygenesis. Monogenesis (or one origin) theory maintains that all tales were ultimately derived from a single source (from one culture) and eventually these stories spread by word of mouth throughout the world. An example of this can be found in the Anansi tales that originated in Africa and spread to the southern United States as the Brer Rabbit tales (Young 2004).

Polygenesis (or many origin) theory maintains that tales emerged independently of each other in different parts of the world. Any similarities in form and content are fundamental proof that all human beings are alike. This theory holds that people everywhere have the same experiences and thus develop the same stories. In the polygenesis theory, elements of each culture are evident in individual versions. Creation myths are an example of polygenesis theory, because virtually every culture has a myth to explain its origins.

Types

Under the broad term *traditional literature* are beast tales, cumulative tales, fables, fairy tales, folktales, fractured tales, Jataka tales, legends, myths, noodlehead tales, pourquoi tales, tall tales, and trickster tales.

Beast Tales

Beast tales feature animals that behave like humans. This type of folktale can be either serious or funny. Unlike fables, there is no explicit moral to the story in a beast tale. Examples of beast tales are "The Three Bears," "Henny Penny," and "The Three Little Pigs." The animals embody various human traits; this feature is also known as anthropomorphism. In a beast tale the animals interact with humans, but the humans are secondary characters. Picture book examples are *The Three Little Pigs: An Old Story* (1988), illustrated by Margot Zemach; *The Bremen Town Musicians* (2007), illustrated by Lizbeth Zwerger; and *Henny Penny* (1979), illustrated by Paul Galdone.

Cumulative Tales

Cumulative tales are simple stories with repetitive phrases. There is not much plot involved, but the repetition and rhythmic structure of these tales is very appealing to children. Events follow each other logically in a pattern of cadence and repetition, sequentially repeating actions, characters, or speeches until a climax is reached. Examples of cumulative tales are "The House That Jack Built" and "There was an Old Lady Who Swallowed a Fly." Picture book examples are *The Napping House* (1984), illustrated by Don Wood; *Bringing the Rain to Kapiti Plain* (1980), illustrated by Beatriz Vidal; *The House That Jack Built* (2000), illustrated by Jeanette Winter; *The Gigantic Turnip* (1999), illustrated by Niamh Sharkey; and *There Was an Old Lady Who Swallowed a Fly* (1997), illustrated by Simms Taback.

Fables

Fables are short prose pieces or verse with a moral ending. The characters are animals and other inanimate objects that take on human characteristics, such as talking and expressing emotions. The form is generally ascribed to Aesop, who developed it in the sixth century BC. Aesop's fables are very well known in the West. Other famous fables include the *Panchatantra*, a collection of fables written in Sanskrit. Picture book examples are *Fables* (1980), illustrated by Arnold Lobel; *Doctor Coyote: A Native American Aesop's Fable* (1987), illustrated by Wendy Watson; *The Lion and the Mouse* (2000), illustrated by Bert Kitchen; and *The Ant and the Grasshopper* (2000), by Amy Lowry Poole.

Fairy Tales

Fairy tales are filled with dreamlike possibility. They feature transformations, magical interventions, fantastic creatures, enchanted forces, and, of course, magic. Fairy tales always have a "happily ever after" ending, where good is rewarded and evil is punished. The scholarly term for fairy tales is *märchen*. Picture book examples are *Cinderella* (2002), illustrated by Ruth Sanderson; *Sleeping Beauty* (2002), illustrated by K. Y. Craft; *Rapunzel* (1997), illustrated by Paul O. Zelinsky; and *Puss in Boots* (1990), illustrated by Fred Marcellino.

Folktales

Folktales feature common people, such as peasants and farmers, and commonplace events. Characters are usually flat, representing an everyman or everywoman. Folktales have tight plot structures, filled with conflict. Cycles of three often appear in folktales. Elements of magic or magical characters may be incorporated, but logic rules, so the supernatural must be plausible and within context. Picture book examples of folktales include *The Little, Little House* (2005), illustrated by Jessica Souhami; *Hansel and Gretel* (1984), illustrated by Paul O. Zelinsky; *Koi and the Kola Nuts: A Tale from Liberia* (1999), illustrated by Joe Cepeda; and *Rhinos for Lunch and Elephants for Supper!* (1992), illustrated by Barbara Spurll.

Fractured Tales

Sometimes called parodies or transformed tales, fractured tales are humorous or exaggerated imitations of an author, a particular traditional tale, or a style. Fractured tales are currently popular in picture book format. Beginning with *The True Story of the 3 Little Pigs* (1989), Jon Scieszka and Lane Smith began a trend that shows no sign of abating. Traditional tales from "Little Red Riding Hood" to the "Three Little Pigs" to "The House That Jack Built" have been retold in a humorous vein in picture book format. Picture book examples are *The Dinosaur's New Clothes* (1999), illustrated by Diane Goode; *Little Red Riding Hood: A New Fangled Prairie Tale* (1995), illustrated by Lisa Campbell Ernst; *The Little Red Hen Makes a Pizza* (1999), illustrated by Amy Walrod; and *Beauty and the Beaks: A Turkey's Cautionary Tale* (2007), illustrated by Mary Jane Auch.

Jataka Tales

Sometimes called birth stories, Jataka are accounts of the previous lives of the Buddha in various animal and human forms. They have been absorbed into the folklore of many countries. Jataka tales have many similarities to the *Panchatantra* and Aesop's fables. Picture book examples are *Buddha Stories* (1997), illustrated by Demi; *The Brave Little Parrot* (1998), illustrated by Susan Gaber; and *Foolish Rabbit's Big Mistake* (1985), illustrated by Ed Young.

Legends

Legends are based in history and embellish the acts of a real person. The facts about and adventures of the person are exaggerated or romanticized, making the individual notorious or his or her deeds legendary. Finn MacCoul, King Arthur, and Robin Hood are legendary figures. Legends are generally associated with a particular place or person and are told as if they were historical fact. Legends, like myths, are stories told as though they were true. Picture book examples are *Finn MacCoul and His Fearless Wife; Arthur and the Sword* (1995), illustrated by Robert Sabuda; *Robin Hood* (1996), illustrated by Margaret Early; *The Pied Piper of Hamelin* (1993), illustrated by Michéle Lemieux; and *Saint George and the Dragon* (1985), illustrated by Trina Schart Hyman.

Myths

Myths attempt to explain the beginning of the world, natural phenomena, the relationships between the gods and humans, and the origins of civilization. Myths, like legends, are stories told as though they were true. Myths are narrative projections of a culture's origins, an attempt by a collective group to define its past and probe the deeper meaning of their existence. With complex symbolism, a myth is to a culture is what a dream is to an individual. Picture book examples are *Atalanta's Race: A Greek Myth* (1995), illustrated by Alexander Koshkin; *King Midas: The Golden Touch* (2002), illustrated by Demi; *Hercules* (1999), illustrated Raul Colón; and *Cupid and Psyche* (1996), illustrated by K. Y. Craft. Creation myths emerge from a culture's desire to define creation and bring order to the universe. Picture book examples of creation myths include *Moon Mother* (1993), illustrated by Ed Young; *The Star-Bearer: A Creation Myth From Ancient Egypt* (2001), illustrated by Jude Daly; *Adam and Eve and the Garden of Eden* (2005), illustrated by Jane Ray; and *The Woman Who Fell from the Sky* (1993), illustrated by Robert Andrew Parker.

Noodlehead Tales

Sometimes called simpleton tales or fool tales, noodlehead tales are humorous stories about absurd situations in which the stupidity or foolishness of the characters plays a central part. The main character in a noodlehead tale usually makes the same mistake over and over until the resolution of the story. Although foolish and bumbling, the noodlehead is often wiser than the other characters, suggesting that the rest of the world is foolish and unable to recognize wisdom. Picture book examples are *Soap! Soap! Don't Forget the Soap* (1993), illustrated by Andrew Glass; *Flossie and the Fox* (1986), illustrated by Rachel Isadora; *Lazy Jack* (1995), illustrated by Russell Ayto; and *Piggie Pie!* (1995), illustrated by Howard Fine.

Pourquoi Tales

Pourquoi tales offer folklore-type explanations for scientific phenomena or aspects of creation, for example, why the leopard has spots or how the stars came to be. The explanation is not scientifically true, and while this type of folktale is often serious, it can also have hilarious aspects integrated into the telling. Pronounced por-kwa, it means "why" in French. The *Just So Stories* by Rudyard Kipling are pourquoi tales. Picture books examples are *Why Mosquitoes Buzz in People's Ears* (1975), illustrated by Leo Dillon and Diane Dillon; *The Great Ball Game: A Muskogee Story* (1994), illustrated by Susan L. Roth; *Why the Sun and the*

Moon Live in the Sky (1968), illustrated by Blair Lent; and *Arrow to the Sun* (1974) by Gerald McDermott.

Tall Tales

Intended to dupe the listener, tall tales are particularly associated with the U.S. frontier, although some other cultures (such as Australia) have similar stories. Tall tales rely on a delicate balance between sober narration and comic exaggerations. American tall tales possess the very essence of the American spirit, complete with outrageous feats and daring heroes. Stories of famous tall tale heroes, such as Paul Bunyan and Mike Fink, were originally passed along through the oral tradition of storytelling. Picture book examples are *Paul Bunyan: A Tall Tale* (1984), illustrated by Steven Kellogg; and *Doña Flor: A Tall Tale About a Giant Woman with a Great Big Heart* (2005), illustrated by Raul Colón. Some tall tales are based on people who actually existed, such as *John Henry* (1994), illustrated by Jerry Pinkney; and *Casey Jones* (2001), illustrated by Allan Drummond. There are several original stories that build on tall tale motifs, including *Library Lil* (1997), illustrated by Steven Kellogg; *Swamp Angel* (1994), illustrated by Paul O. Zelinsky; and *The Bunyans* (1996), illustrated by David Shannon.

Trickster Tales

Trickster tales are humorous stories in which the hero, either in human or animal form, outwits or foils a more powerful opponent through the use of trickery. Anansi the spider is a trickster figure in African folklore; Iktomi, which means spider, comes from the U.S. Plains Indians and is generally in human form; Coyote is a trickster figure from southwestern Native American folklore; and Raven is from the U.S. Pacific Northwest. Picture book examples are *A Story, a Story* (1970), illustrated by Gail E. Haley; *Iktomi and the Boulder* (1988), illustrated by Paul Goble; *Raven: A Trickster Tale from the Pacific Northwest* (1993), illustrated by Gerald McDermott; *Nail Soup* (2007), illustrated by Paul Hess; and *Maui and the Big Fish* (2003), illustrated by Frané Lessac.

CONCLUSION

Format and genre are two important aspects to consider when examining picture books. Picture books feature a rich variety of genres and subgenres, ranging from animal stories to tall tales. Although the picture book itself is a format, there are also various types of formats used in picture books—pop-up books and board books, for example. Analyzing books for both their physical aspects (format) and content (genre) helps readers evaluate the vast picture book canon.

ENDNOTES

1. Although most textbooks refer to "picture book" as a genre, this negates the importance of what Maria Nikolajeva and Scott refer to as "picturebook paratexts." They include much of what is in this chapter. Also, whereas I make a distinction between "format" and "genre," Nikolajeva and Scott include "format" as one of the "paratexts."

2. Some sources report that *The Cat in the Hat* has 223 words, but according to http://www.seussville.com, the first beginning reader had 236. In 2007, Project 236 celebrated the 50th Anniversary of *The Cat in the Hat*.

3. In a capstone project, Storybook Online for scholars, Majid Amani and Janet Weigel examined the potential for children's e-books. They identified several key issues that have direct bearing on the future success of children's e-book publishing endeavors. Their capstone project can be viewed at http://zonorus.marlboro.edu/~mamani/capstone/index.html.

Chapter 5

The Art of the Story

A picture book is a dialogue between two worlds: the world of images and the world of words.

—Leonard S. Marcus, *Ways of Telling*

As for the rest of us, we have never quite gotten over our absolute fascination with the dance of words and pictures, and the spell they cast.

—John Cech, "The Dance of Words and Pictures"

In This Chapter
• How Picture Books Work
• Reading Pictures
• Visual Interest
• Picture–Text Relationships
• Narrative Structures
• Character Development

Chapter 1 explored some of the ways that picture books have been broadly defined. As far as picture–text balance, there can be anywhere from no words in wordless books to hundreds in picture storybooks. This chapter more closely examines the picture–text relationships and how these words and images interact, working either with or against each other. The chapter also discusses some of the ways illustration adds to, complements, or contradicts a story, as well as how some illustrators and designers create visual interest and the rate at which stories unfold.

HOW PICTURE BOOKS WORK

The relationship between the text and pictures is a delicate one. Martin Salisbury (2004) says, it is a "unique and sometimes complex one." Salisbury states that text and pictures should complement one another, rather than duplicate or cancel one another out. Often the words exist before the images, but the way an illustration develops can also have an effect on the story, requiring an adjustment to verbal narrative. Salisbury, who has illustrated several children's books in addition to teaching illustration to aspiring artists, says that the relationship between verbal and visual is constantly shifting and changing to reach that perfect balance. Sometimes a sentence will trail off or words may be ambiguous because the picture is filling in gaps. At other times it isn't even necessary to use words. For example, in a scene in which the sun is shining, it may not be necessary to state that verbally. On the hand, an image of light, such as the sun, may also represent hope or happiness, in addition to being a source of illumination.

Consider the quote by Leonard S. Marcus that opens this chapter. Although Marcus's use of dialogue as a metaphor only scratches the surface in explaining the complex relationhip between pictures and text, it does introduce the notion of a conduit, a channel that opens up to explain the interaction that occurs when pictures and text merge. Marcus's use of the word "dialogue" is intriguing because it nicely summarizes the magic that happens in a picture book. Terms used to describe the picture–text relationship in picture books are often used interchangeably. For example, some scholars use the word pairing "verbal–visual," whereas others refer to the "word/image" pairing. For the most part, this chapter uses "picture–text."

When discussing the picture–text relationship in picture books, the role of the reader or viewer is inextricably entwined with both the verbal and visual narratives as they unite to tell the story. One theory, the "reader-response theory,"[1] asserts that responsibility for making meaning of a story falls on the reader and the process of reading rather than on the author or the text. In other words, the reader, not the author, determines meaning. Furthermore, meaning is continuously revised as readers compare their reactions with those of other readers. In addition, the picture–text relationship can result in different meanings for different readers. Readers approach texts and make meaning by filling in gaps between what is implied and what is stated (Nodelman 1990). As far as picture books are concerned, the reader is also involved in making meaning from the pictures.

In each reading situation, the dynamics of the setting (or context) affect how and what is seen in a picture book. Consider a librarian reading a book to a storytime group. Her attention is focused on the text (as the reader). The children (as listeners/viewers) play a different role. Freed from the linear text on the page, they are able to focus on the nonlinear story being told through the pictures and the words they hear (see figure 5.1). In fact, each child is formulating the story differently, filling in details based on experience and previous knowledge. Sometimes the gaps between the text and the picture are intentional.

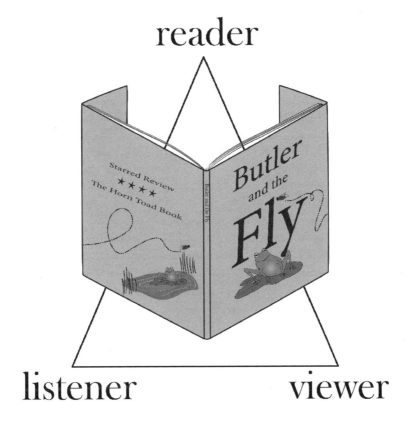

Figure 5.1. The reader/listener/viewer triangle addresses the different ways individuals approach a picture book. The reader focuses on the text; the listener/viewer focuses on the illustrations.

READING PICTURES

As readers, our response to picture books is often difficult to articulate. However, most picture books follow continuous narrative patterns, one thread from the narrative, with illustrations complementing or contradicting the text.

Text is linear and fixed. People read from left to right, top to bottom. And although typography may play with typeface and size, the story itself remains linear in the sense that readers start at the beginning and read sequentially to the end. In contrast, pictures are nonlinear. The eye fixes on a point in an illustration and moves about in a pattern, often predetermined by the illustrator, although the viewer may be unaware this is happening. Whereas single pictures can be considered nonlinear rather than linear, the series of illustrations that make up the book is linear. In other words, readers have to see the illustrations sequentially to make meaning of the story. Each illustration is generally dependent on the one that preceded it, as are the ones that follow. Variety adds visual interest. By alternating angles and views, and close-ups and views from varying distances, an illustrator adds variety and stimulates the reader to turn the page (Salisbury 2004). Illustrators can control the continuity of the illustrations through picture sequence and page spreads.

Picture Sequence

When illustrations are all at eye level, facing the viewer, a picture sequence can become static. Illustrators create variety by altering the way readers look at a page.

For example, in *Madlenka* (2000) illustrator Peter Sís varies his presentation of the protagonist by varying the angles and views from which readers see Madlenka. In one scene, readers see Madlenka at eye level, but from a distance she appears small. In the next illustration Sís moves in closer and readers have an enhanced view. The story is about Madlenka's loose tooth and her journey around her block in New York City to show it to her neighbors. Readers follow her journey from multiple perspectives, from atop a building and looking from across the street.

Picture sequence is an important element of the picture–text relationship. The order of events, or picture sequence, also helps the reader establish a sense of order. For example, in figures 5.2 and 5.3 the text is: "Butler was hot, so he jumped into the pond to cool off." In figure 5.2, a reader might feel unsettled because the sequence of events does not complement the text.

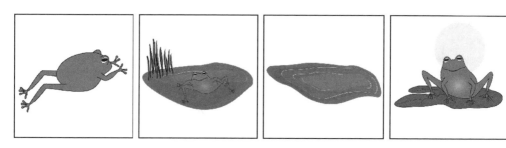

Figure 5.2. This sequence feels unsettled. In the first frame we see Butler jumping for no apparent reason, in the second frame Butler is swimming in the pond, in the third frame we see an empty pond, and in the fourth frame Butler sits under a hot sun. A reader may have a difficult time connecting the series with the narrative.

Illustrations work like film. When a sequence in a movie is odd or disjointed, perhaps jumping from one actor to another, it is disturbing, which may make the viewer feel unsettled. Like a movie, harmony of the sequence in a picture book is important. Generally each successive illustration in a picture book should relate to the one that preceded it and lead to the one that follows. In figure 5.2 the images have an unsettled feeling. A reader might ask why Butler is jumping in the first frame when the text begins "Butler was hot." Of the four frames, which one best correlates to the text? In this case, it is the fourth frame. Moving the frame with Butler swimming to the first position is logical (see figure 5.3).

   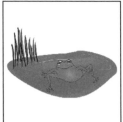

Figure 5.3. This sequence feels more settled. It follows the narrative because in the first frame Butler sits under a hot sun, in the second frame a pond inspires him to cool off, in the third frame he is jumping toward the pond, and and in the fourth frame Butler is swimming in the pond.

Page Spreads

As discussed in chapter 2, there are two types of page layouts: single- and double-page. Single-page illustration is confined to one page, with large blocks of text placed opposite a page with art. This is common in picture books with longer texts, or what many professionals refer to as picture storybooks. Used often in various forms of traditional literature, this type of layout accommodate the longer narratives that are a hallmark of folk literature. In *Little Red Riding Hood* (1983) illustrator Trina Schart Hyman used this layout to great effect. Incorporating elaborate borders that complement and border the text, Hyman was able to take the familiar story to new heights. Double-page illustrations are spread across both sides of an open book. This type of layout is used often for landscape views or scenes. For example, in *The Creation* (1994) illustrator James Ransom punctuated single-page spreads with double-page scenic spreads, including a scene of a canyon and a rocky cliff overlooking the ocean. In *Round Is a Mooncake* (2000), illustrator Grace Lin chose to use double-page spreads throughout the entire book.

Sometimes an illustrator or a designer may have a specific reason to use all double-page or single-page spreads. Unless an illustrator has a specific reason to not alternate page layouts, a combination of layouts stimulates interest. For example, in *Rosie's Walk* (1968) illustrator Pat Hutchins used double-page spreads throughout the entire book. In this case, it makes a powerful statement because readers familiar with the book know that the power of the book is Hutchins's illustrations, in which the crafty fox lurks behind Rosie during her morning walk. In almost all of the illustrations, the fox is featured on the left-hand side of the page spread, which adds to the reader's anticipation. Had Hutchins incorporated a different approach, for instance alternating between double-page spreads and single-page spreads, the book would have lacked the drama it has in its current form.

In *Piggies* (1991) Don Wood and Audrey Wood used double-page layouts throughout the entire book, except the last two pages. The story, which is a variation of the traditional rhyme "This Little Piggy," recounts the adventures of 10 little piggies that dance on the fingers and toes of a child preparing for bed. In each double-page spread, the child's left hand is on the left-hand side of the page and the child's right hand is on the right-hand side of the page, which is brilliant;

readers feel as if they are looking at their hands. On the last two pages, the child folds her hands and quietly puts the 10 little piggies to sleep with gentle kisses. This is an example of very effective use of double-page layout.

In most picture books, however, there are both single-page and double-page spreads. In *Officer Buckle and Gloria* (1995) illustrator Peggy Rathman employs mostly single-page spreads and pages made up of small vignettes. However, several key scenes are laid out as double-page spreads. In particular, the scene in which a television news team videotapes Officer Buckle's speech shows him through the eyes of the audience. The scene features an auditorium of children watching the police officer and Gloria on the stage. The double-page spread adds drama because readers see the stage from the vantage point of the audience.

A picture book lies open when read, so even if an image is isolated to just one page, the illustrator considers how it works in a two-page spread. Both single-page and double-page spreads depend on the drama of turning the page. As stated previously, an illustration depends on the page opposite it as well as the page that precedes it. When two single-page spreads are laid out in a left-to-right spread, it helps build the story visually. Figure 5.4 shows the left-hand side only of a left-to-right spread. Taken out of sequence, this page only tells us part of the story. What happens next? How does this picture relate to the next page?

Figure 5.4. In a left-to-right page spread, two single illustrations are connected by text, and in this case, the fly's trail. Without the right-hand page, the reader is left wondering what happens.

Figure 5.5 features both sides of the left-to-right page spread. Two single-page spreads are connected by the text and the fly's trail. On the left-hand side is the text, "The fly flew up . . ."; on the right-hand side is the rest of the sentence, "and down." Readers know what happens after the fly flew up: he flew down.

Figure 5.5. Viewing the pages together, readers know that after the fly flew up, he flew down. In this case the narrative is strengthened by the double-page spread.

In figures 5.4 and 5.5 the example is a left-to-right layout. If figure 5.4 were on the right-hand page, readers might be inspired to turn the page to find out what happens next. Not only do readers wonder what the end of the sentence is, they also want to follow the visual cue of the fly's trail. In figures 5.6 and 5.7 (p. 112) the illustrations have been changed, which creates drama. Simply by changing the layout, a different mood is created.

Figure 5.6. The text reads, "The fly flew up." To find out what happens, readers have to turn the page. The text, as well as the fly's trail, encourage readers to turn the page.

Figure 5.7. Readers were prompted to turn the page. The sentence that began on the previous page is completed. In addition, the trail leads to the fly.

VISUAL INTEREST

Visual interest means just that, keeping the illustration visually interesting. An illustration should draw readers in, inviting them to explore. A well-done picture book is worth pondering; in fact, the great ones beg to be read again and again. This chapter has already discussed how using single- and double-page spreads and picture sequence creates variety. An illustrator can stimulate readers by creating visual interest. Illustrators have several tools at their disposal to create visual interest: drama, pace, panels, and framing (Salisbury 2004).

Drama

Drama, also known as rising action, is the action or tension that carries the story forward. In traditional narrative structure, dramatic tension marks the beginning of a story as conflict moves toward a climax.

In illustration, drama can be indicated through an action that is halfway complete. For example, in *Harold and the Purple Crayon* (1955) Harold draws a mountain so that he can search for his room. On the opposite page, Harold is perched atop a mountain, crayon in hand. Illustrator Crockett Johnson creates a situation in which Harold is placed in danger. Readers have no idea what Harold's fate is until they turn the page to view the illustration that shows Harold tumbling, but not down the mountain, because he never drew the other side. Instead, Harold falls through space, his purple crayon ready to create an alternate reality. This series in the book presents Harold with a situation that is initially unresolved. Until the reader turns the page, the action is incomplete. Likewise, in figure 5.8 the fly hovers over a pond. A reader may or may not identify that the green area is actually a toad sitting on a lily pad in the middle of the pond. Figure 5.9 is the page that comes after the page in figure 5.8. In that illustration the fly, as well as the reader, is closer to the green object in the lake.

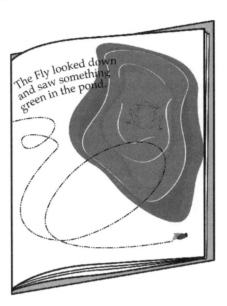

Figure 5.8. The fly hovers over the lake, looking down. Like the fly, readers may not realize that the green in the lake is actually a toad.

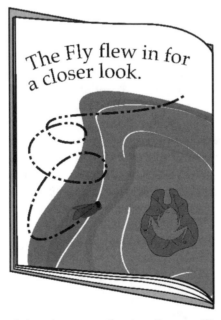

Figure 5.9. This illustration is what readers see as they turn the page. The fly has moved in for a closer look. This angle provides visual interest because it draws the reader closer, into the image.

Pace

Another way an illustrator creates visual interest in the story is through pace. To keep the reader engaged and intrigued, composition must never become stale. By pacing the illustrations, the story can slow down, giving the narrative a chance to build and the reader an opportunity to engage in the story.

With only 32 words, Pat Hutchin's *Rosie's Walk* (1968) takes about a minute to read—that is, if you focus on the text, or the verbal element. When readers focus on the illustrations, or the visual element, they realize that an entirely different story is being told. Hutchins manages to slow down the pace of the story with the illustrations. The fox is never mentioned in the text, but is always ominously present. Also, with two exceptions, the fox is always on the left-hand side of the double-page spreads, which indicates to the reader there will be a shift in the action. Although this predictability may seem somewhat static, Hutchins actually manages to create a sense of anticipation. When readers see the fox, the pace of the story slows so they can comprehend the action in the illustrations with the text. K. Y. Craft, who is known for her lush illustrations populated with sparkling jewels and period fashion, often controls the pace in her picture books with one-page spreads interspersed with double-page spreads. The one-page spreads are balanced with pages of text with illuminated borders that pick up details from the illustrations.

Illustrators can control the visual pace of the story by alternating views, exploiting white space, and avoiding repetitive composition (Salisbury 2004). That is, 32 illustrations that all look similar are boring, in contrast to illustrations that vary as the reader turns the pages. In *The Three Pigs* (2001) illustrator David Wiesner does a brilliant job of using white space to create a multifaceted story. In fact, he has two pages that are completely white, void of text and pictures. He is also adept at using panels to create variety. In *Jazz* (2006) illustrator Christopher Myers exuberantly mixes up compositions with single-page spreads facing text-only pages with double-page spreads, and by changing the horizontal, left-to-right orientation to vertical for a key scene. Myers's stylized figures appear against vivid backdrops in which brushstrokes create an intensity that make readers want to tap their feet to the rhythm inherent in the text and transmitted through the art. Figure 5.10 shows four types of composition that illustrators might use to add visual interest to illustrations. The first is created using two small vignettes; the second is text without adornment, which can be effective when used properly; the third is three panels stacked vertically; and the fourth is a single-page illustration without text.

Figure 5.10. Used together in variety of ways, different page compositions add visual interest and prompt readers to turn the page.

Panels

Sometimes an illustrator breaks an illustration into panels for effect. Panels add visual pacing or rhythm to the story and allow the illustrator to achieve artistic statements not possible in a single- or double-page spread. Panels are an effective way to show various aspects of a character's personality.

Panels allow illustrators to establish time and movement. Martin Salisbury (2004) cites illustrator Alex Deacon's use of panels in establishing time and movement in *Slow Loris* (2002). The loris, an animal that is known for being slow, is the principal character in Deacon's book. In the opening scene, Slow Loris is shown in the upper right-hand corner of six frames that spread across two pages. In each of the frames, Deacon shows time passing as everything in each panel changes, expect for Slow Loris, who barely changes position. In figure 5.11 panels are used to show three different aspects of Butler's personality. In the top panel he is relaxed, in the middle panel he is excited and energetic, and in the bottom panel he is calm and quiet.

Figure 5.11. Three different aspects of Butler's personality are revealed through the use of panels.

Framing

Another method used by illustrators is framing. When an illustration presents a figure or object entering or leaving a frame, that creates a sense of time and movement. Furthermore, framing can connect the current page with the preceding page and invite the reader to turn the page to see what is going to the following page. In figure 5.12 Butler enters on the left and leaves on the right. Readers do not know where he has been or where he is going.

Figure 5.12. An illustrator can create a sense of time passing through the use of framing to prompt a reader to turn the page.

PICTURE–TEXT RELATIONSHIPS

Chapter 1 examined some of the ways that picture books have been broadly defined using the idea of picture–text balance. As previously discussed, picture books have illustrations on every page, with art almost dominating the text; picture storybooks also have illustrations on every page, but with larger blocks of text; and in illustrated books the text dominates the page, with pictures playing a supporting role. In all three cases, illustrations are pivotal to the story, but to a different extent. The definitions do not address the picture–text relationship. This chapter takes a closer look at picture–text relationships and considers how these relationships work with or against each other. It also examines some of the ways illustration adds to, complements, or contradicts a story.

Several scholars have attempted to explain the dynamics of the picture–text relationship, and in the process have introduced new ways of thinking about picture books. In chapter 1 it was stated that there are many ways to define what a picture book is, and there have been just as many attempts to define the relationship between the verbal and the visual in picture books. Although there are several ways to characterize the picture–text relationship, this guide focuses on the symmetrical, complementary, and contradictory. However, understanding how other critics have defined the relationship is also beneficial.

In *Ways of the Illustrator* (1982), one of the first works that explored the picture–text relationship, scholar Joseph Schwarcz describes a "verbal-visual" narrative, further broken down into *congruency, elaboration, specification, amplification, extension, complementation, alternation, deviation, and counterpoint.*

In *Narrative Symbol in Childhood Literature* (1990) Joanne Golden describes five different types of visual–verbal relationships in picture storybooks: 1) text and picture are symmetrical; 2) text depends on picture for clarification; 3) illustration enhances, elaborates text; 4) text carries primary narrative, illustration is selective; and 5) illustration carries primary narrative, text is selective.

In *Looking at Pictures in Picture Books* (1993) Jane Doonan, perhaps influenced by Schwarcz, echoes some of his definitions when she explores picture–text relationships. Her terms, though similar to Schwarcz's, vary somewhat: *elaborate, amplify, extend, complement, contradict,* and *deviate.*

In "One and Inseparable: Interdependent Storytelling in Picture Storybooks" (1999), Denise Agosto simplifies matters by using the terms *parallel storytelling,* in which the pictures and text tell the same story simultaneously, and *interdependent storytelling,* in which both picture and text are considered concurrently.

Scholars Maria Nikolajeva and Carole Scott (2001, 2006)[2] use the following terms to describe the verbal–visual interaction in picture books: *symmetrical, enhancing, complementary, counterpointing,* and *contradictory.* They define a symmetrical relationship as one in which words and pictures tell the same story. In an enhancing interaction, pictures amplify words, or the words expand the picture; in a complementary one, the enhancing interaction is significant, almost dynamic. In a counterpointing relationship, pictures and text collaborate to communicate because neither can tell the story alone. In a contradictory relationship, which is an extreme form of counterpointing, words and pictures seem to be in opposition to one another. Further, Maria Nikolajeva and Carole Scott place emphasis on the one-word spelling "picturebook" because it is distinct "from picture books, or books with pictures."

The picture–text relationship can change from page to page; that is, the balance between them in a picture book is never completely symmetrical, complementary, or contradictory. Further, there are picture–text relationships that are easy to characterize, but others require a deeper examination of the complex codes within. For example, the characterization in a picture book may be complementary to the illustrations, but the plot and setting may be contradictory (Nikolajeva and Scott).

The majority of illustrations in picture books have a symmetrical or complementary relationship with the text, meaning that the relationship is either redundant or that picture and/or text fill in the gaps in the other.

In a symmetrical picture book, the words and images tell the same story. Although readers may pick up a few hints from the pictures that aren't in the text; for the most part the relationship is equal.

In a complementary picture book, the pictures add to or amplify the text, or vice versa, with the words adding meaning to the pictures. The relationship is a more complex dynamic.

In a contradictory picture book, the words and pictures seem to be in opposition to one another. This ambiguity challenges the reader to mediate between the text and pictures to establish a true understanding of what is being depicted.

Symmetrical

Several scenes in *The Snowy Day* (1962) are examples of a symmetrical relationship; that is, the text and pictures basically tell the same story. In the opening sequence in the book the protagonist, Peter, sits on his bed looking out the window. The first sentence reads, "One winter morning Peter woke up and looked out of the window." Details, such as the color of the bedspread (tan) and the walls (red), are auxiliary and not essential to the narrative but are gleaned from the illustrations. Readers know that Peter has awakened. Even though the text doesn't say he sat up in bed, it is apparent that he is sitting up in bed. Without the pictures, readers might or might not assume he is still lying down.

The most significant thing readers learn from the pictures that is not indicated in the text is that Peter is African American. Although this book is often heralded as one of the first picture books with a child of color as the main protagonist, that detail is not tied to the plot.

In figure 5.13 the picture and text are symmetrical. The text indicates the fly flew up and down, which is supported by the movement of the fly's trail. There are other elements in the picture, but they do not add to or take away from the text.

Figure 5.13. In a symmetrical picture book, the words and images tell the same story. In this example, the text indicates the fly flew up and down, which readers can also see by following the movement of the fly's trail.

Complementary

Several illustrations in *Harold and the Purple Crayon* (1955) offer examples of complementary relationship. In the opening page spread, Harold is looking over his shoulder with the text: "One evening, after thinking it over for some time, Harold decided to go for a walk in the moonlight." On the left-hand side is a series of purple squiggles, which look as if they were drawn out of boredom. The text has not yet indicated that Harold is carrying a purple crayon, but the illustration lets the reader know. Although his face is not overly expressive, readers can identify from his expression that he is thinking.

After Harold has had his fill of adventure, he decides it is time to go home. He draws window after window, but somehow none is right. Finally he sees the moon framed inside one of the windows he has drawn and realizes this window will take him home. Although it isn't overtly stated, the reader recognizes that it is the same window that was seen on the first page of the book.

In figure 5.14, in the text on the left-hand side of the double-page spread readers learn that the fly wants a friend. On the right-hand side of the spread, which is dominated by the thought balloon, are two additional characters that may or may not be friends. And though the pictures of an elephant and a pig are present, the reader doesn't know what role they play in the story.

Figure 5.14. In a complementary picture book, the pictures add to or amplify the text, or vice versa, with the words adding meaning to the pictures. In this example, the reader learns that the fly wants a friend. However, whether or not the pig and elephant are friends is not indicated.

Contradictory

In *Rosie's Walk* (1968) there are actually three stories: the one the words tell, the one the pictures tell, and the one they tell together. The opening page spread provides an example of a contradictory relationship. On the surface, the story is simple. The narrative in *Rosie's Walk* consists of 32 carefully chosen words. On the right hand page, are the words, "Rosie the hen went for a walk." The illustration features typical objects readers might expect to see on a farm, such as a barn and milking cans. Readers already know that Rosie is a hen, but the text does not offer any details. Without the pictures, the color of her feathers is unknown. So far, readers assume that this is a case of complementary picture–text relationship. However, on the left-hand side of the double-page spread a fox appears. Hutchins never mentions the fox in the text; it is through the illustrations that readers are introduced to the second character. In this case, the illustration elaborates on the text and even contradicts it. This is no ordinary walk—Rosie is, in fact, in danger. The text is a simple, rather dull story. On the other hand, the pictures tell of a dangerous but clumsy fox and a clever, mischievous hen. Hutchins never reveals that Rosie is aware of the fox; she may be. A number of interpretations are possible: some readers may think Rosie is mischievous and aware the fox is following, whereas other readers may view Rosie as unaware of the danger.

In figure 5.15 both sides of the double-page spread contradict the text. Although the text on the left-hand side indicates that fly flew the up, the opposite is true. The contradiction is further amplified by the fact that the text with the word "up" is located on the bottom of the page. The reverse is true for the right-hand side of the spread.

Figure 5.15. In a contradictory picture book, the words and pictures seem to be in opposition to one another. In the example both the placement of the text and the direction of the fly creates ambiguity that the reader has to sort out.

NARRATIVE STRUCTURES

There are several types of narrative structure in picture books: continuous, double, split, and multiple, with continuous narrative being the most frequently encountered (Nikolajeva and Scott 2001, 2006).

Continuous Narrative

Continuous narrative involves one character or object portrayed in two or more places on the same page or page spread. In *Whistle for Willie* (1964) illustrator Ezra Jack Keats uses a double-page spread to show Peter in two different settings. Peter is larger on the left-hand side of the page spread; on the right-hand side a smaller Peter is present. The same sidewalk appears in both pictures, although Peter appears twice. This gives readers a sense of time and movement, moving the narrative forward without stating that time has actually passed (Schwarcz 1982). Likewise, in figure 5.16 the fly starts in the upper left-hand corner of the page. Although the text does not indicate that time has passed, the picture seems to imply that it has.

Figure 5.16. The fly is shown small and gets progressively larger to demonstrate the passage of time, or that the fly is flying toward the reader.

Double and Split Narrative

Double narratives feature two scenes with different characters or settings on the same page or page spread, also known as the field of action or picture space. Split narratives involve two episodes in the same setting, with different characters on the same page or page spread.

In *Why Mosquitoes Buzz in People's Ears* (1975), the Dillons illustrate split narrative through the character of the python. The python talks to the iguana on one page, while on the next page he has crossed the gutter to slip down the rabbit hole—all on the same length of tail with two heads.

Figure 5.17 is an example of double narrative. Both the toad and the fly address the reader. However, the background of each panel is different, which indicates that the two events are not happening simultaneously even though they are on the same page.

Figure 5.17. In the left-hand panel, Butler is shown against a dark background that simulates night. The fly is shown in a daytime setting. Although both characters address the reader, the different background places the narratives at opposite times of the day.

Multiple Narrative

Multiple scenes with different characters or settings on the same page or page spread are found in some picture books. This technique is called multiple narratives. Multiple narratives are the most sophisticated storylines, requiring careful examination and attention from readers.

Black and White (1990) by David Macaulay is an example of a multiple narrative (Goldstone 1999). The story has four potential individual narratives: "Seeing Things," "Problem Parents," "A Waiting Game," and "Udder Chaos." On each page four different narratives occur simultaneously. Although the four narratives can be read independently of each other, this is really a book about connections. In fact, the author/illustrator explains this when he adds a warning in one of the opening sequences: "careful inspection of both words and pictures is recommended."

It is difficult to read *Black and White* one time through and be finished or satisfied. Aware of the narrative complexity inherent in his book, Macaulay includes a preface: "This book appears to contain a number of stories that do not necessarily occur at the same time. Then again, it may contain only one story." Figure 5.18 is an example of a simple multiple narrative showing the fly at various points in the story on the same page. In figure 5.19 a more complicated narrative involves disparity in the images. Unlike figure 5.18, in which readers can see a connection, the action in figure 5.19 is ambiguous.

Figure 5.18. This four-panel layout is a simple multiple narrative. Readers view the fly traveling in different directions at the same time even though the action is not happening simultaneously.

Figure 5.19. This three-panel layout is a more complicated multiple narrative. Readers must make connections in the visual narrative based on the images alone.

CHARACTER DEVELOPMENT

Characters are usually presented through their actions, dialect, and thoughts, as well as by describing them. Authors and illustrators use point of view to bring the character to life.

Point of View

Point of view depends on who the narrator is and how much he or she knows. In picture books, this creates an interesting dynamic, because readers encounter both visual and verbal points of view, which aren't necessarily the same. There are three points of view that can be presented: first person, second person, and third person.

The first person point of view uses "I." A character tells the story from his or her perspective. *Eloise* (1955) is an example of a first person narrative. "I am Eloise/I am six." So begins the beloved story of the precocious little girl who lives at the Plaza Hotel in New York City.

The second person point of view uses "you." The author speaks directly to the reader. Although traditionally rare in picture books, characters frequently speak to the reader in many contemporary postmodern books. One picture book example is David Wiesner's *The Three Pigs* (2001), in which the pigs actually stop the narrative to address the reader.

The third person point of view uses "he," "she," or "it." The author tells the reader about the characters. Miss Clavell's troupe of 12 girls and their adventures in *Madeline* (1939) are told though a third person narrator.

Convincing characters are essential to any story, and are fundamental to the success of picture books. A cute, appealing character is not enough—the picture book character must be engaging and real.

Some critics assert that picture book characters cannot be fully realized in 32 pages. David Shannon's title character in *No, David!* (1998) doesn't speak, yet readers feel as if they know him very early in the narrative. No one could argue that the character is cute or even appealing, with his large, round head and razor-sharp teeth, yet he resonates with readers for his refreshing simplicity and honesty.

According to illustrator Martin Salisbury (2004), good characters emerge when an author and illustrator have a keen sense of human nature, even going so far as to say they need to have voyeuristic tendencies. Although that may sound odd, what he means is that an observant person notes the intricacies and commonalities that human beings share. Furthermore, he or she is able to apply those observations to strong, vibrant characters, in both text and pictures.

Educator Walter Sawyer (2003) states that great characters possess qualities that make them both endearing and memorable. Outstanding characters do not have be extraordinary or have special powers. Consider, for example, Shannon's character David. The reason he connects with children is probably that they see a child very similar to themselves in environments they recognize. That's not to say that characters in extraordinary circumstances don't resonate, because they do. Kay Thompson's Eloise, a rich, pampered, and privileged child, is as popular today as she was when she was introduced in 1955. Few children live the luxurious life that Eloise enjoys, but there is still a quality about her that connects with children.

There are several types of characters in picture books.

Round versus Flat

Round (or three-dimensional) characters are depicted in a very detailed and realistic way. Protagonists are normally round characters. Antagonists are often round as well, although villains may also be almost farcically flat. The wolf in *The True Story of the 3 Little Pigs* (1989) is round, although also deliciously wicked and funny.

A flat (or two-dimensional) character is distinguished by its lack of detail and nuance. Although the description of a flat character may be detailed, the image of the character has little detail and usually just emphasizes one characteristic. Background characters are often flat.

A number of stereotypical, or "stock" characters exist in picture books. These characters are often the basis of flat characters, though elements of stock characters can be found in round characters as well. Examples are a grocer in a market setting or children in books set in schools. These characters may be featured in the illustrations and not mentioned in the text, or they be mentioned in the text and not featured in the illustrations.

Supporting characters are generally flat, as most minor roles do not require a great deal of complexity. Experimental literature and postmodern fiction often intentionally make use of flat characters, even as protagonists.

Dynamic versus Static

A dynamic character is one who changes significantly during the course of the story. What kind of changes make a character dynamic? Usually the changes are internal. They may be changes in insight or understanding, in commitment, or in values. Changes in circumstances (such as where the character lives), even physical circumstances (such as the character's size), do not apply unless they result in some change within the character's self. By definition, the protagonist is nearly always a dynamic character.

In contrast, static characters do not generally undergo significant change. Whether round or flat, their personalities remain essentially the same throughout the course of the story. This treatment is similar to that of secondary characters, and it lets them serve as thematic or plot elements. Supporting characters and major characters other than the protagonist are generally static, though exceptions do occur.

Inanimate Objects

Picture books are filled with inanimate objects, often personified to resemble humans. Readers are drawn to the inanimate objects as if they were human because they allow for an exploration of human emotion, however detached. Classic characters such as the train in *Little Toot* (1939), Mary Ann from *Mike*

Mulligan and Steam Shovel (1939), and the house from *The Little House* (1942) resonate with readers. In *The Little Red Lighthouse and the Great Gray Bridge* (1942) the lighthouse and bridge don't speak, but they are given human characteristics and, like the house in Virginia Lee Burton's *The Little House*, they have semblances to the human face. In both books, tough subjects are tackled, but the use of inanimate objects creates sympathy that may not occur with human characters. In *The Little House*, progress and a changing landscape threaten the house. Readers empathize with Virginia Lee Burton's character, following her on her journey through changing seasons and across years, building a relationship with the house in the same way the house builds a relationship to the land.

Several notable contemporary titles employ objects in this way, including *I Stink* (2002) by Jim McMullen and Kate McMullen. The loud, boisterous trash truck is full of life and vitality, even issuing a loud burp in the middle of the narrative. In *Fireboat* (2002) Maira Kalman tells the story of a forgotten fireboat built in 1931 and decommissioned in 1955, as the needs of New York City changed. On September 11, 2001, the *John J. Harvey* is called into service once again. Though Kalman personifies the fireboat in the text, it is done sympathetically and with compassion to honor New York City.

Animal Characters

Animal characters in literature have a long and rich tradition, from the early fables of Aesop to the tales of the Grimm brothers. Human qualities are often projected onto or ascribed to animals through story. Animals often represent extremes in human nature (Salisbury 2004). Consider some phrases used to describes humans: "sly as a fox," "quick as a rabbit," and "quiet as a mouse." When we are hungry we claim to be "hungry as a horse," and after we eat too we claim to have "eaten like a pig." Some animals, such as horses and eagles, represent strength and dignity, while other animals, namely wolves and rats, are often assigned the negative characteristics of humans In fact, wolves tend to be portrayed in a less than flattering light. In most versions of "Little Red Riding Hood," the wolf is portrayed as deceitful, dangerous, selfish, and wicked by turns. In other fictional accounts, the wolf usually does not fare much better. In most versions of the "Three Little Pigs," the character of the wolf suffers numerous indignities. Jon Scieszka and Lane Smith gave the wolf an opportunity to tell his version of events in their classic parody of the old English tale in *The True Story of the 3 Little Pigs* (1989), but somehow the wolf still ended up being made a fool. He does not fare much better in David Wiesner's Caldecott-winning version, *The Three Pigs* (2001).

According to Martin Salisbury (2004), animal characters free authors and illustrators from needing to be specific about age, gender, class, and race. Perry Nodelman (1990) suggests that characters based on rabbits, mice, and pigs are common because they are small enough to express the trauma children experience in the world of adults. Animals in picture books talk, walk, dress, and otherwise behave like humans. There is usually little or no magic because the animals have human characteristics that render them capable of extraordinary feats. Settings can be imaginary or contemporary.

Because animals often represent children, animals in picture books are often cute and cuddly. Domestic animals such as dogs and cats are prominent in picture books. Martin Salisbury (2004) suggests that this may be because they are comforting and familiar. Not that there are not a few cats with attitude, namely Skippyjon Jones in *Skippyjon Jones* (2003) and Kitty in *Bad Kitty* (2005). Though not cute or cuddly, there are just as many mice and pigs gracing the pages of picture books. Kevin Henkes is known for his mice books, which include *Lilly's Purple Plastic Purse* (1996) and *Sheila Rae, the Brave* (1987). Ian Falconer's Olivia, from *Olivia Saves the Circus* (2002) and *Olivia Forms a Band* (2006), is a pig.

Although mice, rabbits, and pigs are most common, there is an array of unusual animal characters in picture books. There are books with donkeys, namely *Sylvester and the Magic Pebble* (1969); crocodiles, including *Lyle, Lyle Crocodile* (1973) and *I, Crocodile* (1999); cows, including *Click, Clack, Moo: Cows That Type* (2000) and *A Particular Cow* (2006); gorillas, including *Good Night, Gorilla* (1994) and *Gorilla* (1985); rats, including *That Pesky Rat* (2002) and *Hooway for Wodney Wat* (1999); bats, including *Stellaluna* (1993) and *Bat Loves the Night* (2001); and bears, including *Bear Snores On* (2002) and *Very Hairy Bear* (2007).

Though it is commonly accepted that animal characters in picture books often represent children and display human characteristics, other animal stories feature animals in their natural setting, such as *Bashi, Elephant Baby* (1998), which is about a baby elephant in its natural habitat. In a trilogy of picture books, author Krista Ruepp and illustrator Ulrike Heyne tell the adventures of a young girl named Anna and her horse, Prince. In *Winter Pony* (2002), Prince leaves her to join a herd for a short time; in *Runaway Pony* (2005), Prince returns to the family farm; and in *Anna's Prince* (2006), the horse is four years old—old enough to ride.

Some animal characters resonate so strongly with readers that they spawn series. Lucy Cousins's Maisy is a mouse that is extremely popular with preschool-aged children. In addition to picture books, Cousins has created board book editions and other toy formats[3] and a television show produced by Nickelodeon. In *Bear Snores On* (1992), in which the title is a refrain repeated throughout the narrative, a bear sleeps soundly thorough the revelry of the other forest animals, that is, until the other animals realize there is a problem. Written by Karma Wilson and illustrated by Jane Chapman, the book has spawned four other titles in the series. Jane Yolen and Mark Teague's How Do Dinosaurs series, which features dinosaurs behaving (and misbehaving) in ways very similar to children. The series began with *How Do Dinosaurs Say Goodnight* (2000); the most recent offering is *How Do Dinosaurs Go to School?* (2007).

CONCLUSION

One of the most unique aspects of picture books is the picture–text relationship, the way the verbal and visual elements work together and against one another in the picture book format. Having explored picture–text relationships, readers can identify elements that help them begin to look at picture books in a new, exciting way. The art of the story is as important as the story itself. This chapter explored narrative structures that exist in text as well as pictures. Characters must be not only believable, but also consistent. Characters that resonate with readers are those that exhibit these characteristics. The picture–text relationship, the narrative structure, and the characters of picture books all have a tremendous impact on the reading experience.

ENDNOTES

1. There are many other literary theories, including Marxist, feminist, postcolonial, postmodern, etc. It is beyond the scope of this book to explore other theories. For readers interested in other theories, I suggest *The Nimble Reader: Literary Theory and Children's Literature* (McGillis 1996) and *A Reader's Guide to Contemporary Literary Theory* (Selden et al. 1997)

2. In *How Picturebooks Work* (2001) Maria Nikolajeva and Carole Scott offer a quick overview of attempts to define picture book types. In a section called "Attempts at a Picturebook Topology," they summarize the work of Torben Gregersen, Kristin Hallberg, Joseph Schwarcz, Perry Nodelman, Ulla Rhedin, Joanne Golden, and Lawrence Sipe.

3. For a complete list of products based on Lucy Cousins's Maisy character, see www.maisyfunclub.com.

Chapter 6

Development, Literacy, and Picture Books

Oh, magic hour, when a child first knows she can read printed words!
—Betty Smith, *A Tree Grows in Brooklyn*

In This Chapter
- Child Development and Picture Books
- Emergent Literacy
- Visual Literacy

Learning to understand and appreciate the stages of child development can be rewarding for educators, librarians, and parents. Knowledge of the theories of cognitive development underlies an understanding of the way children think. In the last 20 years, early childhood educators and librarians have identified the importance of early literacy in child development. Emergent literacy, what children know about reading and writing before they can actually read or write, and visual literacy, the ability to understand and make meaning from images, are the foundations of literacy behaviors. Early exposure to picture books helps children develop both types of literacy skills. Picture books offer an excellent opportunity to support literacy, both emergent and visual, because children are introduced to verbal and visual communication through the narrative art of picture books.

CHILD DEVELOPMENT AND PICTURE BOOKS

Educators and librarians often use picture books to help children conceptualize the physical, socioemotional, and cognitive development of children. Almost every children's librarian has been asked, "Do you have a book about . . ." or "I am looking for a book to help my child . . ." . Libraries offer theme-based lists, and parenting magazines routinely feature bibliographies that address developmental issues. Picture books supply a natural context for developmental theories, and the illustrations often mirror a child's developmental progress through memorable, and lovable characters (Hansen and Zambo 2005).

Identifying picture books with well-drawn characters that complement the development of children and theories of child development can be a useful tool. For example, parents seeking to help their child detach emotionally from a favorite toy or blanket might find Kevin Henkes's *Owen* (1993) useful. In *When Sophie Gets Angry—Really, Really, Angry . . .* (1999), illustrator Molly Band creates a protagonist who resonates with readers. The bright palette and childlike art capture Sophie's emotional development in an accessible and playful way.

However, one of the ironies of working with picture books and children is that readers often encounter picture books with protagonists who are preoperational (ages two through seven) but stories that only an operational child (ages seven through eleven) can understand. During the preoperational stage, children are not able to think logically, but with the development of language they can describe the world through images and symbols. Preoperational children are egocentric but are beginning to take a greater interest in objects and people. During the operational stage children are able to complete mental operations without aids. For example, they can add, subtract, multiply, and divide without counting on their fingers. The preoperational child was able to count from one to ten, but the concrete operational child understands that "one" stands for "one object." The primary characteristic of the concrete operation stage is *reversibility*. Concrete operational children can reverse their direction of thought. For example, they recognize that something can be added as well as subtracted. Consider, for example, *Owen* (1993). Owen, a four-year-old mouse, is still attached to his no-longer-fuzzy blanket named Fuzzy. Owen's parents take the advice of Mrs. Tweezer, the next-door neighbor, who offers ideas for helping Owen part from his blanket. Owen is at the preoperational stage; he is developing language and views the world through images and symbols. For Owen, the blanket is a symbol of comfort. He does not understand that the blanket could be problematic in his future development. A concrete operational child can identify that the blanket is problematic, whereas a preoperational child sympathizes with Owen.

Understanding the difference between a preoperational child and an operational child is challenging. Parents and adults who work with children are more familiar with observable milestones, such as the fact that babies learn to crawl around six months and learn to walk around one year.

Learning to understand and appreciate the stages of child development can be rewarding for educators, librarians, and parents. Scholars Evelyn Arizpe and Morag Styles (2003) assert that an understanding of the theories of cognitive development of both Jean Piaget and Lev Vygotsky help us understand the way children think. With regard to visual literacy, neither Piaget or Vygotsky specifically refers to the way children view or sort images, but familiarity with the work of both psychologists is still beneficial.

Piaget identified four stages of cognitive development: *sensory-motor* (birth through age two), *preoperational* (ages two through seven), *concrete operational* (ages seven through eleven), and *formal operational* (eleven through sixteen). All children pass through these stages, but not at the same rate. Each stage lays the foundation for the next. Each is qualitatively different, meaning that it involves a change in nature, not just quantity. For example, understanding Piaget's developmental stages explains why an infant needs help turning pages between the ages six and twelve months, and just a few months later, at twelve to eighteen months, is able to turn pages independently.

Lev Vygotsky offered an alternative to Piaget's stages of cognitive development. His theories became a major influence in the field of psychology and education. The basic principles underlying Vygotsky's framework are that 1) children construct their own knowledge, 2) development cannot be separated from social context, 3) learning can lead development, and 4) language plays a central role in mental development (Woolfolk 2004).

Piaget believed that children learn through experience. He theorized that children are born with and acquire schemas, or concepts, that through experience develop hypotheses based on their actions. Vygotsky concurred with Paiget's idea of learning though action, but placed the emphasis on language. To Piaget, perception was subordinated to action and tied to developmental stage. Thus, according to Piaget, younger children are not capable of seeing the world in the same way as older children and adults. Vygotsky, on the other hand, believed that children's development interacts with their social and cultural experience, and that perception, action, and speech are necessary for the acquisition of language (Arizpe and Styles 2003).

In addition to stages, Piaget also used terms specific to development, such as *spatial egocentrism*, which refers to a child's difficulty differentiating between two perspectives of the same object. In *Harold and the Purple Crayon* (1955), a young boy perhaps three years old decides to take a walk. After Harold has had his fill of adventure, he decides it is time to go home. He draws window after window, but somehow none is right. Finally, he sees the moon framed inside one of the windows he has drawn. To Harold's way of thinking, this is the same window that readers see on the first page of the book. The reader knows this is not the case, but as a child displaying spatial egocentrism, Harold sees the two windows as one and the same (Singer and Revenson 1996).

Another example can be found in Piaget's definition of *animism*, which is the belief that everything in nature has consciousness and life. Singer and Revenson (1996) provide the following example: "When Christopher Robin, the child in Winnie-the-Pooh, talks to his woodland friends, a donkey, a tiger, an owl, a pig, and a bear, he is engaged in what Jean Piaget has called animism." As do the majority of picture books that feature animal characters, a child engaged in animism readily accepts that animals can and do behave as humans. An example is Olivia, Ian Falconer's character who has resonated with adults and children alike and is the protagonist in five titles. The first in the series, *Olivia* (2002), introduces Olivia, a boisterous and loving character who exhibits many of the traits associated with children.

EMERGENT LITERACY

Literacy is more than just the ability to read and write. It includes the ability to understand and communicate information and ideas and to form thoughts using reason and analysis. The early childhood years are critical to literacy development.

The building blocks for language and literacy begin to develop in the first three years of life. Research shows that children's early experiences with books and stories affect their reading success as they enter school. This process of early literacy development is often referred to as *emergent literacy.*

Zero to Three, a nonprofit organization,[1] defines literacy as "what children know about communication, language (verbal and nonverbal), reading, and writing before they can actually read and write. It encompasses all the experiences children have had with conversation, stories (oral and written), books, and print." The Center for Early Literacy Learning (CELL)[2] defines early literacy as "the knowledge and skills that young children need to read, write, and communicate. Early literacy learning for children from birth through 6 years of age is made up of print and language (spoken and written) learning."

Simply put, emergent literacy, or early literacy, is what children know about reading and writing before they can actually read or write. Beginning in infancy, children are exposed to all sorts of language and literacy. Every day babies encounter sounds that eventually help them form words and sentences. These are the building blocks that lead to reading and writing. From birth through two years old, two keys in a baby's literacy development are vocabulary and print motivation. From age two through the preschool years, print awareness, narrative skills, letter knowledge, and phonological awareness begin to develop.

In recent years, educators and parents have become increasingly motivated to help children develop these emergent literacy skills. Children's publishing has responded to that concern by increasing the number of picture books for younger, emerging readers.

Components of Early Literacy

In 2001 the Public Library Association (PLA) partnered with the National Institute of Child Health & Human Development (NICHD) to form The Early Literacy Initiative. One of the components to emerge from the partnership was a series of handouts that librarians and media specialists could distribute to parents.[3] The Early Literacy Initiative identified six components of early literacy.

Vocabulary

Vocabulary refers to knowing the names of things, and it begins to develop at birth. By 12 to 18 months of age children usually say their first word. By age two most children have vocabularies of 300 to 500 words. By the time they enter school most children know between 3,000 and 5,000 words. Adults can help babies and toddlers develop their vocabulary by talking to them and describing the things in the surrounding environment. Using clear, simple speech and encouraging the noises and sounds babies make also helps develop vocabulary.

Print Motivation

Print motivation is an interest in and enjoyment of books. Children with good print motivation play with books, pretend to read and write, and enjoy being read to. Adults can help babies and toddlers develop print motivation by sharing books and visiting the library.

Print Awareness

Print awareness includes recognizing that writing follows basic rules, such as reading from top to bottom and left to right. Children with print awareness point to the words on the pages of books while adults read. Adults can help children develop print awareness by reading to and with them, and by showing children that they love books and reading.

Narrative Skill

Narrative skill is the ability to understand and tell stories, as well as the ability to describe things. Children need narrative skill to understand the process of learning to read. Children developing narrative skill relate the events of the day as a story. They may also "read" a picture book using past knowledge and picture cues. Adults can help children build narrative skill by encouraging them to describe sequences, such as getting dressed ("First I put on my . . .) or taking a bath (First I fill the tub with water. . .).

Letter Knowledge

Letter knowledge includes learning that letters are different from each other, that they have names and specific sounds. A child developing letter knowledge recognizes a letter and the distinct sound it makes, such as "B" and the sound "buh." Adults can help children develop letter knowledge by pointing out letters in words in books, signs, and labels. Letter knowledge can also be developed through a variety of reading and writing activities using different media, such as crayons, pencils, and magnetic letters.

Phonological Awareness

Phonological awareness is a child's ability to hear and manipulate the sounds in words, such as the /at/ sound in "cat." It includes the ability to hear and create rhymes, to say parts of words, and to put parts of words together to make a new word, such as /h/ and /at/ or /c/ and /at/. Adults can help children develop phonological awareness by playing word games, such as having children find objects that rhyme with a particular word, such as cat.

How Picture Books Fit In

Beginning at six months, babies can focus on pictures in a book. Although they cannot yet make meaning from the pictures, this is a big step to picture recognition, an important early literacy skill. Because their vision is still blurry, newborns seem to prefer looking at brightly colored or high-contrast objects, such as black and white patterns.

At about four months, infants begin to show more interest in pictures in a book, particularly bright colors and shapes. Because they do not yet have picture recognition, infants do not attach meaning to the symbols or recognize that the pictures represent things and ideas. However, a particular page may hold their attention.

At about six months, babies may reach for or grasp a book. This skill is the first way a baby physically explores and learns about books. This is print motivation.

Picture books engage all of these skills, built into a fun format that is ideal for sharing.

Early Literacy Behaviors

Educator and early literacy expert Judith Schickedanz (2001) identifies four distinct early literacy behaviors: book handling behaviors, looking and recognizing, picture and story comprehension, and reading behaviors.

Book Handling Behaviors

Activities related to the way babies or toddlers physically handle books are referred to as book handling behaviors. These include turning pages and chewing on covers. Babies and toddlers may treat books roughly because they view books as toys. They will carry books around and throw them. This is part of their development; as they grow older toddlers learn how to handle books and turn pages without damaging them.

Looking and Recognizing

Looking and recognizing involves behaviors related to how children interact with books, particularly the pictures. Babies may look intently at pictures or laugh or smile at familiar objects. By six months of age, a child may reach out and touch the picture of a familiar object. Toddlers may name objects in a picture and point to pictures and ask "what's that?" These behaviors are the beginning of children's understanding of the role of pictures in books.

Picture and Story Comprehension

Picture and story comprehension refers to behaviors that show an understanding of pictures and events in a book, such as imitating an action seen in a picture or talking about the events in a story. Children may have favorite books or pages in a book. They may also be able to recall events or recognize sequences in the story. Adults can encourage participation by letting children turn pages and encouraging comments or questions.

Reading Behaviors

Reading behaviors are children's verbal interactions with books and their increasing understanding of how print works in books. Babies may babble or make other sounds. Toddlers might repeat phrases or reach out and run their fingers underneath the words, as if they are reading. They may also recite familiar books aloud by reciting from memory as they view the illustrations.

From Picture Books to Board Books

Many picture book titles are now being reproduced as board books, which are ideal for small hands—or for a parent balancing a baby in one arm and trying to hold a book with the other hand. Board books are made of laminated cardboard pages, with sturdy, with rounded edges. To a baby board books are toys, so parents should not be concerned about how a baby handles a board book. However, just because a title is in board book format does not mean it is suitable for every baby

Board books are durable and can be chewed on. It is normal for babies to put things in their mouths—including books. In fact, experts now consider chewing on books to be significant to the development of reading (Schickedanz 2001).

Libraries usually only have basic board books in their collections, because pull-the-flap and pop-up books do not hold up well through multiple circulations. Touch and feel books retain stains and germs, creating sanitary issues. And babies love to put their fingers in their mouths.

Board books are good for toddlers because, while they are showing more interest in the picture and narrative, books must be as mobile as a toddler. A two-year-old carries a book around the house much the same as a blanket. By using board books as transitional objects toddlers learn how to handle picture books as they grow older.

In the last decade publishers have responded to the demand for more board books. On the one hand, this is great because there are more titles to choose from than ever before. On the other hand, not all titles are suitable for board book format. In addition, not all publishers use the format to its best advantage (Horning 1997a). Many picture books have been reduced in size and printed on sturdy boards, ignoring the fact that the text is just too wordy for the board book format. Although the reduced format and sturdy cardboard pages make them ideal for children under three, not all titles have the appeal that engages children. For example, a title with a long narrative does not work well in board book format. When sharing books with babies and toddlers, their hands are constantly reaching out to turn the page, whether or not the adult is finished reading the words on the page. The time it takes to read 25 words or more per page is too long for children at this stage. Also, certain media or illustrative techniques, such as watercolors, are not suitable because the edges are blurry and fuzzy and children have trouble distinguishing the objects. Bright colors and defined shapes on a solid background are best.

In board books that have been created from a picture book, often the illustrations from the original picture book edition are omitted to make room for the text. The popular *Guess How Much I Love You* (1994) is available in a variety of formats, from board book to paperback. The premise of the story is lovely and the message is appropriate for babies—a timeless refrain of "guess how much I love you" makes the book a popular choice as a gift book—but the small board book format doesn't do justice to the story or to Anita Jeram's soft watercolor illustrations. In addition, the publisher reduced the page count from 28 to 20 to accommodate the board book format. Although the entire text is intact, some of the illustrations were omitted. Librarian Kathleen Horning says that the board book edition of *Guess How Much I Love You* pales in comparison to the original picture book format.

Another example of a picture book that was probably not the best choice for a board book edition (2004) is Chris Raschka's *Charlie Parker Played Be Bop* (1992). As a picture book it was successful as a biographical account of the jazz musician's contributions to that musical format. Raschka decorated the pages with pictures of birds as homage to Charlie (whose nickname was "Bird"), but the artistic embellishment is lost on toddlers, who are not familiar with Parker's history. Although the text is rhythmic and the text is formatted to accentuate the bouncy refrain, the book is not for younger children because the story is beyond the comprehension of a baby or toddler.

Educator Kathleen Odean (2004) also questions the misuse of the board book format. She acknowledges the strengths of the format, citing many pioneers, including Helen Oxenbury and Tana Hoban. She cites the works of author Byron Barton, originally issued in picture book format, as suitable for the board book format because Barton's illustrations have bold color and little detail. Another author with a style similar to Barton's is Todd Parr. Eric Hill's <u>Spot</u> titles feature bright colors and clearly identifiable objects, which make them suitable as well.

Horning (1997a) acknowledges that although misguided, publishers have only been attempting to feed demand for books for babies. She points out that most consumers are misled by the format and that librarians and parents buy familiar titles in board format because they are available rather than suitable.

Successful board books have shared characteristics. Pacing is appropriate to the story; word count is limited. There is not a magic formula for the number of words per page, but it is usually 10 or fewer per page. Babies and toddlers love familiar objects, bright colors, and high contrast.

A number of popular characters from picture books have been adapted for board book editions, including David Shannon's self-titled character, Ian Falconer's porcine heroine Olivia, and Kevin Henkes's mouse characters, namely Lilly, Sheila Ray, Owen, Wemberly, and Julius. Ian Falconer created a series of board books based on his best-selling series about Olivia. The titles include *Olivia's Opposites* (2002) and *Olivia's Counts* (2002). Rather than just adapting the picture books, Falconer instead created unique board book titles featuring Olivia.

In his board book series Kevin Henkes uses the popular characters from his mouse books. The first in the series is *Sheila Rae's Peppermint Stick* (2001), which features the star of *Sheila Rae, the Brave* (1987). Other board book titles by Henkes include *Owen's Marshmallow Chick* (2002), *Wemberly's Ice-Cream Star* (2003), *Lilly's Chocolate Heart* (2003), and *Julius's Candy Corn* (2003).

David Shannon created a series of board books featuring his popular character David, protagonist from *No, David!* (1998). The <u>Diaper David</u> series includes *David Smells!* (2005), in which David discovers the five senses, and *Oops!* (2005), in which David finds himself in a few sticky situations and learns five new words.

Types of Picture Books for Emerging Readers

John Locke (1632–1704) and Jean Jacques Rousseau may have helped define childhood, but it is the publishers, editors, and educators—not to mention the authors and illustrators—of the twentieth century who have increased the focus on books for children and their needs. A plethora of books have been created especially for emerging readers. In fact, many publishers have created imprints especially for infants and toddlers. For example, Little Simon, an imprint of Simon & Schuster, and the My First series from Dorling Kindersley are imprints that target younger children.

There are several types of board books for emerging readers: high contrast, touch and feel, novelty (pop-up, life-the-flap), songs and rhyming, concept, and bathtub.

High Contrast

High contrast picture books have a striking balance between the object and the background. That is, the main object on the page is easily discernible from the background. Perhaps the best example of this is *White on Black* (1993) by Tana Hoban. Hoban placed everyday objects (e.g., buttons, fish, boats) on each page and silhouetted them against a black background. She reversed the concept for *Black on White* (1993).

Touch And Feel

Touch and feel books have textured surfaces, ranging from fuzzy to smooth. They invite participation and stimulate tactile curiosity. Materials used in touch and feel books include fur, velour, sandpaper, mirrored paper, and foam. *Fuzzy Fuzzy Fuzzy!* (2003) by Sandra Boynton is an example of a touch and feel book. Perhaps the most popular touch and feel book is the classic *Pat the Bunny* (1940) by Dorothy Kunhardt. Generations of babies have rubbed the bunny's fur and hesitantly touched daddy's scratchy beard. Books in DK Publishing's My First Touch and Feel series feature textures and colorful images of common objects.

Novelty

Novelty books encourage exploration and inspire curiosity. From pop-up to lift-the-flap books, these books beg to be picked up and explored. *Where's Spot?* (1980) by Eric Hill spawned a series based on the lovable dog and engendered a whole cast of characters. *Where's Spot* has sold over four million copies in 65 languages. Unfortunately, novelty books are often roughly handled and can easily tear.

Songs and Rhyming

These books feature popular chants and rhymes paired with colorful photos and simple illustrations. Babies love hearing the same sounds and stories over and over again. Soothing, rhythmic repetitions mimic the sound of the human heartbeat.

Concept

Concept board books, like concept picture books, feature simple concepts in an accessible format. Unlike picture books, concept board books have few, if any, words. The focus is on very basic concepts: colors, shapes, animals, letters, and numbers. The <u>My First</u> series from Dorling Kindersley, also known as DK Publishing, is very popular.

Bathtub

As the name implies, bathtub books are water resistant. Small children enjoy playing with these in the tub. Because they are made of plastic, they are great for infants, who take a lot of pleasure in chewing on them.

Predictable Books

Predictable books, also called pattern books, are stories that feature repeated language patterns—repetition of words, phrases, sentences, and refrains—throughout the text. Particular phrases with strong rhyming and rhythm create a predictable text that propels the story forward. Illustrations feature repeated elements and backgrounds that create continuity. *Brown Bear, Brown Bear* (1967) is probably the most famous predictable title. The text begins with the phrase, "Brown bear, brown bear, what do you see? I see a red bird looking at me." In each successive page the animal from the second sentence is moved to the beginning of the next sentence (e.g., "Red bird, red bird, what do you see? I see a yellow duck looking at me," and so forth.). Predictable books invite children to make predictions about upcoming textual elements (words, phrases, and sentences) and pictorial elements (line, shape, color, value, texture, and space).

Chain or Circular Story

In a chain or circular story the plot is interlinked so that the ending leads back to the beginning. *Why Mosquitoes Buzz in People's Ears* (1975) by Verna Aardema, *Oh, Look!* (2004) by Patricia Polacco, and *If You Give a Mouse a Cookie* (1985) by Laura Joffe Numeroff are examples of chain or circular stories.

Cumulative Story

In a cumulative story, previous events are repeated each time a new event occurs. *Hattie and the Fox* (1987) by Mem Fox, *Mr. Gumpy's Outing* (1971) by John Burningham, and *One Fine Day* (1971) by Nonny Hogrogian are cumulative stories.

Familiar Sequence

Picture books with familiar sequences are organized by recognizable theme, such as days of the week. Examples are *Today Is Monday* (1993) by Eric Carle and *Chicken Soup with Rice* (1962) by Maurice Sendak.

Pattern Stories

In pattern stories scenes are repeated with some variation. Examples are *The Doorbell Rang* (1986) by Pat Hutchins, *The Runaway Bunny* (1972) by Margaret Wise Brown, *The Carrot Seed* (1945) by Ruth Krauss, and *Suddenly!* (1995) by Colin McNaughton.

Question and Answer

In a question and answer book, the same or similar question is repeated throughout the story. Examples are *Brown Bear, Brown Bear* (1967) by Bill Martin Jr., *Where Is the Green Sheep?* (2004) by Mem Fox, *What Do You Do with a Tail Like This?* (2003) by Robin Page, and *Knock! Knock!* (2007), which features the work of 14 popular picture book illustrators. Each illustrator tells and illustrates a different knock knock joke.

Repetition of Phrase

In picture books with repeated words or phrases, the repetition drives the narrative forward. Examples are *Bear Snores On* (2002) by Karma Wilson, *Hug* (2000) by Jez Alborough, *No, David!* (1998) by David Shannon, *It Looked Like Spilt Milk* (1947) by Charles B. Shaw, and *Silly Sally* (1992) by Audrey Wood.

Rhyme

In rhyming books, words, refrains, or patterns create a rhyming scheme that invites participation. *Sheep in a Jeep* (1986) by Nancy Shaw, *Barnyard Banter* (1994) by Denise Fleming, and *Is Your Mama a Llama* (1989) by Deborah Guarino are rhyming books.

Songbooks

Many traditional songs have been adapted to predictable picture book format. The familiar songs encourage children to sing along. Examples are the old Appalachian counting rhyme, attributed to Olive A. Wadsworth; *Over in the Meadow* (1971), illustrated by Ezra Jack Keats; the traditional circle song *Farmer in the Dell* (2004), illustrated by Ilse Plume; and *Old MacDonald Had a Farm* (1990), illustrated by Glen Rounds.

Picture Books and Babies

Reading provides a special opportunity for parent and baby to spend time together and bond. From birth babies recognize voices and find comfort in hearing the soothing tones of parents or loved ones reading to them.

Sharing books with babies helps nurture a love for books and reading. Reading provides a baby with rich language experiences. When read to, babies often try to imitate the adult who is reading.

Because a baby is attracted to different sounds, reading aloud to babies helps them attach meaning to those sounds. For instance, a child associates the word "meow" with the image of a kitty. By nine months a baby begins to understand simple words.

Books and reading also provide visual stimulation for the baby. Books give babies an opportunity to develop their vision by focusing on objects. A newborn's sight is the least developed sense at birth. A newborn's eyes can track movement, but for a very short distance, only 9 to 12 inches from the face. Because an infant's eyes cannot focus, objects and people appear fuzzy. By three months infants can see out of the corner of their eyes (peripheral vision). They can follow an object moving in a circle, like the mobile hanging above the crib. Eventually they develop the ability to focus on an object. Between two and six months infants' ability to follow an object with their eyes strengthens and they are able to focus on objects. They also can see color and depth. By six months the area of the brain that sends and receives messages about what the newborn sees is developing. Eventually an infant's vision is as clear as an adult's.

In addition to being a visually motivating experience, reading to a baby also stimulates the baby's brain development. Reading provides babies with their first literacy experiences. Research has shown that an early start with reading and books is linked to a child's later success in learning to read.

Ten Tips for Sharing Books with Babies

- Select books that can babies can touch and chew, such as cloth books or board books. Choose titles with rounded corners and avoid ones with pointed edges.

- Touch your baby when sharing books.

- Pick books with bright colors, high contrast, and familiar objects.

- Books should have one object per page/one word per page.

- Vary the selection by choosing books that provide tactile experiences, such as flaps to raise, surfaces to touch, and holes to poke fingers through.

- Babies like to handle books, so choose interactive books with flaps they can lift and cut-outs they can poke their fingers through.

- Pick a quiet time and a comfortable space for reading. If a baby is fussy or does not show interest, do not force him or her to share books.

- Read every day, several times a day, even if it is only for a few minutes.

- Babies respond to different voices and sounds, so be inventive and enthusiastic when reading.

- Hold your baby on your lap and the book so that your baby can see the pages clearly.

Picture Books and Toddlers

Books can nurture a toddler's love for books and reading. Sharing literature with toddlers builds a foundation for literacy. Through the shared experience of reading, toddlers learn how to handle books, such as how to turn pages. Reading with a toddler also develops early literacy skills, such as print awareness, or the understanding that print moves from top to bottom and left to right.

Sharing books with toddlers gives them an opportunity to participate in the story experience. Reading to and with a toddler provides rich language experience. Toddlers' vocabulary grows through the repetition of words and phrases, which is why books with rhymes are ideal.

Perhaps most important, picture books provide toddlers with their first experience of art and how stories and illustration work together.

Ten Tips for Sharing Books with Toddlers

- Select books that can toddlers can handle, such as cloth books or board books. Choose titles with rounded corners and avoid ones with pointed edges.

- Select books with bright colors and familiar objects to help toddlers build vocabulary.

- Select books with repetition: sound, rhythm, or rhyme.

- Select books that provide tactile experiences such as flaps to raise, surfaces to touch, and holes to poke fingers through.

- Encourage toddlers to participate by letting them "read" the story and act it out.

- Linger over the story, pointing out words and pictures.

- Let toddlers participate by turning the pages and give them time to respond.

- Toddlers have limited attention spans. Don't force reading time, but rather read several simple, short books throughout the day.

- Place your child on your lap or next to you during reading time. Hold the book so your child can see the pages clearly.

- Make books and reading a regular part of every day.

VISUAL LITERACY

The human eye is constantly bombarded with a myriad of colors, shapes, textures, and patterns. If a person were to close his or her eyes and then open them, certain colors and patterns might have an impact, but the majority of the visual stimuli would be difficult to recall.

Humans learn to analyze, evaluate, and interpret information from a variety of visual media, including text, photographs, art, film, and the Internet. In the information age, information is increasingly visual.

The brain sorts through the visual cues, imprinting images. Sensory preceptors are not passive; they actively sort and assess the endless stream of visual stimuli. From the millions of visual cues, individuals select and use what is most meaningful (Wade and Swanston 2001). The human brain responds to and sorts through the cues; with a little cooperation, the eyes and brain communicate to make sense of the visual miasma (Wade and Swanston 2001).

Not only are humans constantly bombarded with billions of stimuli, but each individual reacts differently to those stimuli. An individual's emotional state plays a significant role in how meaning is made from visual cues. Designers and artists control the way people look at picture books by applying elements to elicit specific responses from viewers.

Literacy refers to the ability to read and write; developing literacy means learning to make meaning from words. So what is visual literacy? In a nutshell, visual literacy is the ability to communicate through and understand images. Developing visual literacy means honing the ability to effectively analyze, evaluate, discriminate, and interpret messages embedded in images. Visual literacy allows people to actively participate in making meaning of images instead of being passive receptacles. Put simply, visual literacy is the ability to understand and use images.

Why Is Visual Literacy Important?

In the last decade scholars have explored how we "read" pictures. They contend that the complexity of the picture–text (or the verbal–visual) relationship requires readers to call upon cognitive skills. It is now acknowledged that picture books can have multiple meanings and multiple discourses, and that the ability to read images is one aspect of visual literacy that is needed in an increasingly globalized, technological age (Nikolajeva and Scott 2001, 2006).

How is the "reading" of images different from the reading of print? A comprehensive study by two British scholars presents evidence of children's sophisticated interpretation of visual texts. The research reflects findings that suggest that reading images involves a different process than reading words. Scholars Evelyn Arizpe and Morag Styles (2003) conducted a two-year study in which they examined children's responses to picture books.[4] Their research concluded that children are very sophisticated when viewing images. They found that children ages four through eleven were able to make meaning from complex images on many levels: literal, visual, and metaphorical.

In print, readers rely on text to relay the message. In an image, the visual cues help decode the message.

Visual communication is the transfer of information in a visual form. Gestures, like a smile or a nod or the way a person stands, communicate information. People communicate visually through a variety of media, from television to art to the Internet to advertising. In media, the focus is on the presentation of text, pictures, diagrams, photos, and graphics. Visual presentation is the actual presentation of information.

Visual literacy is the ability to understand and make meaning from visual stimuli. A visually literate person understands how visual elements contribute to the meaning of the whole. Visual literacy is the ability, through knowledge of the basic visual elements, to understand the meaning and components of the image.

What may be most interesting about images is the way that these two-dimensional, flat objects represent our three-dimensional world. In a composition, every component and aspect that makes up the picture—from line to value to texture—works together to create an allusion, association, or experience for the viewer. For example, in *The Garden of Azgazi* (1979), Chris Van Allsburg uses tone and texture to create tension between reality and illusion. In the story, Alan Mitz, has strayed into a garden filled with eerie topiary sculptures, made all more disturbing through Van Allsburg's intricate drawings. Even after Alan escapes, he is haunted by the spell of Azgazi's garden.

Pictorial Elements

Text is linear: it moves from left to right, top to bottom. When reading text the eyes move linearly, back and forth, line after line. Images are nonlinear. Eyes may dart around a composition, trying to make sense of the visual message. Created by the hands of a competent, talented artist, the illustration guides the eye through a planned and intentional path. For example, the eye may be drawn to a splash of color in the lower-left hand corner of a dark background. Arrangement of objects on a page from the lower left-hand corner to upper right draws the eye upward. From that point, a composition leads the eye to another part of the picture.

As they learn to read, children are introduced to letters, words, spelling, grammar, and syntax—the elements of literature and literacy. The same is true of visual literacy. Like sentences and stories, images are compositions, and compositions have parts. To put it another way, visual images have their own grammar. Some of the basic elements important to visual literacy were explored as art elements and design principles in chapter 3. As discussed there, the elements of art are basic components used by the artist in creating a work of art. They are color, line, perspective, shape, space, texture, and value. The principles of design are the arrangement of visual elements in an illustration. They include balance, contrast, emphasis, harmony, movement, rhythm, and unity.

ELEMENTS OF ART

Color: setting, theme, or mood

Line: direction and guiding the viewer's eye across the page

Perspective: illusion of depth on a two-dimensional surface

Shape: basic outlines that define and enclose space

Space: the relative size, measurement, and dimension of objects

Texture: the surface characteristic of the composition; can be optical or tactile

Value: the presence or absence of light, saturation of color

PRINCIPLES OF DESIGN

Balance: stability, visual weight

Contrast: abrupt, unexpected

Emphasis: focal point, direct attention

Harmony and variety: visual interest, accentuating

Movement: motion, action

Rhythm: repetition, pattern

Unity: completeness, synergy

In addition to using principles of design or art elements, an illustrator also considers picture space. Readers look at a picture and see the subject or main idea immediately; what may be less obvious is composition. How did the illustrator manage to capture the scene that gives the viewer that immediate knowledge of what the picture is about? There are hundreds of things happening simultaneously that create a first impression when readers look at a picture. Often the objects in the compositions are immediately obvious. What is often overlooked is the space around the objects.

For example, in *Where the Wild Things Are* (1963) there is a boy (Max), who the reader knows is precocious by the way Sendak has drawn him. In the illustration in which Max is sent to his room, Max's head is slightly turned up and his arms are folded across his chest in defiance of his predicament. There are other objects in the room—bed, dresser, and rug—but the visual emphasis is on Max. Sendak's use of space around the illustrations is commonly mentioned when critics attempt to define what makes illustrations in a picture book work. He uses white space to propel the narrative forward, as Max journeys to the land of the Wild Things.

Chapter 3 explored picture space and composition. Picture space is the depth of space, which includes the objects and space around them. Composition is the way the elements are organized. As a child, artist Uri Shulevitz (1997) says he was only aware of the objects in the picture, what he calls the visible aspect of the picture. In his example of a tree, he recalls seeing the tree but not space around the tree or between the branches. Gradually he became aware of invisible space around the tree. He learned there was a hidden structure that organized the picture. The invisible space or "nothingness" plays a very important role in how pictures work. According to Shulevitz, all elements, whether hidden or visible, work for or against the picture. Uri Shulevitz's journey from seeing "nothingness" to an appreciation of the way a picture works was crucial to his development as an artist. A child developing visual literacy progresses through a similar process.

Artist Molly Bang explored picture composition in *Picture This: How Pictures Work* (1991, 2000). Using the story of "Little Red Riding Hood," she examined the aspects of composition. Already a successful illustrator when she wrote the book in 1991, Bang admits in the preface that she was not really sure how pictures worked. Her quest to understand led to the publication of the book.

Bang slowly added color, experimented with scale, explored the effects of size, and manipulated shapes as she negotiated composition and picture space. She discovered that geometric shapes create emotions she didn't feel with organics shapes. She used sharp angles and lines to create drama, while at the same time building a narrative.

Bang ultimately identified 10 principles that she visually communicated thorough a series of illustrations designed to illustrate what she learned as she built the pictures for her book. For example, on pages 68–69 she explored the effect background has on a composition, which corresponds with the sixth principle she identified. She placed a dark object in a light background and paired it with a light object on a dark background. Her analysis was that lighter backgrounds make viewers feel safer, while dark ones imply danger. On pages 70–71 Bang explored shape, which corresponds with the seventh principle she identified. She paired a an image with jagged edges to one with curved edges. Her analysis was that viewers are more scared looking at jagged edges, which impart feelings of fear, as opposed to curved objects, which impart feelings of calm and comfort.

Many of the principles Bang explored in her book are some of the art elements and design principles covered in chapter 3. Bang put them into context by exploring the way they changed the story of "Little Red Riding Hood." When she added triangles to the wolf's mouth, he became dangerous. When she changed the color of his eyes from white to red, he was absolutely menacing.

Figures 6.1 through 6.5 (pp. 146–47) were created to illustrate a few of Bang's principles. In figure 6.1 a light object is set on a dark background, which conveys fear, danger, and impending doom. On the other hand, a dark object on a light background conveys safety and security. In figure 6.2 a jagged shape is placed opposite a curved shape. The jagged shape conveys extreme emotion, such as anger, whereas the curved shape is calming. In the first two frames of figure 6.3 horizontal and vertical shapes are placed next to one another; the horizontal shape is stable while the vertical shape is energetic. In the third frame, a horizontal shape is placed across the top of two vertical shapes. According to Bang, when a horizontal shape is placed on top of a vertical shape, it dominates the energy and instability vertical shapes have and makes a picture more stable. In figure 6.4 two frames, one with an object in the upper half of the picture and one with an object in the lower half, are an example of what Bang calls the "emotional horizon" of the picture space. The emotional horizon separates the picture space in the top and bottom. The top half feels joyous and free, whereas the bottom half feels heavier and constrained. People tend to notice shape before color when all objects are the same color. When two colors are present, people sort by color. Bang says people associate the same color more strongly than the same or similar shapes. In the first frame of figure 6.5, all the objects are black. In this case, the natural tendency is to sort by shape. In the second frame, there are black and gray objects. In this case, the inclination is to sort by color. Therefore, when asked to group the objects in the first frame, most people would divide the objects by shape: triangles and circles. However, in the second frame, because color is a stronger influence, most people would sort the objects into black and gray groups.

Figure 6.1. The left-hand side has a light object on a dark background, which implies fear or danger. The right-hand side has a dark object on a light background, which conveys safety.

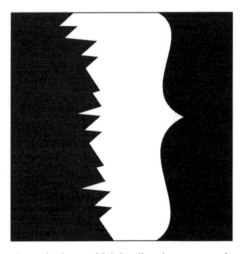

Figure 6.2. The left-hand has jagged edges, which implies danger or perhaps anger. The curved edges on the right-hand side convey a feeling of calm and comfort.

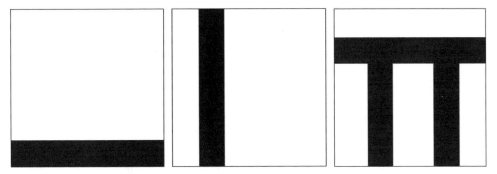

Figure 6.3. Horizontal shapes are stable; vertical shapes are active. When they are combined, the horizontal shape dominates the frame, creating stability.

Figure 6.4. Placing an object in the top half of the picture space creates a feeling of joy; placing an object in the bottom half creates a feeling of sadness.

Figure 6.5. People associate the same or similar colors more strongly than they associate the same or similar shapes.

> For interactive examples of the way shapes, color, and size affect composition, please visit www.picturingbooks.com.

The impact of a story without pictures is different than that of one with pictures. Let's take another look at *Where the Wild Things Are* (1963). In this book, words are often placed on a white space without pictures. In addition, there is a series of pages without any words at all. Maurice Sendak says the pictures in *Wild Things* quicken the pace of the story. For Sendak, to quicken means that the creator fully understands his story, then gives life to that through illustration. In other words, the illustrations do not exist to support the text, but rather extend it and give the story new meaning.

Picture Books and Visual Literacy

Illustrations play an integral role in picture books. When used concurrently with other curriculum, picture books can help children develop strong visual literacy skills. Illustration is the heart of a picture book. Images beat with life and energy, taking a story from the mundane into a whole other realm. In addition to illustration, composition and design establish the setting, define characters, extend or develop the plot, and provide a different perspective. A child with strong visual literacy skills is able to use these tools to make meaning from the text, enhancing and extending the reading experience.

When pictures and words come together in a picture book, synergy is the result. The two join forces, creating a visual experience. The text, linear and sequential, helps readers understand the story. It moves along line after line, page after page, building comprehension. The illustrations are a series of images and details that assail the eye simultaneously (Schwarz 1982). Through picture books, readers learn to follow linear text and nonlinear images simultaneously. These two synchronize in the drama of turning the page to create a unique reading experience.

Perhaps the reason that scholar Barbara Bader's words, with which chapter 1 of this book opens, are so frequently cited is that it is difficult to find a way a better way to describe the magic moment when text and picture meet and merge.

When reading a picture book, eyes and brains work in linear fashion with the text and at the same time in a nonlinear fashion with the images. Illustrations in a picture book work sequentially, either working with or contradicting the text. In addition, different viewers interpret the illustrations on different levels (Schwartz). The illustration on page one leads to page two, and so forth. In other words, with each turn of the page, readers get another piece of information, a little more drama, and a little more action.

The combination of or contradiction between the narrative and the illustrations offers variations for content, context, and form (Schwartz). Some books incorporate metaphor and symbolism that raise their status to the heights of the sublime. Books like those by Maurice Sendak work on multiple levels. On one level, *Where the Wild Things Are* (1962) is a story of a naughty boy sent to bed without his supper. On a visual level, Sendak uses white space to show Max entering his dream and then returning home again. Aside from Anthony Browne, author of *Voices in the Park* (1998), *The Shape Game* (2003), and *Zoo* (1993), Sendak is probably the most studied picture book illustrator in the world.

What is learned from great illustrators?

- Readers gain a greater understanding of the relationship between text and illustrations.

- Readers explore and interpret ideas, themes, and issues expressed visually.

- Readers identify and understand metaphor and symbolism.

- Readers develop an awareness of the role of an illustrator and how the illustrations of a text are constructed.

- Readers explore the media and illustrative techniques that enhance the reading experience.

How can picture books help build visual literacy?

Picture books are ideal for helping children develop visual literacy skills. They are defined by their illustrations, and sometimes the true meaning of the story is only accessible through pictures, such as in wordless picture books. Through picture books children can develop visual literacy by using the illustrations to explore, reflect, and critique the story. Through picture books children

- learn to read images;

- explore how images make meaning;

- develop an understanding of the picture–story relationship; and

- explore and interpret ideas, themes, and issues expressed through images.

> *"What is the use of a book," thought Alice "without pictures or conversation?"*
> —Lewis Carroll, *Alice's Adventures in Wonderland*

CONCLUSION

From a child's birth, picture books play an important role in the development of literacy. Emergent literacy or early literacy is what children know about reading and writing before they can actually read or write on their own. From birth through two years old, two keys in a baby's literacy development are vocabulary and print motivation. From age two through the preschool years, print awareness, narrative skills, letter knowledge, and phonological awareness begin to develop.

Visual literacy is the ability to understand and make meaning from images. A visually literate person understands how visual elements combine and express meaning. Through knowledge of the basic visual elements, children develop stronger visual literacy skills.

Picture books offer an excellent opportunity to support literacy, both emergent and visual, because children are introduced to verbal and visual communication simultaneously.

ENDNOTES

1. Zero to Three is a national nonprofit multidisciplinary organization that exists to inform, educate, and support adults who influence the lives of infants and toddlers. The Web site is www.zerotothree.org.

2. The Center for Early Literacy Learning (CELL) is a research-to-practice center funded by the U.S. Department of Education, Office of Special Education Programs, Research to Practice Division. CELL promotes the adoption and sustained use of evidence-based early literacy learning practices, especially for children, birth to five years of age, with disabilities, developmental delays, and at-risk environments. The Web site is www.earlyliteracylearning.org.

3. The series, Parent's Guide to Emergent Literacy, was developed by Dr. Russ Grover Whitehurst, professor of psychology at the State University of New York, and Dr. Christopher Lonigan, associate professor of psychology at Florida State University. The handouts are well organized and useful to anyone interested in an overview of emergent literacy.

4. Arizpe and Styles conducted their research in Great Britain. They spell picturebook as one word.

Chapter 7

Picture Book Issues

The best books break down borders. They surprise us—whether they are set close to home or abroad. They change our view of ourselves; they extend that phrase "like me" to include what we thought was foreign and strange.

—Hazel Rochman, *Against Borders: Promoting Books for a Multicultural World*

In This Chapter
- Multicultural Picture Books
- International Picture Books
- Controversial Picture Books and Censorship Challenges
- Classic Picture Books
- Reissues
- Good Intentions

Picture books may seem an innocuous form of literature, impervious to controversy and conflict. But the opposite is often true. Issues of authenticity and portrayal in multicultural and international literature continue to elicit debate, with the criteria and eligibility for awards joining the fray. Once taboo subjects such as homosexuality, divorce, and death are common subjects in picture books. Today, almost no subject is forbidden for children's literature, picture books in particular. Classic picture books, rife with stereotypes and inaccuracies, struggle to find a place in the children's literature canon. This chapter explores some of the more common issues surrounding picture books.

MULTICULTURAL PICTURE BOOKS

Historical Overview

From 1878, when Randolph Caldecott published his first picture book, *The Diverting History of John Gilpin*, until the publication of *Stevie* (1969), multicultural issues were notable for two reasons: (1) the absence or token presence only of children of color and (2) the inaccurate portrayal of children of color. That is not to say that the problem has disappeared, or that everyone—authors, illustrators, editors, reviewers, and critics—should not rigorously fight and remain alert to the false and harmful representations in multicultural picture books. However, it can be said that things have changed.

In her classic article, "The All-White World of Children's Books," noted educator Nancy Larrick (1965) exposed the lack of color in children's books and the often false, intentional or not, representation of minority cultures. Her study revealed that only four-fifths of 1 percent of the 5,000 titles published in the three previous years either included or mentioned African American culture.

In the years following Larrick's study, more picture books were published that featured children of color, but they often lacked authenticity and cultural substance. When characters of color were included, they were often stereotyped. One common criticism of *The Snowy Day* (1962) is that Peter's mother is portrayed as overweight. However, it was not just the characters that were slighted in these books; cultures and traditions were also inaccurately portrayed. "I is for Indian" and "I is for igloo" were commonplace in alphabet books. This is a blemish on the otherwise rich tradition of children's book publishing and the children's literature canon.

During the 1980s and 1990s a tremendous effort was made to authentically and accurately portray various ethnic cultures. Authors, illustrators, editors, reviewers, and critics realized that portraying contemporary Latino characters wearing sombreros and huaraches and Asian Americans eating rice was not only hurtful but also inaccurate, lacking in both substance and honesty. The multicultural picture book canon began to evolve, but progress was slow. Early efforts to increase the number of multicultural titles resulted in an influx of folktales to introduce other cultures to children (Horning 1997b).

Multicultural children's literature received more attention during the 1980s. The number of authentic multicultural titles published each year was small compared to the total number of books published. In 1985 the Cooperative Children's Book Center documented the number of children's books written or illustrated by African Americans and published in the United States. Only 18 of the roughly 2,500 trade books published that year were by African American authors and illustrators, not much of an improvement from when Larrick conducted her study 20 years earlier. (The figures are approximate because, although the CCBC receives copies from the major trade book publishers, it does not receive every book published in a given year.)

In 1990 over 5,000 titles were published for children and young adults; of those only 51 were written and/or published by African American authors (Lindgren 1991). According to educator Merri V. Lindgren, at that time it was even harder to find titles by Asian Americans, Native Americans, and Latino Americans.

Meanwhile, the 1990s saw the beginning of a debate about who should write and illustrate books about people of color. One creator, artist Tom Feelings, made his case clear: "Truly authentic multicultural books are created—written and illustrated—by people who belong in the race, culture, or nation of origin which is reflected." Critics vary in their opinions about this, and the issue is not yet resolved.

Even today, more than 40 years after the issue was first brought to light, there is a great discrepancy in the numbers of authors and titles by multicultural authors, and the quality of multicultural literature, though much better, is still a topic that raises as many questions as it answers.

People outside the represented culture too often overlook or forgive inaccurate details, although not intentionally. For example, *Brother Eagle, Sister Sky* (1991), illustrated by Susan Jeffers, has been controversial for its depiction of Native American culture. Doris Seale of Oyate, an organization that works to address the accurate and honest portrayal of the lives and histories of Native American cultures, recognizes that Jeffers's previous body of work included "beautifully illustrated books for young children," but nonetheless painstakingly outlines the inaccuracies in Jeffers's book.

Although *Brother Eagle, Sister Sky* has been a children's best seller for years—by 1999 it had sold almost 500,000 copies—the book did not garner universal praise. Patricia Dooley, reviewing it in *School Library Journal* (September 1991), said, "Alas her entire stock of characters appears to have come from the Sioux Central casting" and notes that the text is not "well served by images that ignore the rich diversity of Amerindian cultures." In her response to Dooley's review, illustrator Susan Jeffers stated that her research for the book was extensive. However, Seale asserted that Jeffers's extensive research was not the issue. According to Seale, "Native nations are not interchangeable."

Defining Multicultural Literature

Defining multicultural literature is difficult; attempting to isolate it to just picture books is even harder. To begin with, there really isn't a single definition of *multicultural literature*. It seems to mean different things to different people. For some it is books by and about people of color.[1] For others it is books that cross cultures and are not limited to those by or about people of color.[2] Furthermore, there are scholars who ponder the place of other marginalized groups based on social class, disability, gender, religion, and sexual orientation, to name a few issues. How do we deal with groups that some might argue are even more marginalized than groups who are denigrated because of race or ethnicity? That argument is beyond the scope of this book. This section explores the topic from a racial/ethnic perspective. Despite the disagreements, or attempts to reach a consensus, do not underestimate the role that naming or defining plays in children's picture books.[3] A definition that is meaningful and applicable to a given situation can help readers make informed decisions about selection and use; understanding different perspectives and positions helps readers clarify and refine a course of action.

There are two types of definitions worthy of consideration here: literary and pedagogical.[4] A literary definition describes the literary merit of a work, whereas a pedagogical definition describes the role of multicultural literature in education.

Scholars constantly analyze issues of literary quality versus insider knowledge. This book does not attempt to explore the issue in detail. Readers are encouraged to pursue the subject further by examining the books and articles listed in appendix C.

Literary Definition

In the literary definition there are two types of multicultural literature: explicitly and implicitly multicultural. Explicitly multicultural literature is openly multicultural in its approach. The setting is usually multicultural, such as a predominantly Latino neighborhood or perhaps a character adapting to an environment in which his or her ethnicity plays a central role (e.g., the first African American child to attend a segregated school). An explicitly multicultural book may also be about a minority culture and how a character interacts with or lives within the mainstream society. An example is *The Story of Ruby Bridges* (1995), which is the biographical account of African American girl who attends a segregated school in New Orleans in 1960.

In contrast, implicitly multicultural literature is dependent on insider knowledge. An author or illustrator may intentionally include references that require the reader to discover certain challenging aspects of the text, which can lead to a deeper understanding of the work. An example of an implicitly multicultural book is *Nappy Hair* (1997) by Carolivia Herron. Herron, an African American author and educator, wrote *Nappy Hair* as a celebration of her cultural heritage. When she heard about a teacher in Brooklyn, New York, who was fired and branded a racist for reading *Nappy Hair* to her class, Herron was astounded. Shocked by the situation, the author stated, "The idea that the book is racist is ridiculous. This book is a wonderful celebration of nappy, African-American hair" ("NYC Removes Teacher 1998). The use of the word "nappy" in both the title and repeatedly throughout the book created controversy because *nappy* is an insider term that is often used in a derogatory manner (Martin 1999). In addition to the word "nappy," the narrative is an example of a type of storytelling called "call and response," which is unique to African American people.

Pedagogical Definition

Educator Rudine Sims Bishop states that "multicultural literature is one of the most powerful components of a multicultural education curriculum" (1997). Rating authenticity as perhaps one of the most sensitive issues in multicultural literature, Sims Bishop stresses the necessity for accurate portrayals of people of color, including values, customs, and familial relationships (1997). Most critics fear that having authors and illustrators from outside of a culture write about the culture leads to representation of people of color as "the other." Critics are also concerned about who controls the representation of people of color in the publishing world (1997). Sims Bishop insists that when children are involved with literature it not only allows them to see the world through a window applicable to their experiences, but it also allows them to see images of themselves mirrored in the texts that they encounter (Smith 1997).

Fear of charges of racism and stereotyping are common for teachers in the late twentieth- and early twenty-first centuries. Sims Bishop asserts that it is impossible to create a tidy checklist to help teachers and others select authentic children's literature. Instead, Sims Bishop pushes for awareness, offering two strategies that can help teachers select appropriate multicultural literature. The first is to be aware of the various types of multicultural literature, including format (e.g., nonfiction, biographies, picture books, novels, and traditional literature). The second is to read extensively in literature by "insiders," which Sims Bishop defines as those from the culture being written about (1997). She asserts that reading literature by insiders helps readers recognize themes, topics, values, social mores, and language—those elements that characterize a culturally specific body of literature (1997).

Who Creates Multicultural Literature?

Who should write the texts?

Who should illustrate the texts?

Who should publish the books?

Who buys the books?

Whom are the books for?

Whose Voice Do We Listen To?

The author?

The illustrator?

The publisher?

The critic?

The scholar?

The child?

Types

In discussing multicultural literature, it is useful to examine some of the types: inclusive or "melting pot," multicultural in content, and multicultural in content and by a member of culture.[5] Not all critics agree on these types, and they may define them differently. The definitions discussed below are based on who wrote and illustrated the books. There are many other approaches. For example, books can be classified by social consciousness and intended reader age group. Readers interested in a comprehensive exploration of multicultural literature should read the works of Rudine Sims Bishop; *Multicultural Literature for Children and Young Adults: Reflections on Critical Issues* (2003) by Mingshui Cai; and *Stories Matter: The Complexity of Cultural Authenticity in Children's Literature* (2003), edited by Kathy G. Short and Dana L. Fox. All are excellent resources for readers interested in a detailed overview of multicultural literature.

Inclusive or "Melting Pot" Titles

Inclusive or "melting pot" titles reflect a world in which differences between cultures are minimal. Most melting pot titles are picture books; thus the differences in the books are often reflected in the illustrations rather than the text (Cai 2002). That is, because the text is not culturally specific, readers only know that a character is of color through the illustrations. Author Vera B. Williams writes and illustrates titles that include people of all colors in ordinary settings, but her books do not address issues or themes of race, culture, or ethnicity. *A Chair for My Mother* (1982) and *More More More, Said the Baby* (1990) are books that feature children of all colors, without addressing cultural background. Melting pot titles feature people of all colors in everyday situations. Children play together oblivious of the distinction of skin color, while adults carry out errands and travel to work.

Multicultural in Content

A second type of multicultural literature is multicultural in content but not by a member of the ethnic group represented. This type includes the work of Chris Raschka (an American author) and Paul Goble (a British author). Raschka has written and illustrated a series of picture books about jazz music, and Goble, who has been intrigued with the Plains Indians all his life, writes about them. The respect they have for the cultures they write about is apparent in the loving words and beautiful illustrations in all of their books. That is not to say that the books are not controversial, but the exquisite attention to detail and research into the topic of each of the books by Goble and Raschka is a strong argument in support of titles written by someone outside of the culture. Ezra Jack Keats's <u>Peter</u> books, which include the Caldecott-winning *The Snowy Day* (1962), are multicultural in content, though they could also be classified as inclusive because although the majority of the characters are African American, the cultural aspect is significantly downplayed.

Multicultural in Content and by a Member of That Culture

A third type of multicultural literature is multicultural in content and is created by a member of the ethnic group represented. Illustrator Allen Say, born in Japan in 1937 to a Korean father and a Japanese American mother, has produced many titles that explore his own life and memories growing up in Japan, as well as the lives of his family. His biographical *Grandfather's Journey* (1993) won the Caldecott Medal in 1994.

The authenticity of multicultural titles not written by a person of the culture represented is often controversial. Many critics maintain that only a member of the culture can accurately depict it. Thus, while many of Paul Goble's titles are praised, they still cause concern. Goble's recent books include long lists of sources that critics Doris Sale and Beverly Slapin speculate may be in response to the Native American community's increasing insistence that they tell their own stories.

Who should write and illustrate multicultural titles is an ongoing debate. Understanding why authenticity and accuracy are important is essential. Reading reviews in major journals is helpful. The children's librarian at the local library can help readers locate articles and research. Organizations such as the Cooperative Children's Book Center (www.education.wisc.edu/ccbc) and Oyate (www.oyate.org) offer resources on their Web sites. However, as the *Nappy Hair* incident shows, sometimes controversy is unavoidable.

Images in Multicultural Literature

Scholar Mingshui Cai (2002) asserts that distinguishing between stereotypes and realistic portrayal is very difficult. Aspects of stereotypes may be true. For example, many migrant workers are from Mexico, but automatically portraying all people of Mexican descent as migrant workers is a stereotype. Cai asks, "If showing African Americans eating fried chicken, watermelon, or spareribs is a stereotype, does it mean it is taboo to detail this is any story?" He uses *Tar Beach* (1991), illustrated by Faith Ringgold, as an example. There are several scenes in the book that feature these elements. Cai asserts that it is not problematic because Ringgold is African American. Had the illustrator not been of the culture represented, it may have been viewed as problematic.

Cai asserts that society must be vigilant regarding stereotypes, detecting and dissecting existing ones, and examining news ones that arise (2002). He says caution should be taken to thwart stereotypes that serve the dominant culture, but at the same it is necessary to make sure that realistic portrayals of cultures are not mistakenly considered stereotypes. The *Nappy Hair* situation is one example. The confusion over the representation of the dominated culture, in this case African Americans, and the celebration of culture and family history resulted in a controversial situation.

Images in picture books are particularly troublesome in classic picture books. Many classic picture books distort and denigrate ethnic cultures. An example is *The Five Chinese Brothers* (1938), which portrays Asians with bright yellow skin and slanted eyes. For readers not of the culture portrayed, it can be difficult to understand why particular books, titles now considered classic and much loved, are problematic.

Issues

Multicultural Awards

In a bold and daring article, "Slippery Slopes and Proliferating Prizes: Questions about the Creation of Three Book Awards Based on Race or Ethnicity" (2001), author and editor Mark Aronson questioned the wisdom of culture-specific awards, that is, awards that are directly tied the author's or illustrator's ethnicity He focused on awards created and regulated by the American Library Association (ALA). ALA, which had already established two such awards—the Coretta Scott King Award, for contribution by an African American author or illustrator, and the Pura Belpré, for contribution by a Latino author or illustrator—was at that time developing an award for Asian American authors and illustrators.

Aronson contended that having "awards in which a book's eligibility is determined by the race or ethnicity of its creators is a mistake." He asserted that this is not the way to bring multicultural books to the attention of the public; that it is wrong to evaluate the books not on their merit but rather on extraneous standards such as skin color.

Consider the work of Chris Raschka, who is white. Raschka's *Yo! Yes?* (1993) is an almost wordless picture book, with only 34 words. With deceptive simplicity, Chris Raschka integrates multicultural aspects of two boys from different backgrounds broaching friendship. Although the book has been celebrated (in fact it was a Caldecott Honor winner) and is a lovely story of two cultures meeting, it would not be eligible for the Coretta Scott King Award. Neither would Raschka's innovative picture book biographies *Mysterious Thelonious* (1997) and *Charlie Parker Played Be Bop* (1992), or his collaborations with bell hooks, *Be Boy Buzz* (2002) and *Happy to Be Nappy* (1999), all featuring African American themes and characters.

After the article was published, the *Horn Book* received a flood of letters, some supporting Aronson, most not. The journal also ran a response by author and editor Andrea Davis Pinkney in the 2001 September/October issue, "Awards That Stand on Solid Ground." Pinkney asserted that to "allow white authors to become eligible for these awards is to turn that tapestry into a monochromatic blanket it used to be."

Shortly after Aronson's article was published and Pinkney's response printed, the world changed. After September 11, 2001, Aronson decided he didn't want to nitpick about differences. In a poignant response to the criticism, Aronson wrote his own letter to the editor that reads, "The terrible loss of life makes our disputes seem silly while making the cause of decreasing the barriers between us all the more essential."

In a time when publishers are producing more multicultural literature, there is still a lot of work to be done. The Cooperative Center for Children's Books (CCBC) has been keeping statistics on the number of books by and about people of color since 1990. Although the number of published titles has increased, the combined number of books published by authors and illustrators of color is still clearly inferior to those by white authors and illustrators.

Evaluating Multicultural Literature

Multicultural is a fairly new word that is being used with increasing frequency. Since the late 1980s and early 1990s, when political correctness first reared its ambiguous head, people have struggled with its definition (Rochman 1993). Unfortunately, it is often incorrectly applied, used to describe people of color without regard to culture or race. When applied to literature, the term is often used to show only positive images of minority cultures, ignoring the aspects that make people human. In its most authentic form, it is an area of literature that focuses on the reality of various cultures, showing both the positive and the negative aspects of a culture (Rochman 1993).

Beyond the definitions, purposes, and trends of multicultural children's literature are the evaluative measures that readers can familiarize themselves with. Being familiar with and selective about the relatively small number of multicultural books is crucial. Readers can educate themselves to identify stereotypes and negative images, which helps them assess literary quality. Several researchers and reviewers of children's multicultural literature have identified criteria they believe to be important in selecting books for the multicultural classroom. The following checklist is culled from several sources.

Features of Quality Multicultural Literature

- Avoids distortions or omissions of history.

- Avoids negative or inaccurate stereotypes of the ethnic group being portrayed.

- Avoids titles with derogatory words used to describe the characters and culture (e.g., "savage" in the case of Native American).

- Represents various perspectives of the given culture.

- Features characters who use speech that accurately represents their oral tradition.

- Portrays women and the elderly accurately within their culture.

- Portrays familial relationships accurately.

- Avoids elements that would embarrass or offend a child whose culture is being portrayed.

- Is created by an author and/or illustrator with the qualifications needed to deal with the cultural group accurately and respectfully.

- Has illustrations that do not generalize about or include stereotypes (e.g., characters of the same ethnic group do not all look alike, but show a variety of physical attributes).

Educator Rudine Sims Bishop (2003) suggests that those who want to become adept at evaluating literature about different cultures read extensively in the literature written by "insiders," those writing about their own culture and experiences. Once immersed in the work of authors and illustrators writing about or drawing images of their own cultural group, a reader has a solid basis for comparison with books by authors whose ethnicity is unknown.

Publishers of Multicultural Literature

Although many publishers issue multicultural literature, here are two that specialize in it:

Lee and Low: An independent children's book publisher specializing in multicultural themes. It is the company's goal to meet the need for stories that children of color can identify with and that all children can enjoy. The Web site is www.leeandlow.com.

Children's Book Press: Nonprofit publisher of bilingual and multicultural children's literature that shares stories reflecting the traditions and cultures of African American, Asian American, Latino, Chicano, and Native American communities. The Web site is www.childrensbookpress.org.

INTERNATIONAL PICTURE BOOKS

J. K. Rowling isn't the first children's author to have an international impact. Before the Harry Potter phenomenon, many other authors wrote books that became global phenomena. There were C. S. Lewis's *The Lion the Witch, and the Wardrobe* (England), L. Frank Baum's *The Wonderful Wizard of Oz* (America), and Astrid Lindgren's *Pippi Longstocking* (Sweden), to name just three. Many books now considered classics have been published in numerous languages. *Winnie the Pooh* (A. A. Milne) has been translated into more than 25 languages, and *The Little Prince* (Antoine De Saint-Exupéry) has been translated into 37.

International children's literature is a broad topic. Because the subject of this book is picture books, the discussion of international issues focuses on the picture book format and related issues. However, it is useful to have a framework regarding international children's literature as a whole.

International literature is distinct from multicultural literature. As far as American audiences are concerned, multicultural literature has traditionally been books by and about African Americans, Asian Americans, Latino and Hispanic Americans, and Native Americans. Although titles by and about Jewish and Muslim cultures are sometimes included, the majority of the dialogues and the research centers on these four cultures. (It would be interesting to find out how most countries define exactly what "multicultural" literature is.)

Defining International Literature

International children's literature refers to the body of books originally published in one country and later published in another country. International books can be subdivided into the following categories:

- *Translated works*: Books originally written in one language and translated into another language. This includes copies originally written in English and translated into other languages and vice versa. Marcus Pfister's *The Rainbow Fish* (1992) was originally published in Sweden in German. It has been translated into 40 languages and has sold more than 15 million copies worldwide.[6]

- *Nontranslated works*: Books originally written and published in one country and later published in another country that speaks the same or a similar language. Examples are a book originally published in France in French and later published in Canada also in French and a book originally published in Australia in English and then later in the United States also in English. *Possum Magic* (1990) by Mem Fox, was originally published in Australia and published in the United States in the same year.

One of the pleasures of reading a picture book from another country is that it retains a sense of place. It can be said that a book is only international if it was published in a country other than one's own, but that leaves out a large body of works. Consider the following in a definition of international literature:

- Books written or illustrated and set in a country other than the one in which the author or illustrator resides. Ann Grifalconi has illustrated some lovely books set in Africa, including *The Village of Round and Square Houses* (1986) and *The Village That Vanished* (2002). Author Isaac Olaleye, born in Nigeria in 1941 currently makes his home in West Virginia. His first book for children, *Bitter Bananas* (1994), was set in Africa and acclaimed by critics for its novelty and energy. It was based on a story he heard growing up. He continues to draw on his childhood in his picture books, which include *The Distant Talking Drum: Poems from Nigeria* (1995) and *In the Rainfield: Who Is the Greatest?* (2000).

- Books written or illustrated by individuals who have immigrated to another country. For example, Gennady Spirin, whose lushly illustrated titles include the fairy tale *Jack and the Beanstalk* (1999) and *Martha* (2005), an old family story, was born in Russia but now lives in the United States. Peter Sís, who was born in Prague in what is now the Czech Republic and moved to New York City in the 1980s, is another internationally known illustrator. Three of his titles have won Caldecott Honors: *Starry Messenger* (1996), *Tibet Through the Red Box* (1998), and *The Wall: Growing Up Behind the Iron Curtain* (2007).

The last category is particularly important because it can be said that the work of Spirin and Sís, as well as other authors and illustrators who have immigrated, has been influenced by their culture of origin and nationality. Their work is infused with their experiences growing up in a culture different from the one they currently reside in.

Publishing International Picture Books

Most publishers of translated books care about broadening the horizons of children. Publishing translated books is expensive and time consuming. In addition, the titles often fail to perform financially and are unsuccessful in the marketplace. Stephen Roxburgh, publisher of Front Street books, attributes this to "insular mind-set visible everywhere in our American culture" (Roxburgh 2004). He finds the lack of interest in international literature rather confusing, especially considering the attention given to multicultural education in the last few decades. He says, "At its best, multicultural education acknowledges and celebrates diversity in our culture. But it falls way short of the mark in acknowledging and celebrating the integrity of other cultures" (Roxburgh 2004).

So why, after 25 years of questionable success, does he continue to champion translated children's books? Roxburgh believes that international books offer a way of seeing the world that may otherwise be unavailable. He says that in order to truly appreciate what international literature has to offer, we "must leave the familiarity and comfort of our culture."

Several publishers specialize in translated children's literature. One is Kane/Miller, a small independent publishing company that specializes in translated picture books. The company believes that children's books should "comfort and challenge, that they should awaken the imagination and the conscience." It publishes books that bring the "world closer to a child and the children of the world closer to each other." Kira Lynn, Kane/Miller's publisher, is very passionate about her independent publishing company. The most popular title published by Kane/Miller is *Everyone Poops*, written and illustrated by Taro Gomi. It has sold over one million copies since it appeared in 1993. The Web site for Kane/Miller is www.kanemiller.com.

Another leading publisher of international picture books is North-South. Chronicle Books in San Francisco, California, distributes North-South's titles in the United States. The parent company is NordSüd, one of the outstanding publishers of picture books for the international market. In addition to picture books, the company also has a wide array of board books and merchandise based on award-winning characters such as Rainbow Fish, Little Polar Bear, and Davy the Rabbit. The goal of NordSüd's founders was to build bridges—bridges between authors and artists from different countries and between readers of all ages around the world. The Web site for NordSüd is www.nord-sued.com. North-South's Web site is www.northsouth.com.

Issues

Portrayal and Authenticity

When selecting and introducing books from other countries, it is not enough for a book just to be from another country. Books representing other countries should portray the culture authentically. When books lack authenticity, readers are misinformed, which can lead to misconceptions—about the culture and the people.

As with multicultural literature, a persistent question for international books is the origin of the creator. Here again, some critics (and creators) believe that only a person of the race, culture, or nation of origin being depicted should be the creator of the book. On the other side of the argument is the view that a well-researched work reflects values and traditions of a culture, regardless of the race or nationality of the creator. What about the people who review international books? Can an "outsider" understand and appreciate all of the cultural norms being presented in the book? Although these questions may seem unanswerable, it is important to be aware of the issues and differing opinions (Hearne 1991). As with multicultural literature, there is no perfect answer. The best approach is to gather as much information as possible about the publisher and read book reviews. The children's librarian at the local library and PR departments at publishing companies can be helpful resources. Ultimately readers must decide for themselves, but armed with the right information, they can become more comfortable choosing international picture books.

Although some of Roxburgh's (2004) comments are dismal, there are several journals that make a point of reviewing international picture books. Selecting culturally sensitive titles that are free of bias can be challenging. Fortunately, many tools are available to help readers make informed choices. Journals, such as *Bookbird: A Journal of International Children's Literature*, and organizations, such as International Board on Books for Young People (IBBY), which has representative sections in over 65 countries, provide guidance for those interested in international literature. To learn about other organizations that promote international literature, see IBBY's Web site at www.ibby.org.

Translation

Translation is not just the transposing of words from one language into another. It is a complex process that involves a strong knowledge of both languages and a sense of both spoken and written words, their rhythms and their associations. Translators have the responsibility of creating an accurate version of the original work, retaining its spirit.

In "Eight Ways to Say You: The Challenges of Translation," Cathy Hirano, who translated the 1997 Batchelder award winner *The Friends* by Kazumi Yumoto from Japanese into English, offers a very interesting and thought provoking perspective on the translating issue: "Translation of literature is far from mechanical, and [. . .] requires fairly strenuous cultural and mental gymnastics" (1999).

According to Hirano, apart from the challenges posed by the grammatical structure, which often differs from one language to another, there is the writing style. Writing styles are influenced by language, which are very hard to place in a different context and frame of reference.

With literature, the form and the content are equally important to both the reader and the author. Accordingly, the translator needs to capture the essence, the style, and the tone of the source language and make the translation understandable to someone from a different background and culture. As Hirano puts it, the translator must have the ability "to become the author in another language" (Hirano 1999).

There are instances when a simple word is loaded with a great amount of cultural significance that does not have an easy equivalent in the other language. For instance, the slang word *bum* is often used in the United States to describe an irresponsible person, whereas in Great Britain it is used humorously to refer to the derrière. It can be tricky to translate an idea into a language that has multiple options. For example, the word *radical,* which can mean fundamental or extreme, could be difficult for a translator to convey. Sometimes, in order to remain faithful to the original tone and spirit of the storyline, the translator needs to be creative, transposing a meaningful aspect into its closest equivalent in the other language, due to the simple fact that there is no "perfect" parallel. Humor can often be hard to translate, especially when it appears in the form of culturally specific jokes or puns. Sometimes the translator needs to go to extremes, erasing parts of the original joke and replacing it with different elements that convey the original spirit in a more meaningful manner. Hirano explains the difficulty of translating humor in "Eight Ways to Say You" (1999).

In general, nonfiction is considered to be easier to translate than fiction, having more readily accessible language equivalents. Poetry is perceived as the most difficult, because of the specific rhyme, rhythm, and language patterns that characterize it (Freeman and Lehman 2001).

The American Library Association (ALA) established the Batchelder Award in 1966. It has been awarded annually since 1979. Named for Mildred L. Batchelder, a former executive director of the Association for Library Service to Children, this award honors translated children's literature. The award is presented to an American publisher for an outstanding children's book originally published in a foreign language and translated into English. The award acknowledges and encourages American publishers to seek out superior children's books and bring them to American children. Any book published in the previous calendar year is eligible.

Translating Images

The translation of illustrations poses a unique set of problems. It is a topic that is not often discussed, perhaps because pictures are seen as universal and able to translate without words, such as an arrow paired with a symbol of a train to direct travelers to a train station. Scholar Emer O'Sullivan[7] (2006) states that because pictures are often viewed as being capable of "transcending linguistic and cultural boundaries," art in picture books is often seen as exempt from translation. However, he believes that the picture–text relationship is not exempt, especially in the case of picture books. O'Sullivan suggests that the ideal translation should consider not only the significance of the original text, but also the interaction of the verbal and visual elements and the gaps that readers fill in, making the reading experience interactive and exciting. The gaps in the verbal–visual elements require readers to make the same effort in a translated work as they would have to do in the original version.

According to O'Sullivan, picture books pose a special challenge for translators because of the interaction of illustration and story. Translators are faced with the complex situation of translating the intricate interplay of the picture and text. The pictures in the original text, a situation that can be hard to reconcile, may influence a translator (O'Sullivan 2006).

The strong sense of place in picture books with particular settings creates additional problems. In "No Red Buses Please: International Co-Editions and the Sense of Place," illustrator Martin Salisbury (2006) challenges some of the constraints placed on illustrators whose books are pending publication: "The setting didn't need to be familiar to the reader; the work of these artists was and is widely adored by those for whom this was often a first introduction to the visual detail of a particular location." His article was written in response to editors who, in an effort to tackle markets outside their own countries, ask illustrators to omit cultural details, such as Britain's red buses, from illustrations.

> *For me as a child pictorial representations of unfamiliar landscapes and architecture made books that much more intriguing.*
>
> —Martin Salisbury,
> "No Red Buses Please: International Co-Editions and the Sense of Place," *Bookbird*

Globalization

In the world of children's literature, *globalization* refers to the process of altering a foreign text to suit audiences in other countries. The danger of this practice is that cultural identity is reduced and homogenized. Even British and Australian English are sometimes modified for American readers, which some professionals find unnecessary and demeaning to children. A good example of this is the Harry Potter series. In "Foreign Goods: An Essay," Michael Patrick Hearn quotes Arthur A. Levine, publisher of the Harry Potter series in America: "I wanted to make sure that an American kid reading the book would have the same experience that a British kid would have" (2000). However, by removing British phrases and idioms, some say he did exactly the opposite. Scholar Eve Tal states that "by choosing to translate books with universal themes to which American children can relate, publishers homogenize children's literature to fit a universal American standard, from the vocabulary changes between the American and British editions of Harry Potter, to the choice of books that portray 'universal,' i.e. American, portrayals of childhood" (Tal 2004).

In a provocative two-part article, "This is Not What I Wrote! The Americanization of British Children's Books," author Jane Whitehead (1996, 1997) decries the process of globalization after encountering several favorite titles that had been "Americanized" for children in the United States. The title of the article comes from the note British illustrator Amanda Vesey's emphatically scribbled in the flyleaf of the U.S. edition of *The Princess and the Frog* (1985), which was given to Whitehead: "This is NOT what I wrote." Whitehead examines Catherine Anholt's and Laurence Anholt's *Tiddlers* (U.K. edition), which became *Toddlers* (1993) in the

United States. *Tiddler* is a Victorian nursery word that means minnow and stickleback, and derives from *tiddly*, which means small. British parents would know what tiddler means. In that example, altering the title made sense because American parents would not have the background needed to understand the reference. However, lines of the text had to be rewritten in the American edition also because the word "nappy" is problematic in the United States. In Britain the word "nappy" means diaper. Thus, the line in the British edition, "I am sad, I am happy, I want Mum to change my nappy" was changed to "I am sweet, I can stand on my own two feet." Apparently the Anholts were not able to work the word "diaper" into a rhyme.

Another children's book, *Possum Magic* (1990), takes a different approach—it includes a glossary of Australian words and a map marking the cities visited by Hush and Grandma Possum, which made it unnecessary to alter the text.

In the end, although perhaps beneficial to a publisher's bottom line, removing references and images of a foreign country usually defeats the purpose of international exposure.

> *Books originally written in another language and published in another country aren't about assimilation into American culture. They don't have anything to do with America. They present lives that are not premised on our assumptions and don't focus on our cultural concerns.*
>
> —Stephen Roxburgh, "The Myopic American"

How Picture Books Cross Borders

A book originally published in another country that crosses the border to reach a new market must bypass various obstacles—from language barriers to licensing and publication rights. In addition to translation, which was discussed previously, there are two primary ways in which international books find new markets: book fairs and copublication.

Book Fairs

One of the premiere international book events is the annual Bologna Children's Book Fair in Italy. Since 1962, the fair has provided children's book publishers from all over the world with an opportunity to meet and make contact with the international community of children's book professionals. There are also book fairs in London, the Czech Republic, Zimbabwe, Frankfurt (Germany), and Buenos Aires, Argentina. Literary agents, publishers, and editors from around the world attend book fairs to exhibit their wares, negotiate licensing rights, and make publication deals. Publishers may sell rights world rights or negotiate on a per country basis.

Copublication

Copublication is an agreement between two or more publishers to share the initial costs of publication, such as editorial, production, and advertising. Sometimes copublishing is done on a one-time basis; at other times it becomes a relationship that evolves over time with numerous publications. Two successful arrangements in the United States are between Front Street Books and Lemniscaat in the Netherlands, and Farrar, Straus & Giroux and R & S books, the American counterpart of Rabén & Sjögren in Sweden.

As Martin Salisbury pointed out (2006), constraints placed on illustrators whose books are part of a copublication contract are a negative aspect of such arrangements. Elements such as Britain's red buses are hallmarks of place that are often sacrificed for a publisher to market a book in several countries simultaneously.

Celebrating International Illustration

Since 1967, on or around April 2, readers celebrate International Children's Book Day (ICBD) to inspire a love of reading and call attention to children's books. This date was chosen because it is Hans Christian Andersen's birthday, and his works were among the first children's books to cross borders and land in the hands of children around the world. Each year a different national section of the International Board on Books for Young Readers (IBBY) sponsors the international meeting of the ICBD. Members from that section decide on a theme and invite prominent authors and illustrators to write a message and design a poster to promote the celebration. The materials are used to promote books and reading. Several IBBY Sections promote ICBD through the media and organize activities in collaboration with schools and public libraries. Some sections coordinate the ICBD with children's book week or other special events related to books and reading.

World Book and Copyright Day was designated by UNESCO in 1996 as a worldwide celebration to promote books, reading, writing, and the protection of intellectual property and is celebrated in more than 100 countries around the world. World Book and Copyright Day is about helping children explore the pleasures of books and reading by providing them with the opportunity to have a book of their own. It is not just for children; the aim is to encourage everyone, at whatever age, to enjoy the pleasures of reading. It is celebrated on April 23, the date on which both Miguel de Cervantes, the author of *Don Quixote*, and William Shakespeare, died in 1616, making it a significant date in literary history.[8]

> For a complete list of winners and links to the award Web sites, visit www.picturingbooks.com.

Tips for Selecting International Picture Books

- Look for illustrations that are authentic to the setting of the book.

- Seek books that appeal to children. Don't be afraid to expose children to ideas and cultures different from their own.

- Watch out for books in which the text or illustrations have been "globalized." Remember, removing references and images of a foreign country defeats the purpose of international exposure.

- Avoid titles with stilted narratives, which may be an indication of a hastily translated book.

CONTROVERSIAL PICTURE BOOKS AND CENSORSHIP CHALLENGES

Adults write and illustrate picture books. Adults review picture books. For the most part, adults also select and purchase books for children. In the case of librarians, purchases are made for a collection. All too often the books adults choose are based on their ideology of childhood (Dresang 2003), that is, what adults think children want to read about. It is an imagined set of ideals, based on how adults think children see the world. Or perhaps they are superimposing their memories of childhood on the experiences of the children they know.

Often perception and reality clash, creating controversy. Examples are the case of the teacher in Brooklyn who read *Nappy Hair* (1997) to her classroom or a parent who fondly remembers *The Five Chinese Brothers* (1938) and wants to share the book with his or her children.

So what makes a book controversial? Is it the topic? Is it the portrayal? Is it stereotypes? Is it the language? Further, who determines whether a book is controversial? The teacher? The parent? The reviewer? The reader?

Sometimes an issue or theme creates controversy. There are certain topics that are controversial by nature: sexuality, death, war, and drugs. One of the first picture books to feature homosexual content was *Heather Has Two Mommies* (1989). Published by Alyson Wonderland, an independent publisher of picture books with gay and lesbian themes, the book tells the story of Heather's life in a nontraditional home. It was released in a tenth anniversary edition in 1999. Alyson Wonderland also published *Daddy's Roommate* (1990) by Michael Willhoite and its sequel, *Daddy's Wedding* (1996), two titles that explored the world of a child whose father realized he was homosexual after being married and having children. Mainstream publishers also publish titles with homosexual themes, but the homosexuality is implied rather than stated. One example is *And Tango Makes Three* (2005), which is an adoption story about Roy and Silo, a male penguin couple who parent an egg from a mixed-sex penguin couple. According to the American Library Association, it was the most challenged book in 2006, with 546 challenges (American Library Association 2007).

Death is another controversial topic. There are many books that address the subject, but one that created a stir was *Arlene the Sardine* (1999). On the surface it is a story of dreaming, with the goal to become a sardine—as in a canned sardine. The story begins when Arlene is still a brisling, a small fish swimming "this way" and then "that way" with her "ten hundred thousand friends" in a river. Of course, in order to achieve her dream, Arlene has to die. In fact, the bright, colorful picture book by Chris Raschka, a Caldecott-winning illustrator, makes adults squirm, perhaps because it tackles the subject so openly and honestly. Arlene's eagerness to make the journey is plain: her goal is to become a sardine, and if that means death, Arlene is just fine with that.

Arlene Sardine received a lot of attention, probably due to a negative review in *Booklist*, a respected book review journal. Although the *Booklist* staff commented positively on the design and illustrations, calling them "jaunty" and noting the "blocks and splashes of color," the review went on to imply that only a seasoned illustrator such as Raschka could "get away with getting something like this published," and if the book had been submitted to a publisher by an unknown illustrator, it would have been rejected. "And rightfully so," the reviewer concluded. On the other hand, *Publishers Weekly*, said, "Raschka delivers an uplifting message that death is a regenerative part of the life cycle," and *School Library Journal* praised it with words like "charm" and "provocative," but called it "an acquired taste." Addressing a topic like death in a children's book will always be tricky, and perhaps adults should consider other means to address the inevitability of death. For adults who want to use literature as a springboard from which to discuss death with children, a picture book may be the ideal means—whether it is *Arlene the Sardine* or not.

As previously noted, *Nappy Hair* by Carolivia Herron was at the center of a heated controversy in the late 1990s. In 1998 a young white teacher named Ruth Sherman at PS 75 in Brooklyn read *Nappy Hair* to her predominantly African American and Hispanic American classroom. Sherman states that she used the book as a tool for "teaching self-esteem and pride." Parents of the children in Sherman's classroom disagreed. She was initially fired and threatened by angry parents, but later reinstated and exonerated (Charges of Racism Stun" 1998).

What happened? What did Sherman do that caused so much controversy? The story was picked up by CNN and the Associated Press wire almost immediately. It turns out that Sherman's students liked the book so much she made black and white photocopies of parts of the book for the children to take home. By doing this, she took the book out of context and detached the narrative from the illustrations. The illustrations by Joe Cepeda are filled with bright, bold colors. Brenda, vivacious and full of life, bounces from page to page in a green dress with a bright yellow stripe. In fact, in virtually every illustration, Brenda is portrayed as a happy, well-adjusted child. The black and white photocopies Sherman sent home robbed the book of some of its power.

One might ask, was the editor concerned about the word "nappy" but decided to go forth with publication anyway? Did both Herron and Knopf (the publisher) believe that the world was ready to use the term freely and without negative connotation? Was the book accepted by the publisher because, despite the controversial word, the author represented the ethnic group featured in the book? Would the book have been published if the author had been white? Scholar Michelle H. Martin believes that *Nappy Hair* can foster discussions about ethnic topics, especially those that are rarely mentioned outside of family and community (1999).

The book received several glowing reviews, but *Horn Book* did not review it. In an editorial, *Horn Book*'s editor, Roger Sutton (1999)., explained the journal's decision not to review *Nappy Hair*:

> It wasn't that we didn't like it. That exuberant call-and-response text, Brenda's willful head of hair, the candid defiance of both words and pictures—what's not to like? Here's the thing, though: we didn't know if we were allowed to like it.

Controversy and censorship challenges are probably inevitable, especially in relation to pictures that accompany the text. After all, most adults wish to protect children from harm. The work of an author or illustrator with the best intentions can still be perceived as harmful and negative. Recall that Carolivia Herron wrote *Nappy Hair* as a celebration of her heritage. When Marc Aronson wrote openly and honestly about a topic he felt needed to be addressed, it took courage to stand his ground. From that discussion came a dialogue that will be revisited again in years to come.

Educators and parents can educate themselves, learning to evaluate picture books and be prepared to discuss (even defend) opinions. Readers should rely on their judgment, rather than hearsay, when determining whether a book is appropriate or inappropriate for a child.

It takes courage for writers and publishers to publish books that feature controversial ideas. Authors and illustrators could err on the side of caution and avoid topics such as death, homosexuality, and violence. But is that really the answer? It is through controversy that questions are asked and new ideas are formed. Today, blatant and malicious misrepresentation is not acceptable. However, if we remove books we don't approve of or lock them away in a drawer, are we cheating children of a viable means to ask questions and seek answers?

CLASSIC PICTURE BOOKS

The issue of which books are designated as classics and used in education and children's literature programs is worth exploring. Obviously, what constitutes a classic is as open to definition as the term *multicultural*. Is a book a classic because it is loved by generations of children? Is it a classic because it has been translated into other languages? Is it a classic because it is still in print after many years? All of these characteristics are marks of very successful books, but does that make them classic?

As far as multicultural portrayal and accuracy are concerned, most titles from the 1930s through the 1960s are problematic. Consider, for example, *Mei Le* (1938), *Pedro, the Angel of Olvera Street* (1946), *Crow Boy* (1956), *Nine Days to Christmas* (1959), and *The Snowy Day* (1962). In both *Nine Days to Christmas* and *Pedro, the Angel of Olvera Street*, male characters are portrayed wearing *zarapes* (serapes), long, brightly colored shawls, and huaraches, handmade Mexican sandals with flat heels and woven leather tops. Both of these items are often used negatively to portray Latino cultures and were not commonly worn at the time the books were published. It is an outsider perspective and at best a nostalgic view of the culture (Cortes 1992).

Many of these titles are considered classics because they are Caldecott winners or honor titles. Their place in the picture book canon is an issue that provokes controversy, with strong feelings on all sides. It is a dilemma. On the one hand, these titles are symbolic of picture book history, but on the other, they feature harmful stereotypes.

One such problematic title is *The Five Chinese Brothers* (1938). Why might an amusing story about five brothers raise concern? Asians and Asian Americans (insiders) immediately identify the problems inherent in Claire Huchet Bishop's retelling of the old Chinese folktale. Helping people who are not of the culture (outsiders) understand the flaws is the challenge. *The Five Chinese Brothers* is often criticized for its portrayal of Asian culture. It was published in 1938, when four-color processing was still the primary means of printing, which may or may not account for the yellow skin tone of the brothers. In virtually all of the illustrations, the eyes of the brothers are squinted and slanted in an almost comical fashion. Educator Jonda C. McNair comments on this title in a provocative article, "But the Five Chinese Brothers Is One of My Favorite Books" (2003). The title came from discussions about this and other books considered to be classics when she introduced the idea of the controversial insider/outsider debate to a predominantly white class of preservice teachers in a course she taught. Another issue that McNair faced was classic versus inaccurate. McNair used journaling as a means to help her students understand why a title like *The Five Chinese Brothers* is problematic. However, McNair believes that children's literature, even when it includes stereotypes and inaccuracies, can be a valuable tool for educators to use in raising social critical consciousness.

Another book that has been the issue of much debate and fodder for scholars is *The Story of Babar, the Little Elephant* (1933). Why might a simple story of an elephant be problematic? Is it because Babar's mother dies in a rather violent way? Or maybe because hunters and guns are part of both the narrative and the art? Although those criticisms are valid, the primary reason *Babar* is criticized is that it is seen as a book that promotes imperialism and colonialism. Postcolonial theory states that differentiation of peoples is reflected in and reinforced by language and metaphor. Critics say that these messages of superiority and inferiority are subtly embedded in the text of *Babar* (Malarte-Feldman and Yeager 1998). Consider some of the words from the text: power, king, princess, portrayal, savage, civilized, wealth, and poverty. Another tenet of postcolonial theory is that race and ethnicity have been used in ways that have empowered the dominant culture and oppressed the weak one. In the book, Babar represents the oppressed and Old Lady represents the empowered.

Educator Herbert Kohl actually advocated burning *Babar* in his 1995 essay "Should We Burn Babar." His harsh criticism prompted other critics to respond in its defense. Although some felt that *Babar* was indeed a story that illustrated "*mission civilisatrice*" or the French version of the "white man's burden," they advocated sensitizing children to subtle, embedded messages in the text. (Malarte-Feldman and Yeager 1998).

When *The Story of Little Black Sambo* by Helen Bannerman was published in 1899, it was welcomed because there were so few picture books for children (Midori 2007). Bannerman, wife of a Scottish doctor, wrote the story for her two daughters when she was living in India with her family. On the surface, *Little Black Sambo* is the story of a clever little boy who not only manages to escape two hungry tigers, but also gets a hearty breakfast. The book quickly established itself as a classic. However, like *Babar*, *Sambo* is seen as a product of imperialism and colonialism.

Originally published in Britain in 1899, it crossed the Atlantic and was published in the United States by Frederick A. Stokes. That version, the Grant Richards edition, was just as popular as the original. However, not all American children read or owned the same edition (Bader 1976). The original story and pictures by Bannerman never went out of print, but a host of other versions began to appear, with degrading, stereotyped caricatures of the main character. Most libraries had the Stokes edition on their shelves, but the cheap knock-offs were also plentiful.

In the 1960s, during the civil rights era, *Little Black Sambo* came to represent an image African Americans were fighting to change. For many years, the term *Sambo* was used disparagingly to describe African Americans (Bader 1976).

In 1990 HarperCollins reissued *Little Black Sambo* in its original format, with "The Only Authorized American Edition" emblazoned on the front. In 1996 two adaptations of *Little Black Sambo* were published. *The Story of Little Babaji*, with illustrations by Fred Marcellino, retained Bannerman's text, with the exception of changing the characters' names to Babaji, Mamaji, and Papaji. Marcellino also set the story in India, not Africa. *Sam and the Tigers*, written by Julius Lester and illustrated by Jerry Pinkney, set the story in a mythical Southern town called Sam-sam-sa-mara, "where the animals and the people lived and worked together like they didn't know they weren't supposed to." Author Julius Lester and illustrator Jerry Pinkney, bothered by the racist associations of the characters' names and the stereotypes engendered by Bannerman's original story, say they were inspired to retell the story of Sambo because they were drawn to the little boy's humor. In fact, in the foreword Pinkney explains that working on *Sam and the Tigers* was a sort of catharsis for him, a way to exorcise images that had haunted him throughout his life.

In the debates about the place of classics in today's society, one of two positions is usually taken. The first includes reading a book in context, noting its shortfalls; the second is to avoid the title altogether. Do we remove *The Story of Little Black Sambo* from the shelf and replace it with Julius Lester's *Sam and the Tigers*, or keep both versions? Do books like *The Story of Babar* reinforce ideas of domination and oppression, as some critics claim, or can we have these titles on the shelf, keeping in mind the context within which each book was written? These are difficult questions that librarians, educators, and parents must face, and there is no magical answer that will satisfy everyone.

There are many other books besides those discussed here that have come to be seen as problematic. Issues of accuracy, authenticity, and stereotypes plague classic titles. Many titles may be favorites for nostalgic adults, but are they relevant in today's world? Is that enough for a book to be a classic? When readers have reason to question classic picture books, what's the best way to begin? Lester, Pinkney, and Marcellino chose to retell Sambo's story, paying homage to the book while updating and addressing it negative aspects. What, if any, limitations do we place on classics titles?

One strategy is to pair a controversial book with a title that promotes a more positive image. In the case of *Little Black Sambo*, that might be *The Story of Little Babaji* or *Sam and the Tigers*. If readers have issues with the depiction of the hunter in *The Story of Babar*, they can compare and contrast the portrayal of hunters in *The Hunter* (1994), illustrated by Paul Geraghty, and *Bashi, Elephant Baby* (1998), illustrated by John Butler, which offers an opportunity to see a realistic portrayal of elephants in the wild.

Classic titles are often viewed through twentieth-century eyes. It is easy to impose our social sensibilities on the past. However, fearing the past is not an answer. Controversial picture books can be used to address differing perspectives and changing social issues. Classic picture books, like titles about controversial issues, should be explored and questioned—in the same way a new release is. Parents should determine whether a particular book is appropriate for their children. Librarians should determine whether controversial titles are added or retained in the collection. Educators should decide whether a book is appropriate for classroom use. Seeking the opinions of respected critics and reviewers is helpful, but in the end every individual brings a different perspective to a book. Finding the balance is not always an easy task, but it is a worthy endeavor.

REISSUES

In recent years, many publishers have reissued classic picture books. Of course many, such as *Goodnight Moon* and *Curious George*, never went out of print. However, until a few years ago a number of the early Caldecott titles were difficult to get copies of.

In 2003 most of Maurice Sendak's early works once again became available. For Sendak fans this was exciting, especially for libraries that had been mending classics that had long been out of print. Collectors who had mollified themselves with paperback editions now had the opportunity to get hardback editions of much of Sendak's early work.

The *Horn Book* regularly publishes a feature by Terri Schmitz called "Recommended Reissues," which highlights old favorites once again in print. Schmitz'slisted new offerings are worth looking for. In her March/April 2007 column, she alerted readers that two of the *Anatole* books by Eve Titus books are once again in print. Illustrated by Paul Galdone, both titles were Caldecott Honor books.

Schmitz (2007) objects to publishers who alter or change text, apply the picture book treatment to novels, or abridge longer books into smaller editions. For people who have fond memories of a particular book, a reissue that has been altered can be very disappointing. Drawing on her experience as an independent bookseller, Schmitz sympathizes with publishers, saying she knows that they have bottom lines to attend to, but she laments the alterations nonetheless.

GOOD INTENTIONS

Parents and teachers often turn to picture books to help young children understand a difficult subject or situation or a new experience. In fact, some lesser quality books are attempts to use books as therapeutic aids. In a provocative editorial in 1996, *Horn Book* editor Roger Sutton stated, "These books are aimed at a picture book audience not because children are demonstrably interested in reading them, or in having them shared in a story hour, but because we think it is important that kids learn some lessons."

In this editorial that is still relevant some dozen years after publication, Sutton asks why the picture book audience needs books to help them cope with suicide, war, and gun control. As noted in chapter 1, there was a time when moral tales were all children had to read. Although some picture books published today are a far cry from the didactic tales of the nineteenth century, it is a shame that picture books are sometimes viewed simply as bibliotherapy tools. Sutton remembers a request for a book to help a child get over the fear of lawnmowers, which prompted him to ask, "Is a book always the appropriate solution?" (Sutton's predecessor, Anita Silvey, had pondered the same issue earlier, stating that there are themes that are "possibly not resolvable in a thirty-two page format.")

There are books, particularly the Arthur series by Marc Brown, which have reputations built on the fact that they are intended to help children get through difficult issues or help them solve problems, for example, *Arthur's Eyes* (1979), in which Arthur's friends tease him when he gets glasses. By the end of the book, Arthur learns to wear his glasses with pride. In *Arthur's Teacher Moves In* (2000), Arthur's teacher, Mr. Ratburn, is coming to stay at his house, and Arthur soon discovers his teacher is just like everyone else. Arthur thinks his problems are over, but when he gets an A on his test, his friends start calling him a teacher's pet.

Another series that handles problems successfully is the Berenstain Bears by Stan Berenstain and Jan Berenstain. The characters have very generic names; in fact, they are known by their role within the family instead of by name: Mama Bear, Papa Bear, Brother Bear, and Sister Bear. In *The Berenstain Bears and the In-Crowd* (1989), Sister Bear and Brother Bear learn how to deal with a bossy new she-cub in town, who tries to take over the playground by putting other cubs down, and in *The Berenstain Bears and the Blame Game* (1997), the Bear Family learn to solve problems without playing the blame game and arguing over who is responsible for every awful situation.

Didactic picture books, which can be defined as those created to specifically teach a lesson, are generally poorly written and illustrated. Although series like Arthur and Berenstain Bears do generally have lessons embedded in the title and content, both the Berenstains and Brown are seasoned authors and illustrators, who deftly manage to tackle topics that children struggle with as they grow, without being overly moralistic. When looking for books to provide lessons to children, it is important to examine them carefully and decide whether the issues are handled in a way that interests and makes sense to a child. And keep in mind that it is not appropriate to turn to books to handle every issue that comes up.

CONCLUSION

The issues explored it this chapter are often contentious, eliciting strong emotions and opinions from many perspectives. Issues of authenticity and multicultural and international literature are continuously debated, never seeming to be resolved. Classic titles, often rife with stereotypes, present other problems. Respect for the picture book canon must be balanced with respect for the social and cultural groups represented and today's readers. The challenge for authors, illustrators, publishers, educators, librarians, and parents is finding a balance that promotes titles representative of the world in which respect for differences is both embraced and celebrated.

ENDNOTES

1. The Cooperative Children's Book Center (CCBC) defines multicultural literature as "books by and about people of color." Available at www.education.wisc.edu/ccbc/books/multicultural.asp (accessed July 2008).

2. In *Against Borders: Promoting Books for a Multicultural World* (1993), Hazel Rochman writes that the "best books break down borders. They surprise us." She also states that they "change our view of ourselves; they extend the phrase 'like me' to include what we thought was foreign and strange."

3. Mingshui Cai asserts that the debate over the definition is not "just bickering over terminology in the ivory tower of academia, but rather concerned with fundamental issues of a sociopolitical nature."

4. See Mingshui Cai's *Multicultural Literature for Children and Young Adults: Reflections on Critical Issues* (2003) for a detailed overview of multicultural literature.

5. Mingshui Cai explores several classifications in *Multicultural Literature for Children and Young Adults: Reflections on Critical Issues* (2003), including by "context and intended audience," by "cultural specificity," and by "geographical and cultural boundaries." Each classification is further defined.

6. E-mail correspondence with Matt Navarro, marketing director for North-South books.

7. In "Translating Pictures" in *The Translation of Children's Literature*, O'Sullivan compares the original and translated versions of two picture books: (1) The French *Papa Vroum* (*L'école de loisirs*, 1986) by Michael Gay into the English (*Night Ride*, Morrow, 1987), and (2) the English *Grandpa* (Jonathan Cape, 1984) by Jon Birmingham into the German (*Mein Opa und Ich*, Parabel, 1984).

8. Although both Shakespeare and Cervantes died on April 23, Cervantes's date of death is according the Gregorian calendar. England used the Julian calendar. Shakespeare actually died 10 days after Cervantes. However, because of the discrepancy between the two date systems, UNESCO can correctly claim they died on the same date.

Chapter 8

Exploring and Using Picture Books

In every generation, children's books mirror the society from which they arise; children always get the books their parents deserve.

—Leonard S. Marcus, *Ways of Telling*

There is a child in every adult and an adult in every child, and it is a tragic thing to see them separated.

—Betsy Hearne, *Choosing Books for Children: A Commonsense Guide*

In This Chapter
- Building a Library
- Ages and Stages
- Responses to Literature
- Evaluating Picture Books
- Beyond the Pages

Picture books are commonly used in classrooms and libraries. Many teachers have classroom libraries or book nooks children can visit throughout the school day. Public libraries have entire sections of the children's department dedicated to picture book collections. New library buildings feature reading nooks, and lucky libraries have rooms reserved for story hours. More and more families are building book collections at home. This chapter describes ways to build a picture book collection, how to determine quality and analyze picture books, and how licensing of picture books has allowed picture book characters to go out of the pages of books.

BUILDING A LIBRARY

Distinguishing Between Editions

Picture books are published in different editions. Each edition has its own ISBN (international standard book number), which is a unique 10- or 13-digit number[1] internationally assigned to books for identification purposes and inventory control. The hardbound, or hardback, version is usually published first. In the publishing industry it is called a trade cloth edition and is for sale to booksellers and libraries. Trade editions are published for the general reader, as opposed to targeted markets. Library editions are made with archival paper (which lasts longer than standard paper) and reinforced spines. Public libraries and school media centers often purchase library editions because they can withstand heavy wear and multiple uses. The trade and library edition are often published simultaneously. The spines of both are sewn or stitched, making them more durable than paperbacks.

Most picture books also have paperback versions. Picture book paperbacks are generally the same size as the original hardcover, but the trim size may appear smaller because, unlike hardcover editions, they do not have the cardboard cover boards. In lieu of cover boards, paperbacks have soft covers, usually made of lightweight cardboard. The cheaper versions sold through book clubs are made of lower-quality paper and may deteriorate more quickly than paperback editions purchased from bookstores.

According to Harold Underdown,[2] almost all children's publishers now have paperback imprints, which was not true 20 years ago. For example, the Random House paperback imprint is Dragonfly, Simon & Schuster's paperback imprint is Aladdin, the HarperCollins paperback imprint is HarperTrophy, and Penguin's paperback imprint is Puffin. Underdown asserts that the paperback trend is firmly established and that hardcover editions will never regain their domination of the market. In fact, even libraries, once the primary purchasers of hardbound titles, often make paperback purchases, despite the fact that they have limited shelf life and do not hold up through multiple circulations as hardbound books do.

Other formats for picture books are audiobooks, board book editions, and digital versions.

Audiobook adaptations of picture books generally have both an audio component (a cassette or CD), the narrated version of the story, often with music and other background sounds, and a paperback version of the picture book. Audio components often come in two versions: one with signals, a beep or voice prompting readers to turn the page, and one without.

As discussed in chapter 6, picture books are often released in board book editions as well. Although the format is not always suitable for picture book adaptations, the number of titles increases each year.

Digital picture books exist, but at the time of this writing there is no systematic catalog of books available in digital format, although electronic versions of books do have individual ISBNs. As discussed in chapter 4, a few companies have attempted to raise interest in digital picture books. An early attempt, namely ipicturebooks.com, went out of business in 2002. A new company, Lookybook, founded in 2008, has a goal of digitizing 1,000 books by the end of 2008. The International Children's Digital Library (ICDL) has a Web site that allows readers to read titles online. ICDL also offers reading devices that can be downloaded and allow users to read picture books offline. Only time will tell whether readers embrace digital picture books.

Libraries

Picture books are not cheap; in fact, the price of picture books may be prohibitive for some parents and teachers. Aside from purchasing paperbacks, picture books can be borrowed from public libraries for free. One of the best ways to supplement a personal collection is with picture books from the public library. Checking out picture books from the public library not only gives families and teachers a supplemental source, but the variety is wide and continually updated. Some families keep picture books borrowed from the library on the shelf with their personal collections. The ability to add new books to the collection, if only for the duration of checkout, is fun and exciting.

Most children's librarians say there is nothing more pleasing than helping teachers, daycare providers, or parents find books at the library. Many parents and teachers have special plastic crates or bags that they take to the library, which they fill with dozens of picture books.

Book Clubs and Fairs

One way to introduce children to books is through book clubs. Scholastic Books[3] Clubs are popular in schools. Teachers distribute the order forms, which are usually published monthly, collect and tally student orders, and then wait for the shipment to arrive at the school. There are a number of clubs to choose from:[4]

- Honeybee (toddlers to four years)

- Firefly (preschool)

- Seesaw (grades K–1)

- Lucky (grades 2–3)

Scholastic Books Clubs feature paperback versions of popular picture books, although hardbound titles are sometimes offered. In addition to providing the books, the clubs offer products based on popular book characters, multimedia, and games. The clubs are an affordable way for teachers to build their classroom libraries. Parents can build home libraries as well. Through Scholastic's special promotions, teachers and parents can also earn rewards and other freebies— which is in addition to the low prices and convenience.

Scholastic Book Fairs are events hosted by schools and other organizations, such as daycare centers. The fairs allow the hosting site to generate community involvement and foster a love of books and reading. Administrators and educators are able to promote literacy efforts in a fun and entertaining atmosphere, and a percentage of the proceeds is filtered back to schools. The title selections vary by location, but the assortments are selected by children's book experts. Parents and caregivers have the peace of mind of knowing that they are purchasing titles that have been vetted for quality.

AGES AND STAGES

Picture books are for all ages. There is a plethora of picture books that will intrigue and challenge older readers and adults. Those who regularly read picture books to and with younger children will be directly rewarded by the interplay of the verbal and visual that makes picture books special. Of course, that doesn't mean all titles are suitable for all ages. Traditionally, children begin with board books, move to picture books, step out on their own with easy readers, and plunge solo into novels and nonfiction. Board books and picture books are usually read to children. With each successful transition, another format is left behind. In fact, picture books are often referred to as "bridges to independent reading." Despite the sometimes counterproductive idea that picture books are merely stepping stones to independent reading, picture books do prepare children for reading. However, they are really for all ages and stages.

Chapter 6 explored the developmental stages of childhood and the role of literacy. Understanding what children can do—cognitively, emotionally, and physically—makes selecting books for a collection or personal library easier.

Board books, for example, have enjoyed commercial success because they filled the need for age-appropriate books for babies and toddlers. Choosing books that are suitable for the intended audience is important. Some general questions to ask follow:

- Does the book fulfill an interest or need for the intended audience? If children lack interest or are not challenged by certain titles, then parents or teachers should seek more suitable titles.

- How will the book be used? For entertainment? As a learning tool? Books with built-in toy formats are fun, but not always the appropriate choice.

- How much will the book be used? Hardcover books are more durable than paperback editions. However, board books are even more durable and ideal for babies and toddlers.

If toddlers are the audience, choose books that are durable and able to withstand a little abuse. Toddlers are not deliberately rough with books; they are simply developing book handling behaviors. Board books have fewer pages than standard picture books, and the pages are thicker, making it easy for toddlers to turn pages. Board books are also smaller and easier for a toddler to hold.

Some picture books are especially suitable for younger readers, such as *Hondo and Fabian* (2002), which is a sweet story of the misadventures of a cat and dog that younger children will delight in reading again and again. But with only 10 words or so per page, *Hondo and Fabian* is not a challenging read for an older child. An older child might tolerate the book but quickly become bored.

It can be tough to select a book for a particular age, especially because children develop at different rates. A child might learn to walk as early as 10 months or as late as 18 months. The same principle applies to books: children move from board books to picture books to beginning readers at different rates. Some children are reading chapter books and novels as early as age seven.

On the front flap of the book jacket, publishers often designate an age range as the target audience. The age designations are generally ages zero to three, four to eight, and all ages. The age designations are only guidelines; they should not deter readers from using or purchasing titles for children who fall outside of an age range. No one knows children as well as their parents and teachers. Supplement professional guidance with personal judgment and past experience.

To complicate matters, almost every review journal has differing age designations. *The Horn Book* has the following review formats: picture books, fiction, folklore, poetry, nonfiction, and audiobooks. Within each type there are up to four broad age ranges that are dictated by grade level: primary, intermediate, middle school, and high school.[5] *School Library Journal* separates reviews into two broad categories, preschool to grade 4 and grade 5 and up, which are further subdivided, per the discretion of the reviewer, into PreS–K, PreS–Gr 1, PreS–Gr 2, PreS–Gr 3, K–Gr 1, K–Gr 2, and K–Gr 3.[6] *Booklist* has two categories: younger readers and older readers. *Publishers Weekly* breaks reviews into picture books and fiction, with suggested ages at the end of the review.[7]

A sophisticated book like Graeme Base's *Animalia* (1987) is a good example of a picture book for all ages. One of the most exciting and challenging alphabet books ever published, *Animalia* is perfectly suitable for young readers as well as for adults. There is a lot happening in *Animalia*: from the concrete to the abstract and objective to subjective. An animal and a silly alliterative sentence represent each letter in the book. Surrounding the featured animal are dozens of objects that begin with the featured letter. For example, for the letter "I" the text reads, "Ingenious iguanas improvising an intricate impromptu on impossibly impractical instruments." In the illustration, an iguana is resting on an island clasping an ingot in his claw. Younger (concrete operational) child readers may easily pick out other "I" words: iceberg, ice cream, and iron. Older (formal operational) readers are able to identify "insignia" and "isosceles triangle" because they are able to think abstractly. Proper nouns are represented in the flags from Italy, Ireland, and Israel. The author also used subjective nouns like "idea." Understanding depends on cognitive development, so young readers may or may not identify many objects in the books. Even older readers and adults will be challenged.

Picture Books and Older Readers

Chapter 6 explored the role of emergent literacy and books for babies and toddlers. However, picture books are for all ages, and upper elementary and secondary teachers are realizing the potential of picture books and putting it to use. There are sophisticated picture books suitable for almost every type of curriculum. Picture books are great springboards for learning about almost any topic. There are hundreds of titles that are meticulously researched and illustrated. The illustrations illuminate and expand on the narrative.

For example, dozens of titles explore math concepts beyond counting. Greg Tang and Harry Brigs paired up to create a series of math titles, which include *The Grapes of Math* (2001), *Math for All Seasons* (2002), and *Math Potatoes* (2005). Loreen Leedy is also noted for her innovative and brightly illustrated math titles, including *Follow the Money!* (2002), an overview of the route money takes as it leaves the Federal Reserve, and *Fraction Action* (1994), which introduces the concept of fractions.

Historical picture books are ideal to introduce a specific period, or multiple perspectives on a period in history. For example, if a history class is studying the Civil War, some titles that would complement any lesson plan include Michael McCurdy's illustrated version of the *Gettysburg Address* (1995), which contains the compete text of Lincoln's speech; *Red Legs: A Drummer Boy of the Civil War* (2001), a story about a young boy who, after sitting around the fire of a Union Army encampment one evening, grabs his drum the next morning and marches into battle with his regiment, the Red Legs; and *Moses: When Harriet Tubman Led Her People to Freedom* (2006), a poetic account of Tubman's religious inspiration and the development of the Underground Railroad.

Picture book biographies have many classroom uses. As springboards, they offer a dynamic way to introduce a variety of subjects. Picture book biographies are thoroughly researched and lushly illustrated titles, and make ideal supplemental reading material.

Conforming to the limited page count, picture book biographies offer readers a concise overview of the life of an individual. Titles focus on the highlights or major events in the lives of historical figures, often youth or early years. Some picture book biographies employ traditional narrative structures, such as *Action Jackson* (2002), an account of the brief life of artist Jackson Pollock. The traditional narrative has a formal layout, with text primarily placed beneath the illustrations. Other titles challenge traditional structure and form, such as *John's Secret Dreams: The John Lennon Story* (2004), in which prose and song lyrics merge and tumble across the pages.

Authors and illustrators have created picture book biographies reflecting the diversity and complexity of the world. Of course there are titles about well-known figures, such as George Washington and Martin Luther King Jr., but some writers, particularly Don Brown, write about lesser-known individuals such as Alice Ramsey. His *Alice Ramsey's Grand Adventure* (1997) is a biographical account of a young woman's 59-day drive across America in 1909.

In the last decade picture book biographies have appeared with more frequency. There are hundreds of intriguing picture book biographies for nearly every area of interest. Interested in baseball? Then try *Home Run: The Story of Babe Ruth* (1998) or *Lou Gehrig: The Luckiest Man* (1997). For less familiar aspects of baseball history, try *Players in Pigtails* (2003), which pays tribute to the women's baseball leagues of the 1940s; or *Satchel Paige* (2000), which looks at the life of one of the all-time great baseball players of the Negro Leagues. Chris Raschka has created a dazzling array of picture books with a jazz theme, including *Mysterious*

Thelonious (1997), *Charlie Parker Played Be Bop* (1992), and *John Coltrane's Giant Steps* (2002).

Looking for picture book biographies about women? Try *Rachel: The Story of Rachel Carson* (2003), an account of the biologist and writer whose work was the inspiration for the modern environmental movement; *The Daring Nellie Bly: America's Star Reporter* (2003), which introduces the life of a "stunt reporter" for the New York World newspaper in the late 1800s who championed women's rights and traveled around the world faster than anyone ever had; and *A Voice of Her Own: The Story of Phillis Wheatley, Slave Poet* (2003), the story of the woman who became famous as the first black poet in America.

Many famous poems have been illustrated by noted artists and adapted to picture book format. Susan Jeffers illustrated Robert Frost's *Stopping by Woods on a Snowy Evening* (2001) and verses from Henry Wadsworth Longfellow's epic poem *Hiawatha* (1983). Ted Rand illustrated another of Longfellow's poems, *Paul Revere's Ride* (1990). Ed Young illustrated Samuel Taylor Coleridge's *The Rime of the Ancient Mariner* (1992) and Robert Frost's *Birches* (1988).

Titles by David Wiesner, especially *The Three Pigs* (2001) and *Flotsam* (2006), will also intrigue older readers and adults because they challenge perception and traditional story patterns. Postmodern classics, such as *Black and White* (1990), illustrated by David Macaulay; and *Voices in the Park* (1998), illustrated by Anthony Browne, offer educators many opportunities to explore narrative convention. *Abstract Alphabet: An Animal ABC* (2001), originally published in France as *Animaux*, baffles readers initially because the animals indicated in the subtitle are actually blobs and geometric shapes on a white background. As odd as the picture book appears, it ultimately rouses curiosity.

Only a few titles have been mentioned here, but there are thousands of books suitable for older readers.

> For a more comprehensive list of picture books for older readers, please visit www.picturingbooks.com.

RESPONSES TO LITERATURE

Strategies

There are many ways to approach picture books to learn more about them. Examples are immersion, compare and contrast, and past preferences.

Immersion

Immersion in the vast canon of picture books is one of the best ways to become familiar with picture books. Following are five ways to start:

1. Read everything by one author or illustrator. Go to the library and check out all of the titles by a particular author. Do an illustrator's books change over time? Are books produced at a regular pace? Does the illustrator use one medium and style or many? This approach works best

with authors and illustrators who have established careers, such as Kevin Henkes, known for his strong character development and sense of humor; David Wiesner, three-time Caldecott-winning artist and a master of visual storytelling (his wordless books are renowned); and Jon Agee, often overlooked by award committees but notable for his spare narrative and keen sense of design. After you have become thoroughly acquainted with one illustrator, explore the collection and look for other illustrators who seem intriguing.

2. Read 10 (or 20 or 50) books about the same subject or in the same format. (Types of alphabet books are described in chapter 3.) One of the most popular types of concept picture books is the alphabet book. Locate several alphabet books and compare them. Grab a potpourri of a dozen alphabet books or perhaps several theme-based alphabet books and take a close look at them. What is similar? Do the illustrations strengthen or distract from the letters? Some intriguing alphabet books are *Abstract Alphabet* (2001) and *Bembo's Zoo* (2000). These are very stylized treatments that require readers to ponder. Compare these to ABC titles with simpler constructs, such as *Chicka Chicka Boom Boom* (1989) and *ABC Pop!* (1999). Compare and contrast works with other types of concept books.

Apply the compare and contrast method to artistic media and style. For example, compare and contrast the watercolor illustrations of Emily Arnold McCully, David Wiesner, Jerry Pinkney, and David Small. As noted in chapter 3, naïve art is marked by a childlike quality and is identifiable by the flat, two-dimensional quality it possesses. Some, but not all, artists who employ this style are self-taught. Compare the work of Byron Barton, G. Brian Karas, and Vera B. Williams. See chapter 3 for an in-depth overview of artistic media and artistic style.

Many people are aware of the numerous versions of "Cinderella," but it is not the only work of traditional literature with alternate versions. In the case of "Little Red Riding Hood," there are some versions that are somber, such as the those illustrated by Trina Schart Hyman (1983) and Jerry Pinkney (2007). James Marshall's version, on the other hand, is a hilarious account of the exploits of Red Riding Hood. Hyman's dark palette and Pinkney's distinctive watercolor illustrations address the traditional aspects of the tale, while Marshall's cartoon-style art takes liberties with certain events. Other parody versions of the tale are *Little Red Cowboy Hat: A Southwestern Little Red Riding Hood* (1997) and *Little Red Riding Hood: A New Fangled Prairie Tale* (1995).

Although Red Riding Hood has transformed over the years, the wolf has remained a fearsome and volatile character. Even Ed Young's 1990 version *Lon Po Po: A Red Riding Hood Tale from China* portrays the wolf as greedy and foolish.[8] Young's impressionistic illustrations offer a picture of the wolf that is almost heart wrenching. However, the opening illustration in Young's book shows the muzzle of the wolf as part of the landscape, suggesting that the beast is not evil but an intrinsic part of the world.

3. Read all the books that have won a major award, such as the Caldecott Medal or the Boston Globe-Horn Book Award. Almost every state has a children's choice award. Your local library can help you find information about a particular state award. Explore all the books that were honored in a particular decade, or compare books from two different decades. For example, compare the Caldecott winners from 1960s with the winners from the 1990s. Is there more of one type of picture book that wins in a given decade? Would books that won in the 1960s would win today? There are endless variations on this approach.

4. Read 10 (or 20 or 50) assorted books published in the same year. Do there seem to be any apparent trends? How many were by first-time authors or illustrators? This is the same approach that award committees take. In the case of the Caldecott Award, the committee is charged with the task of determining which picture book published the previous year made the most distinguished contribution in illustration. The Charlotte Zolotow Award acknowledges distinction in writing. It is awarded annually to the author of a picture book published in the United States in the preceding year. Established in 1998, the award honors the distinguished career of Charlotte Zolotow, author of more than 70 picture books, including *Mr. Rabbit and the Lovely Present* (1962), a Newbery Honor book illustrated by Maurice Sendak, and *William's Doll* (1972), a groundbreaking picture book that explored gender.

5. Randomly grab 10 (or 20 or 50) books and explore them. You may discover authors and illustrators who would have otherwise gone unnoticed.

Compare and Contrast

Comparing an unfamiliar book with a favorite title is one way to evaluate the quality of a book. Make a list of your childhood favorites. Can't remember any? Then explore illustrators from the 1950s and 1960s. The collected body of works by Roger Duvoisin, Don Freeman, Leo Lionni, and Crockett Johnson are worth thorough examination. Most of the titles by these illustrators are still in print, in hardcover and/or paperback. Go to the library and see how many are available, check them out, and take them home. Or better yet, find a quiet corner in the library and read, read, read. After reading the childhood favorites, wander around the library and find illustrators with a similar style. Randomly select a stack of picture books and explore the medium used in each book. Which do you prefer? Some readers will feel drawn to soft watercolor illustrations, but others will find that bold color and abstract books are more interesting.

Comparing an unfamiliar book with a book that is noted for a particular reason is a great way to expand your knowledge. For instance, *Bringing Rain to the Kapiti Plain* (1982) is an excellent example of a type of folklore called cumulative literature. Using it as a guide, compare it to other cumulative tales. How do other cumulative tales compare to *Kapiti*? Are they better? The same? This works with any type of book. For instance, you can use *Frog and Toad Are Friends* (1970) to explore other beginning readers' series. Readers interested in photography can explore the works of Tana Hoban and Bruce McMillan. The fruit and vegetable photographs in Saxton Freymann's and Joost Elffers's picture books are clever and delightful. Readers interested in picture book biographies can explore titles by Diane Stanley, Dan Brown, Margaret Early, Shana Corey, and Robert Burleigh.

Past Preferences

Past preferences can be a powerful tool for parents looking for picture books for a particular child. Does a child have a preference for a type of book or subject matter? If a child likes the magical aspect of pop-up books, then another pop-up book would be a good choice. Are stories with pauses for audience participation popular during group reading time? A preschooler teacher will benefit from sharing books that give children the freedom to shout out answers or chime in as the story progresses. Teachers seeking titles to supplement a classroom collection should first review their classroom library. The books that are tattered and torn are most likely the ones the class reads again and again. One option would be to replace the tattered copies and purchase books that are similar.

EVALUATING PICTURE BOOKS

Although you should not underestimate the importance of professional reviews, don't ignore or overlook your gut reaction. Instinct is important and a very powerful tool. With time you can develop an innate sense of what makes a book good or mediocre. The more books you critically assess, the finer your evaluation skills become. You may even develop an intuitive approach to evaluation.

It is true that most picture books are reviewed by at least one major review journal—some titles are reviewed by all of them—but it is important for you to have the ability to articulate a personal opinion. An informed, personal assessment is as important as a professional review. Along with professional reviews, rely on your judgment, experience, and personal response when evaluating picture books

Evaluation can be informal, a quick flip through the pages, or thoughtful, with several readings. It is often helpful to read a picture book in stages: first read the text; second, read the text aloud; third; examine the pictures; and fourth, consider text and pictures together. An analysis includes both the verbal and visual aspects of the story. For example, setting may be described in the text, but it may be that the text allows the illustration to convey setting. In the opening page spread of *The Snowy Day* (1962), the author does not mention the setting except to note that Peter sits up in bed, It is through the illustrations that readers see Peter's bedroom. Chapter 5 examined some of the narrative components in picture books. When you are prepared to approach books in a variety of ways as a reader, you are open to the unexpected—which may result in all kinds of discoveries.

Determining Picture Book Quality

Picture books are not inexpensive. Building a collection is an investment of both time and money. Some publishers are known for their high-quality picture books. However, there are publishers that use cheaper paper and produce a lower-quality product. Knowing how to assess the quality of picture books makes the investment in time and money worthwhile.

- The paper should be of good quality. If the images bleed through from the other side, the paper is not of good quality. Rub a few pages between your fingertips to test thickness. Paper that is thin will tear easily when pages are turned.

- The binding should be tight. Don't buy a copy that has loose stitches or a paperback edition with a cracked or spilt spine.

- If a toy format is built into the design, such as a flap book or pop-up, all parts should be durable. Flip through the pages to make sure all of the parts are in working order.

Remember, if a book is cheaply made and falls apart after just a few readings, your time spent in choosing the book and money spent purchasing it were wasted.

Exploring the Art and Story

Design is the bridge that connects the picture and text in picture books. As discussed in chapter 3, design refers to the overall organization or composition of a work, the arrangement of its parts. Design gives the eye points of reference that lead viewers through the composition. Molly Leach, designer of the seminal *The Stinky Cheese Man* (1992) says she relies on "bold, eye-catching designs, because I don't like it when your eye wanders on the page and has to figure out where to go." The magic that makes a particular book resonate is not an accident. It is the direct result of thoughtful planning and design.

Readers are sometimes so focused on the text and pictures that they overlook the underlying elements of design and the paratexts. These are more fully explored in chapters 2 and 3, but to review, picture book paratexts are the book jacket (flaps, spine, covers) and the front and back matter (copyright age, half-title page, title page, dedication, endpapers). Some picture books, particularly picture book biographies and informational picture books, may include a glossary, table of contents, foreword, afterword, and colophon.

After exploring the book jacket, including the flaps, examine the paratexts for clues to the story. For example, do the endpapers contribute meaning to the text? In *Comic Adventures of Boots* (2002) illustrator Satoshi Kitamura used the endpapers to full advantage. Both the front and back endpapers contain a series of vignettes featuring Boots, the main character. From the moment readers open the book, the adventures begin, and there are three more, punctuated with dialogue balloons and panels that mimic the comic-strip format.

As discussed in chapter 2, a wealth of information can also be found on the flaps. Many designers take advantage of the flaps to include visual clues to the story or display information visually. In *Piggies* (1991) the front flap introduces the five characters: fat (thumb), smart (pointer finger), long (middle finger), silly (ring finger), and wee (pinky finger). In *Math Curse* (1995) the flaps features several math problems, which allude to the math zaniness of the title. The back flap shows a Venn diagram of the books that author Jon Scieszka published with other illustrators, the books illustrator Lane Smith published alone, and the books the pair have published together. The location of the publisher (New York, NY) is written as NY.

Paperback editions do not have flaps, but reviewing the other paratexts, such as endpapers, covers, and title page, will be the same or very similar to reviewing the hardcover edition.

Analysis Strategies

Earlier in this section it was suggested that readers approach picture book evaluation in stages: in the first reading, focus on the text; in the second, explore the text by reading aloud; in the third reading, focus on the pictures; and in the fourth reading, explore how the text and pictures work together. Following are questions to ask while navigating each reading. After examining the book jacket and flaps, you should have a general idea of what a particular picture book is about.

Focus on the Text (read silently)

- Is the story strong without the illustrations?

- Do you notice any patterns in the story or the language?

- Do line breaks feel natural or forced?

- Do the page breaks occur naturally, or are they forced?

- Do some pages have more text than others?

- Are there pages with just text (no pictures)?

Focus on the Text (read aloud)

- Is there rhythm or rhyme?

- Is the language poetic, spare, humorous?

- Is it easy or difficult to read aloud?

- Does the language enhance or detract?

- Is there repetition of certain phrases or sounds?

Focus on the Illustrations

- Do the illustrations tell the story by themselves?

- What is missing, if anything, without the words?

- Do the style and medium add to the illustrations?

- Would another style or medium alter or change the overall mood of the book?

- Does the palette affect the mood of the story?

- Do any specific supporting parts stand out?

- Are there clues on the flaps or endpapers that hint at the contents?

- Is there visual interest? What about drama? Pace?

- Does the page layout add visual interest?

- Does the design support or fight with the illustrations?

- Do the typographic elements support the other design elements?

Explore How the Text and Pictures Work Together

- Would the story be different if it were wordless?

- How do the text and illustrations work together to tell the story?

- Do the illustrations alter or subvert the meaning of the text?

- Does the text fill gaps in the illustrations?

- Do the illustrations fill gaps in the text?

BEYOND THE PAGES

Licensing

In recent decades, picture books have become big business. Chapter 1 briefly touched on licensing. The number of picture book characters that step beyond the pages grows with each passing year. Popular characters such as Kevin Henkes's Lilly, Jean de Brunhoff's Babar, Maurice Sendak's Max and the Wild Things, Beatrix Potter's Peter Rabbit, and Arnold Lobel's Frog and Toad are just a few. More than just stuffed dolls based on the characters, products ranging from posters to coffee mugs to T-shirts to rubber stamps are available. Some businesses, such as Kidstamps, specialize in products that celebrate the art of children's picture books. They offer coffee mugs, T-shirts, rubber stamps, and bookplates. Their products represent the work of more than 40 famous illustrators, including Marc Brown, Kevin Henkes, Arnold Lobel, and Edward Gorey.

By licensing the use of the character, authors and illustrators can earn fees above and beyond the royalties received from their book sales. For people who love particular characters, the idea of collecting is irresistible. In addition, products and services built around popular characters and children can extend the reading experience.

However, licensing has a downside. In a provocative article, "Storyselling: Are Publishers Changing the Way Children Read?," scholar Daniel Hade (2002) looks at issues that have surfaced with the licensing of book characters. In a startling example, he recalls voraciously reading Curious George books when he was a young boy. Although a few licensed products existed, Hades's main exposure to H. A. Rey's character was through books. He imagines that if he were growing up today, he would not only have dozens of original Curious George books to read, but numerous other series based on Rey's character. Hade notes that children today can wake up to Curious George alarm clocks after sleeping on Curious George sheets. They eat breakfast from a Curious George bowl with a coordinating spoon set. Bedecked in a Curious George T-shirt and matching cap, children head off to school with Curious George backpacks. Hade details products bearing the Curious George label that he found available for purchase on Amazon.com, including office supplies (pens, pencils, bookmarks, erasers, calendars), nursery decor (wall appliqués, wallpaper borders, crib sheets, curtains, diaper holder), and jewelry (buttons, key rings bracelets). This is just a sampling; consumers can even purchase a Curious George piñata. And, of course, parents can throw a Curious George theme party complete with tablecloths, plates, napkins, cups, balloons, and party favors.

The downside? Publishers, according to Hade, see children more as consumers than as readers. He is not far off the mark. McDonald's routinely features famous book characters in Happy Meals,® and General Mills, makers of the popular breakfast cereal Cheerios, allowed Scholastic to create a book that looks like a Cheerios cereal box. According to Hade, children consume Cheerios without actually eating them. Hade's research revealed that in 1999, 44 of the 50 top-selling children's hardcover titles featured licensed characters.

Publishing veteran Tom Engelhardt attempted to raise concern about this issue as early as 1991. In his article Engelhardt argued that the new corporate owners of publishing houses Random, owned by Bertelsmann, and HarperCollins, owned by Rupert Murdoch's News Corporation, focus on licensing to such an extent that reading has come to resemble "listening, viewing, playing, dressing, and buying." Englehardt stated that children's books had been liberated from the page, and that reading was becoming just another means of consumption.

Today, the line between book and licensed merchandise has become almost nonexistent. Children are constantly bombarded with images that many cannot even identify as originating in a picture book. The ubiquitous cross-promoting blurs the line between advertisement and entertainment. Hade states that "corporate owners of children's book publishing have successfully turned recreational reading into a commodity."

Sequels and Series

Some characters are so ingrained in the culture that we often forget that they are characters in books. The response to certain characters is often so positive and overwhelming that it is natural for an illustrator to create a sequel. Sometimes supporting characters in books become full fleshed characters in other books.

Consider, for example, Kevin Henkes's mouse books. His most endearing character, Lilly, appears in three books of her own, as well as two other of Henkes's mice books. Ian Falconer's precocious porcine Olivia just appeared in her fourth adventure, *Olivia Forms a Band* (2006).

Jane Yolen and Mark Teague have created a successful series of dinosaur books that began with *How Do Dinosaurs Say Good-Night?* (2000). Other books in the series include *How Do Dinosaurs Get Well Soon?* (2003), *How Do Dinosaurs Eat Their Food?* (2005), and *How Do Dinosaurs Go to School?* (2007). The series is built around playful verse and clever illustrations that build on right and wrong types of behavior. In addition to the picture books, Yolen's and Teague's dinosaur characters have been issued in board books: *How Do Dinosaurs Count To Ten?* (2004), *How Do Dinosaurs Learn Their Colors?* (2006), and *How Do Dinosaurs Play With Their Friend* (2006), and the characters are available as plush toys.

A recent character that has captured the hearts and minds of children is Judith Schacher's lovable Persian kitten, Skippyjon Jones, whose adventures include treasure hunts and encounters with mummies. There are currently five titles in the series, including *Skippyjon Jones* (2003) and *Skippyjon Jones in the Dog-House* (2005).

Picture book series and sequels have both advantages and disadvantages. One disadvantage is that characters that are popular enough to engender sequels are often also subject to licensing. Positive aspects of series are that the characters resonate with children, allowing them to connect with characters over time and through many reading experiences. In picture book series and sequels, children are introduced to characters as toddlers and grow with the character as more titles are published. The familiarity of series characters such as Skippyjon Jones and Curious George allow children to see beloved characters and settings they know well from previous books.

> For comprehensive list of picture books sequels and series, please visit www.picturingbooks.com.

From Page to Screen

Another territory picture books have expanded into is the film industry. Hollywood discovered the potential of children's books early on. Considering the depth and breadth that illustrations add to a story, it is not really surprising that a 32-page book can be adapted into a full-length feature film. The most familiar picture book adaptations are probably the books of Chris Allsburg: *The Polar Express* (1985) was adapted to film in 2004, and *Jumanji* (1981) and its sequel *Zathura* (2002) were adapted to film in 1995 and 2005 respectively. William Stieg's *Shrek!* (1990) has inspired the original movie named after the book and two sequels so far.

Other picture books that have been adapted are H. A. Rey's *Curious George* (1941), adapted to film in 2006; Ludwig Bemelmans's *Madeline* (1939), adapted in 1998; Harry Allard's and James Marshall's *The Stupids Die* (1981), adapted as *The Stupids* in 1996; and William Joyce's *A Day with Wilbur Robinson* (1990), adapted to film as *Meet the Robinsons* in 2007. In 2008 Maurice Sendak's *Where the Wild*

Things Are (1963) and Dr. Seuss's *Horton Hears a Who* (1954) were adapted for the screen.

Numerous books have been adapted for television, some expanded into series. Both PBS and HBO have created series based on picture books. HBO offerings include series adaptations of James Marshall's *George and Martha* and Crockett Johnson's *Harold and the Purple Crayon*. PBS has adapted Norman Bridwell's Clifford books, Marc Brown's <u>Arthur</u> series, and H. A. Rey's Curious George into series.

Movie adaptations often result in a film that looks and feels very different from the picture books they are based on. In the 2000 film version of *How the Grinch Stole Christmas* (1957), director Ron Howard embellished the plot and added new characters to Seuss's classic. Though they are often different than the original picture books, movie versions offer readers an extended experience with beloved characters and settings. However, like licensing, movies based on picture books can result in a multitude of movie tie-ins. This can be good or bad, depending on one's perspective. For publishers, the bottom line remains healthy. Likewise for authors and illustrators. Licensing offers additional income to supplement book royalties.

Original Art and Museums

Other groups profit from picture books as well. There are many businesses, museums, and organizations that specialize in original children's illustration and limited edition prints. These galleries not only celebrate picture books, they also view the individual illustrations as works of fine art. Located in Santa Monica, California, Every Picture Tells a Story represents such artists as Maurice Sendak, Hilary Knight, Garth Williams, David Shannon, Lisbeth Zwerger, Chris Van Allsburg, and Mo Willems. The collection of another gallery, Storyopolis, located in Studio City, California, boasts original artwork from over 150 well-known illustrators, including Mark Teague, David Diaz, Eric Carle, and William Joyce. StorybookArt is dedicated to representing top children's book illustrators in the sale of their original artwork to art and book lovers everywhere.

The National Center for Children's Illustrated Literature (NCCIL) is a nonprofit organization that was incorporated in February 1997 in Texas. The NCCIL provides recognition to the artistic achievements of illustrators and gallery exhibitions of their works. The NCCIL also designs educational programs that relate to illustrations in children's literature in order to stimulate creativity, promote literacy, and increase appreciation for art.

The Eric Carle Museum of Picture Book Art, located in Amherst, Massachusetts, is dedicated to the art of the picture book. Opened in November 2002, the museum's 40,000-square-foot facility houses three art galleries, which feature rotating exhibitions of picture book art from around the world. The museum also has a reading library, gift shop, and research collection. Founded in part by Eric Carle, the celebrated author and illustrator of more than 70 picture books, including the 1969 classic *The Very Hungry Caterpillar*, the museum was the first featuring picture book art that extended its scope beyond collection development by offering workshops, storytimes, and theater presentations inspired by famous picture books. Underlying its many services and events is the mission to inspire an appreciation for and an understanding of picture book art.

Location is an issue, because the museums and galleries mentioned in this section require travel for most readers. Despite the reality that most people will never visit these places, they remain important in the history of picture books. Both The Eric Carle Museum of Picture Book Art and the NCCIL have traveling exhibits that tour the country.[9] Of course, they also have Web sites that you can visit.

> For contact information about the galleries and museums, please visit www.picturingbooks.com.

CONCLUSION

Although they are small, having as few as 24 pages and as many as 64, picture books have stepped beyond their pages in their influence on individuals and culture. Licensing, though it has a downside, has brought many favorite characters from the page to a number of products. Television and movies based on favorite picture books appear with more frequency, solidifying the substance of these thin little books. Digital picture books still struggle to find a place in the industry. It will be interesting to see how they develop and whether they engender new, alternate formats. Picture books are a rich, vital part of the children's literature canon. They have earned a place in the hearts and minds of picture book aficionados. Their unique format is sure to inspire cultural and consumer trends in the future.

ENDNOTES

1. In 2007, the book industry began begin using 13-digit ISBNs to identify all books to expand the numbering capacity of the ISBN system. ISBN-13 has the same identifiers as ISBN-10, except that it has a three-digit identifier preceding the group/country identifier.

2. For a more through exploration of the children's publishing field, please visit The Purple Crayon, by children's book editor Harold Underdown, at www.underdown.org.

3. In 2006, Troll and Trumpet Book Clubs combined with Scholastic Book Clubs. Readers who would like more information should visit the Scholastic Web site at http://teacher.scholastic.com/clubnews/.

4. Scholastic has book clubs for older readers and secondary teachers. The clubs mentioned in this chapter target toddlers through grade 3 and offer picture books and beginning readers.

5. Age designations described in *A Picture Book Primer* are culled from examining the printed versions of the journals, as well as using each journal's Web site. The *Horn Book* staff did not respond to a request for verification. At different points in the journal's history different age designations have been applied.

6. *School Library Journal*'s book review section is divided into sections Pre-School to grade 4 and grade 5 and Up, with the reviewer assigning the appropriate grade level for each individual book. Per e-mail correspondence with Trev Jones, *School Library Journal*'s book review editor.

7. Neither *Booklist* nor *Publishers Weekly* responded to a request for verification.

8. Young dedicated *Lon Po Po: A Red-Riding Tale from China* to " all the wolves of the world for lending their good name as a tangible symbol for our darkness."

9. For information about traveling picture book exhibits, please visit the NCCIL Web site, nccil.org/exhibits/touring/index.htm and The Eric Carle Museum of Picture Book Art Web site, www.picturebookart.org/exhibitions/traveling_exhibitions.

Conclusion

This year, 2008, could very well turn out to be the year that the definition of what a picture book is changes most dramatically. Two books, *The Invention of Hugo Cabret* by Brian Selznick and *Gallop!* by Rufus Butler Seder, both published in 2007, challenge our idea of what picture books are supposed to be. *The Invention of Hugo Cabret* was awarded the Caldecott Award—the first novel that has ever won. Maybe we shouldn't be so surprised that a novel won a picture book award, because in 1982 the Newbery (generally awarded to novels, nonfiction, poetry, and collections) was awarded to a picture book, *A Visit to William Blake's Inn: Poems for Innocent and Experienced Travelers* by Nancy Willard. That wasn't the first time a picture book had been acknowledged by the committee. Other picture books have been honorably mentioned, including *ABC Bunny* (1933) and *Millions of Cats* (1928), both by Wanda Gág. However, at that time the Caldecott Award had not yet been established.

Gallop! introduces a new technology called Scanimation,® which provides an interactive experience in an offline environment. In 1971 the photography in Tana Hoban's *Look Again!,* challenged traditional media techniques in picture books. *Gallop!* is poised to do the same with its Scanimation® techniques.

One can only imagine what early illustrators like Randolph Caldecott (late nineteenth century) and Wanda Gág (early twentieth century) would think of today's picture books. Caldecott is credited with creating the format we know and love today, and Gág is credited with creating the modern picture book. Over the past century, the early production methods of offset presses have yielded to digital methods. Artists formerly restricted to hand-drawn illustration and four-color process can now use any medium they desire. And as in the case of *Gallop!*, new ones are being created all the time.

Digital picture books have existed for a few years. However, early attempts to create successful distribution of digital picture books were not successful. The International Children's Digital Library (ICDL), a nonprofit organization founded in 2002, recently experienced some success, but it does not charge fees and is dependent on outside funding. Another online site that offers digital editions of picture books, Lookybook, was launched in 2008. The creators of Lookybook empathetically state on their Web site, "We'll never replace an actual book in your hands, but we hope to show you new books and help you make informed choices for you and your kids." Books digitized on Lookybook and the ICDL are not interactive in the sense that sounds and animation have been added, but they offer access to a multitude of books in an online environment.

Like other forms of print, some might decry the imminent demise of picture books. In the information age, we may think that digital editions and interactive books somehow offer more than printed books, but far from being static, picture books have a brilliant history and a very vibrant future. Print—not just picture books, but novels, newspapers, and magazines—is often called a dying technology, but in the hands and imaginations of many talented authors, illustrators, designers, editors, and illustrators, it is still a medium of wonder for all ages.

Appendix A

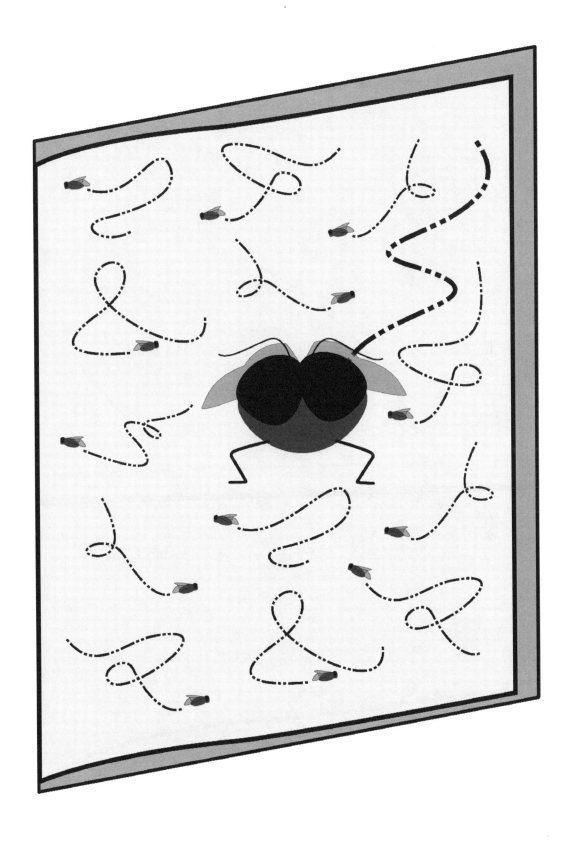

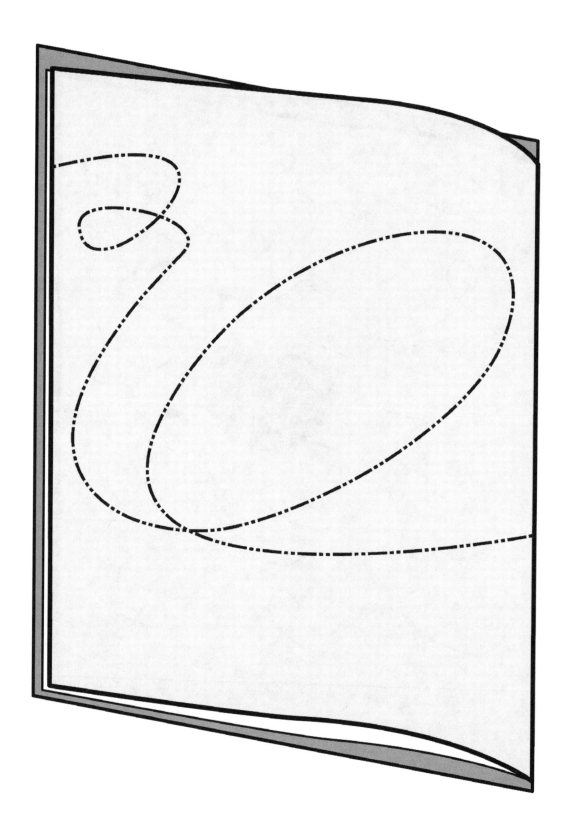

From *A Picture Book Primer: Understanding and Using Picture Books* by Denise I. Matulka. Westport, CT: Libraries Unlimited. Copyright © 2008.

Butler
and the
Fly

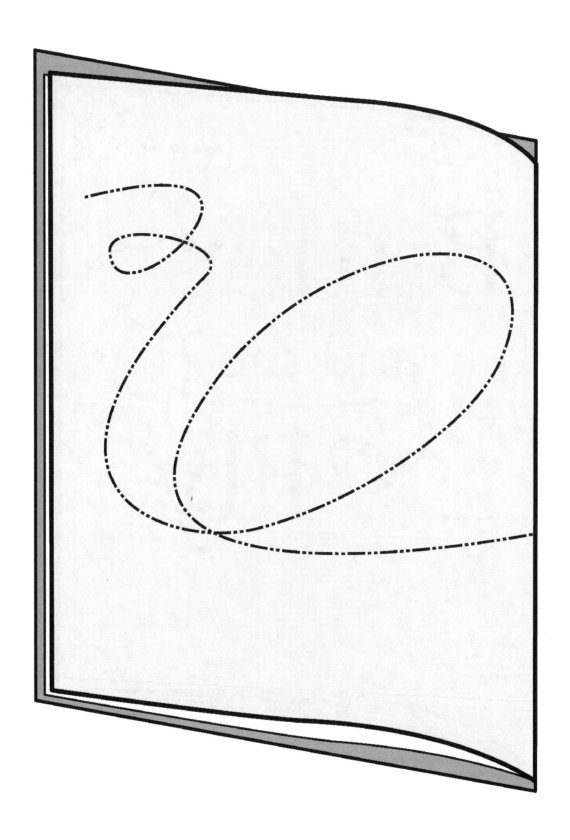

Butler and the Fly

Written & Illustrated by Ivanna Toad

Frog & Toad Books

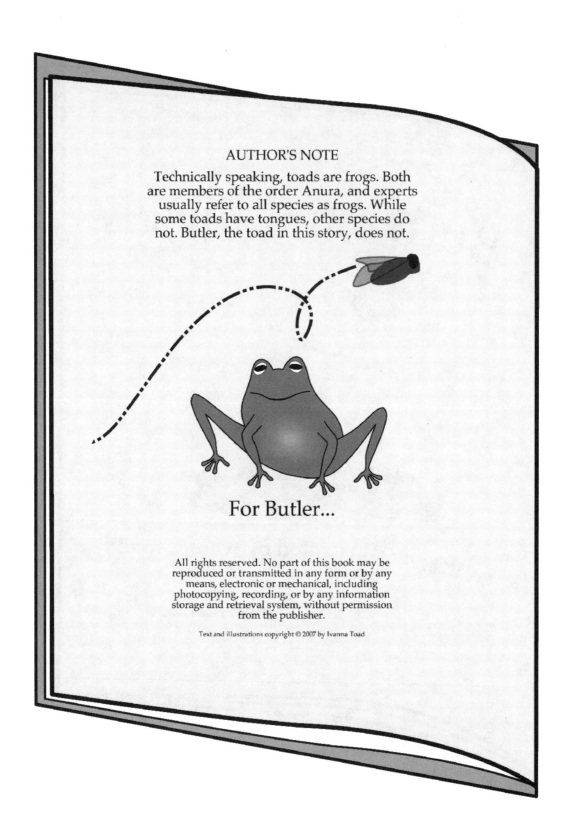

AUTHOR'S NOTE

Technically speaking, toads are frogs. Both
are members of the order Anura, and experts
usually refer to all species as frogs. While
some toads have tongues, other species do
not. Butler, the toad in this story, does not.

For Butler...

The Fly wanted a friend.

Not just any friend...

The Fly flew up…

From *A Picture Book Primer: Understanding and Using Picture Books* by Denise I. Matulka. Westport, CT: Libraries Unlimited. Copyright © 2008.

Looking for a friend.

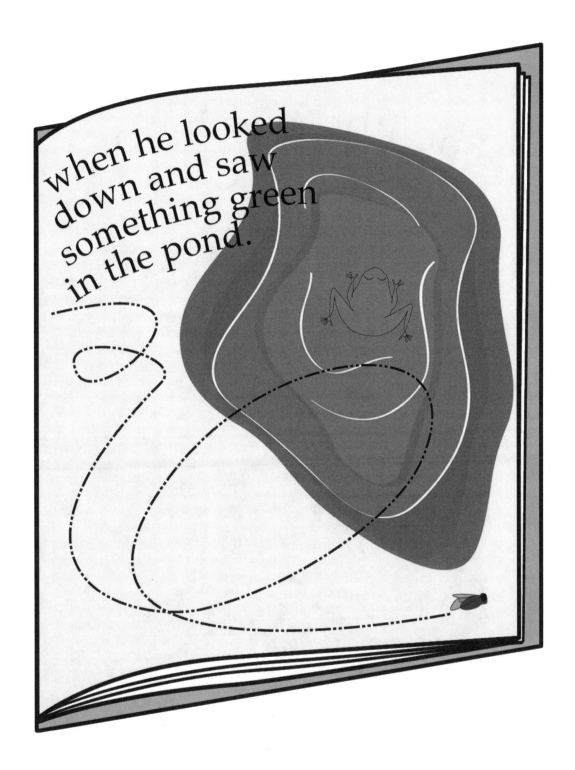

when he looked down and saw something green in the pond.

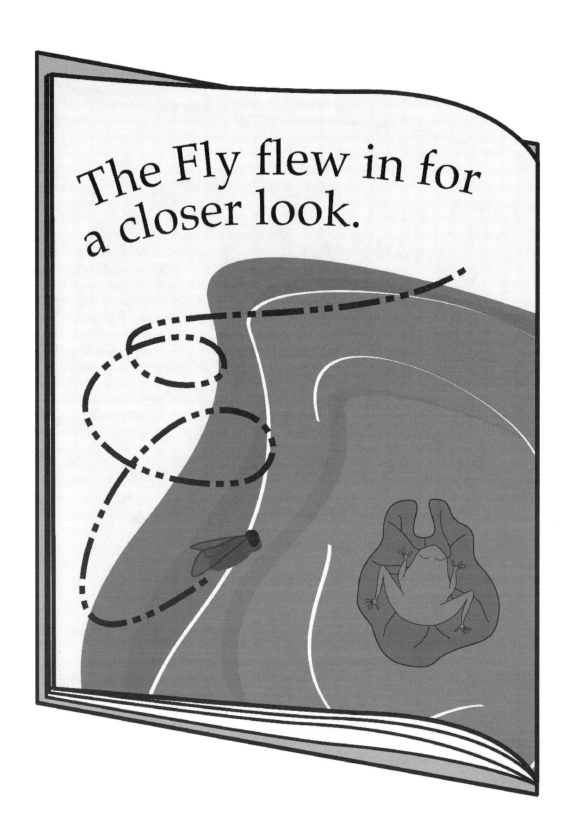

The Fly flew in for a closer look.

From *A Picture Book Primer: Understanding and Using Picture Books* by Denise I. Matulka.
Westport, CT: Libraries Unlimited. Copyright © 2008.

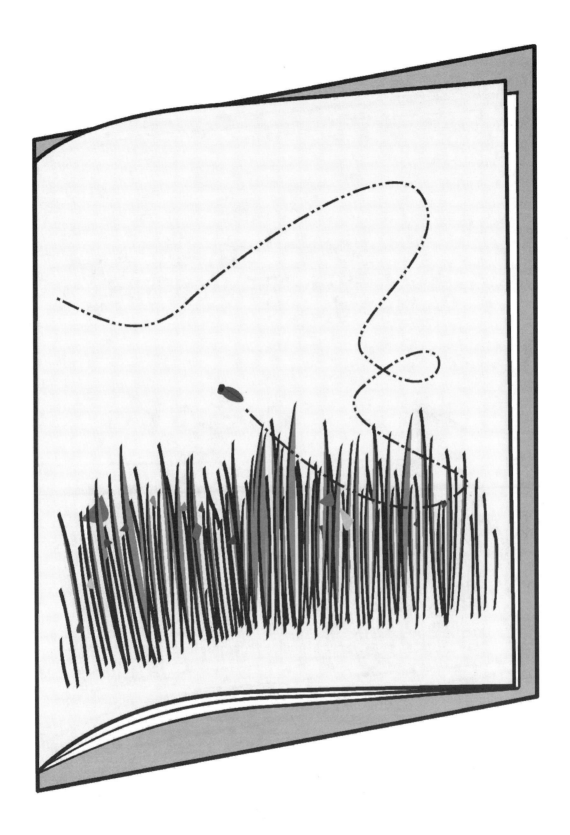

The Fly
had found
a friend.

The Fly had
found Butler.

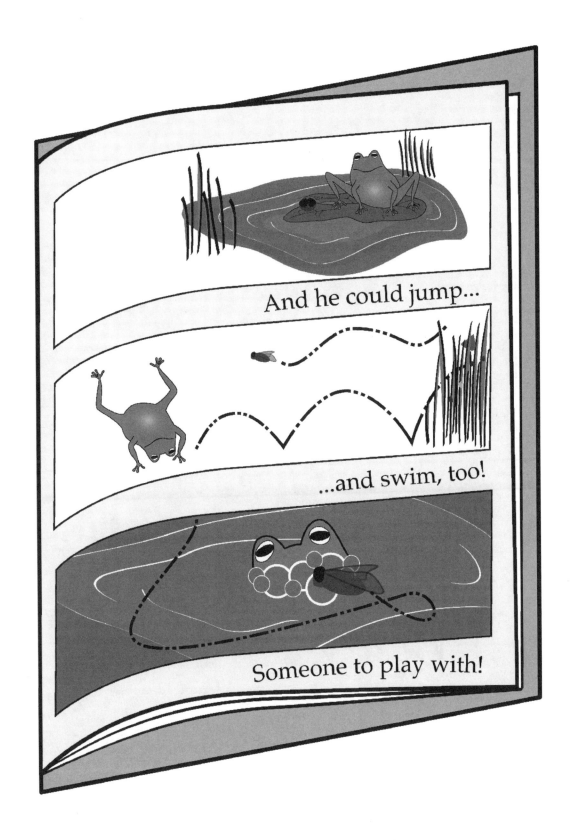

And that's
what they did.

Until it was time to go home...

From *A Picture Book Primer: Understanding and Using Picture Books* by Denise I. Matulka. Westport, CT: Libraries Unlimited. Copyright © 2008.

231

Starred Review

★ ★ ★ ★

The Horn Toad Book

Appendix B: Picture Book Timeline

There are many important dates and figures in the development of picture books. To attempt to include them all is impossible. However, a timeline of major events, important books, and prominent figures is useful. Each entry includes the date of the event, the event, and why it is notable.

DATE	EVENT	NOTABLE FOR
1658	*Orbis Sensualium Pictus—The Visible World in Pictures* published. Written by Johannes Amos Comenius (1592–1670).	Considered to be the first picture book for children.
1744	John Newbery (1713–1767), A Little Pretty Pocket–Book	Although not a picture book, it is often cited as being the first book published for children.
1753	Thomas Bewick born on August 10, 1753 in England, Bewick; died November 8, 1828.	An early engraver who circumvented the problems inherent in wood engraving by using the end grain of the wood instead of the plank, which was softer and reproduced poorly over time.
1792	George Cruikshank born in September 27, 1792; died February 1, 1878.	An early illustrator who made allowances for the wood engraving process by matching his style to the capabilities of the medium, which resulted in higher-quality illustrations.
1812	Edward Lear born in London, England on May 12, 1812; died in San Remo, Italy on January 29, 1888.	His *Book of Nonsense* continues to be the standard for nonsense literature, often imitated, but never surpassed.
1844	*Der Struwwelpeter, or Slovenly Peter,* published. Written and illustrated by Heinrich Hoffmann.	An early example of a book being created to fill a need.
1846	Kate Greenaway born in London, England, on March 17, 1846; died on November 6, 1901.	Greenaway's charming paintings set fashion trends in her time. The major illustration award in the United Kingdom is named in her honor.
1846	*A Book of Nonsense* published. Written and illustrated by Edward Lear.	Continues to be the standard for nonsense literature, often imitated, but never surpassed.

DATE	EVENT	NOTABLE FOR
1846	Randolph Caldecott born in Chester, England, on March 22, 1846; died in St. Augustine, Florida, on February 12, 1886.	Considered the "father" of the modern picture book, Caldecott was a gifted draftsman as well as illustrator. Recognized as the first to realize the potential of the verbal and visual relationship in picture books.
1853	Howard Pyle born in Wilmington, Delaware, on March 5, 1853; died November 9, 1911.	Influential leader of the Golden Age of Illustration. Under Pyle's tutelage, such talented artists such as N. C. Wyeth, Jessie Willcox Smith, and Maxfield Parrish
1862	L(eonard) Leslie Brooke born in Birkenhead, Cheshire, England, on September 24, 1862; died May 1, 1940.	Noted for his pen-and-ink and watercolor illustrations. He was the illustrator of the Johnny Crow series.
1863	Jessie Willcox Smith born in Philadelphia, Pennsylvania, on September 6, 1863; died there on May 3, 1935.	Smith is noted for her *Good Housekeeping* covers, which she painted from 1917 through 1933, and her 12 illustrations for Charles Kingsley's *The Water Babies* (1916).
1865	Frederick Warne company founded.	Warne published *The Tale of Peter Rabbit* by Beatrix Potter, beginning a 40-year partnership that resulted in 22 more books. The partnership evolved into a flourishing merchandising program, the first one based on a children's book.
1865	*Alice's Adventures in Wonderland* published. Written by Lewis Carroll; illustrated by John Tenniel.	The publication heralded a new age of children's books. 1865 is often cited as a pivotal year for children's literature.
1866	Beatrix Potter born in South Kensington, Middlesex, England, on July 28, 1866; died at Hill Top Farm in the Lake District in England on December 22, 1943.	Known for her meticulous research and study of animals, which is reflect in her animal characters.
1867	Arthur Rackham born in London, England, on September 19, 1867; died in Croydon, England, on September 6, 1939.	Noted for his graceful pen line softened with muted watercolors and backgrounds filled with nuggets of imagery. Rackham illustrated such classics as *Peter Pan* in Kensington Gardens (1906) and A *Midsummer-Night's Dream* (1908).

DATE	EVENT	NOTABLE FOR
1870	Maxfield Parrish born in Philadelphia, Pennsylvania, on July 25, 1870; died in Cornish, New Hampshire, on March 30, 1966.	An early illustrator noted for his wash, line, and stipple techniques. Known for the magical, otherworldly quality that permeates his illustrations.
1871	*Through the Looking Glass* published. Written by Lewis Carroll; illustrated by John Tenniel.	Although not a picture book, it had a great impact on the history of children's illustration.
1878	*The Diverting History of John Gilpin* published. Written by William Cowper; illustrated by Randolph Caldecott.	An image from this book inspired the design for the Caldecott Medal.
1882	Edmund Dulac born in Toulouse, France, on October 22, 1882; died in London, England, on May 25, 1953.	One of the major illustrators of the golden age of illustration, Dulac is known for the stylized figures in his illustrations, as well as his elaborate backgrounds and shading of his scenes .
1882	N. C. Wyeth born in Needham, Massachusetts, on October 22, 1882; died on October 19, 1945.	Illustrator of numerous classic children's book, including Robert Louis Stevenson's *Treasure Island* (1911), *Kidnapped* (1913), *The Black Arrow* (1916), and *David Balfour* (1924).
1886	Kay (pronounced "kigh") Nielsen born in Copenhagen, Denmark, on March 12, 1886; died on January 21, 1957 in Altadena, California.	Known for his elongated figures and flattened perspective, Nielsen was influenced by Japanese art, the art nouveau movement, and contemporary Aubrey Beardsley.
1893	The first Children's Room established in the New York Public Library.	A significant development in the changing attitudes toward children, books, and reading.
1897	Marjorie Flack born in Long Island, New York, on October 23, 1897; died on August 29, 1958.	She was best known for *The Story about Ping* (1933), illustrated by Kurt Wiese, and popularized by Captain Kangaroo; it was a trio of picture books about Angus, an insatiably curious Scottish terrier. Historian Barbara Bader says that "Marjorie Flack drew, but not very well; she wrote, but she wasn't a writer; what she had was a feel for stories—situations, for the most part—that would tell well in words and pictures and a knack for dramatizing them: a true picturebook sense."

DATE	EVENT	NOTABLE FOR
1898	Ludwig Bemelmans born in Meran, Tyrol, Austria, on April 27, 1898; died in New York, New York, on October 1, 1962.	The creator of Madeline, a character who still resonates with readers in the twenty-first century.
1899	*The Story of Little Black Sambo* published. Written and illustrated by Helen Bannerman.	Although very controversial today, the book is notable for its humor and lovable protagonist.
1900	*The Wonderful Wizard of Oz* published. Written by L. Frank Baum; illustrated by W. W. Denslow.	Although not a picture book, the pictures in *The Wonderful Wizard of Oz* are notable for their contribution to children's book illustration.
1900	Edward Ardizzone born October 16, 1900, in Haiphong, French Indochina; died on November 8, 1979.	His best known work is the <u>Tim</u> series, featuring the maritime adventures of a young boy. The first book, *Tim and the Brave Sea Captain,* was published in 1936. The most famous of the books, *Tim All Alone,* won the first Kate Greenaway Medal for illustration in 1956. The series ended with *Tim's Last Voyage* (1972).
1902	*The Tale of Peter Rabbit* published. Written and illustrated by Beatrix Potter	One of the first true picture books. Notable for its small format.
1904	Theodor Seuss Geisel born in Springfield, Massachusetts, on March 2, 1904; died in La Jolla, California, on September 24, 1991.	He began his career as a political cartoonist and ended as one of the most influential children's book illustrators in the world. Generations of children have grown up with Seuss's wacky, yet inspired, books.
1910	Margaret Wise Brown born in Brooklyn, New York, on May 23, 1910; died in Nice, France, on November 13, 1952.	Known for her innate sense of childhood and the ability to see the world through the eyes of children. During her short life she published 75 picture books.
1916	Bookshop for Boys and Girls opens in Boston, Massachusetts.	The first independent bookshop for children.
1919	Macmillan establishes a juvenile division.	The first major publisher to establish a juvenile division, with Louise Seaman Bechtel running the ship.
1922	*The Velveteen Rabbit* published. Written by Margery Williams; illustrated by William Nicholson.	Though dated and with a distinctly upper-class British setting, the story endures for its unique perspective on human nature as told from the viewpoint of the toy rabbit.

DATE	EVENT	NOTABLE FOR
1923	*ABC Book* published. Written and illustrated by C.B. Falls	Hailed as an American classic.
1924	*The Horn Book* is founded	It was first journal dedicated to reviewing children's books, is founded
1928	*Millions of Cats* published. Written and illus. by Wanda Gág.	*Millions of Cats* is considered to be the first modern picture book. It won a Newbery Honor medal in 1930, one of the few picture books that did.
1928	Maurice Sendak born in Brooklyn, New York, on June 10, 1928.	Sendak is arguably the most influential picture book illustrator of the twentieth century.
1930	*Angus and the Ducks* published. Written and illustrated by Marjorie Flack.	One of three Angus books by Marjorie Flack.
1932	Quentin Blake born in London, England.	Quentin Blake is the humorous illustrator of numerous children's books and has illustrated more than 300.
1933	*The Story of Babar* published. Written and illustrated by Jean de Brunhoff.	Though beloved by many generations of children, some critics have denounced the Babar books as promoting or justifying colonialism.
1936	*The Story of Ferdinand* published. Written by Munro Leaf; illustrated by Robert Lawson.	Published before the Spanish Civil War and World War II, it featured a pacifist hero who would rather sit in the shade and smell flowers than fight in bullfights
1937	*And to Think That I Saw It on Mulberry Street* published. Written and illustrated by Dr. Seuss.	Dr. Seuss's first book was rejected by 28 publishers before Random House bought the manuscript, beginning a partnership that lasted throughout Seuss's life.
1938	*The Five Chinese Brothers* published. Written by Claire Huchet Bishop; illustrated by Kurt Wiese.	Example of a problematic classic picture book that unintentionally promotes negative stereotypes.
1938	The Caldecott Award established.	It was one of the first major awards acknowledging illustration in children's books.

DATE	EVENT	NOTABLE FOR
1939	*Madeline* published. Written and illustrated by Ludwig Bemelmans.	*Madeline* was initially considered too sophisticated for children. However, Simon & Schuster finally published it in 1939 after several publishers had rejected the book. It spawned five other Madeline books, which were published by Viking.
1939	*Mike Mulligan and His Steam Shovel* published. Written and illustratedby Virginia Lee Burton.	A classic tale about progress and finding a place in the world, with a triumphant resolution. Classic example of strong storytelling supported by illustration.
1940	*Pat the Bunny* published. Written and illustrated by Dorothy Kunhardt.	*Pat the Bunny* has earned a solid reputation as the first book for new babies. Published in 1940, it has sold over seven million copies and spawned numerous other titles and related products.
1941	*Curious George* published. Written and illustrated by H. A. Rey.	An American classic. The first in a series.
1942	*The Poky Little Puppy* published. Written and illustrated by Janette Sebring Lowrey.	The first of the <u>Little Golden Books</u>, which were affordable and the first to be sold in grocery and department stores.
1942	*The Runaway Bunny* published. Written by Margaret Wise Brown; illustrated by Clement Hurd.	Notable for never having gone out of print.
1942	*The Little House* published. Written and illustrated by Virginia Lee Burton.	An early example of a successful integration of text and pictures, with text playing an important part in the design. It was a visually driven book, so Barton balanced the text to accommodate the illustrations.
1945	*The Carrot Seed* published. Written by Ruth Krauss; illustrated by Crockett Johnson.	Maurice Sendak called it "that perfect picture book . . . the granddaddy of all picture books in America." According to Sendak the book was revolutionary and transformed children's book publishing.
1947	*Make Way for Ducklings* published. Written and illustrated by Robert McCloskey.	Winner of the Caldecott Medal in 1948, it has sold over two million copies. *Make Way for Ducklings* was immortalized in bronze. The statute resides in a park on Boston Common.

DATE	EVENT	NOTABLE FOR
1947	*Goodnight Moon* published. Written by Margaret Wise Brown; illustrated by Clement Hurd	Despite an initial poor review from the influential New York Public Library, it became a classic. Parents recommended the book to each other, and it slowly became a word-of-mouth best seller. By 1990 more than four million copies had been sold.
1950	*The Circus Baby* published. Written and illustrated by Maud Petersham and Miska Petersham.	Though not the first picture book by the Petershams, it may be their most recognized. Maud Perersham and Miska Petersham won a Caldecott Medal for *The Rooster Crows* (1945) and a Caldecott Honor for *An American ABC* (1941).
1950	John Lewis Steptoe born in Brooklyn, New York, on September 14, 1950; died there on August 28, 1989.	One of the first prolific authors to write and illustrate books specifically for black children. His settings featured urban landscapes and realistic portrayals of African American children.
1952	The Children's Book Council of Australia established a picture book award (The Children's Book of the Year Awards).	Indicative of the important role picture books play as a format within the children's literature field. Brought attention to Australian illustrators.
1953	Weston Wood Studio founded.	Since 1953, Weston Woods Studios has produced more than 500 animated features based on popular picture books. An early innovator of multimedia picture books.
1954	*The Cat in the Hat* published. Written and illustrated by Dr. Seuss.	The first of a type of book that would become known as beginning or easy readers.
1955	*Harold and the Purple Crayon* published. Written and illustrated by Crockett Johnson.	Critically acclaimed picture book about a boy who uses his imagination to create fantastic landscapes with his crayon.
1956	Kate Greenaway Medal for Illustrators established in United Kingdom by the Youth Libraries Group, a division of the British Library Association.	It is awarded annually for the most distinguished work published in the UK; considered the top British children's book illustration award.
1956	*Harry, the Dirty Dog* published. Written by Gene Zion; illustrated by Margaret B. Graham.	Early critics lauded Harry, as "a timeless personality inviting warmth, involvement and understanding."
1957	Bookbird founded by Jella Lepman and Richard Bamberger.	The first international journal to review children's books.

DATE	EVENT	NOTABLE FOR
1957	*Little Bear* published. Written by Else Holmelund Minarik; illustrated by Maurice Sendak.	The first title in the I Can Read series book gave children a chance to read chapter books and proved that "easy readers" can also be great literature.
1959	*Little Blue and Little Yellow* published. Written and illustrated by Leo Lionni.	Lionni is attributed with being the first illustrator to use collage as a medium in picture books.
1962	*Nutshell Library* published. Written and illustrated by Maurice Sendak.	This four-volume boxed set contains an alphabet book, a book of rhymes, a counting book, and a cautionary tale. Each book measures barely 3 by 4 inches.
1962	*The Snowy Day* published. Written and illustrated by Ezra Jack Keats.	*The Snowy Day* features the first African American protagonist as the central character in a picture book.
1963	*Where the Wild Things Are* published. Written and illustrated by Maurice Sendak.	Many experts consider Sendak's classic to be the "perfect picture book."
1965	Nancy Larrick's groundbreaking article "The All–White World of Children's Books" published in the *Saturday Review of Books*.	The first published critique of the absence of children of color in children's literature, the article highlighted Larrick's five-year study of more than 5,000 children's books.
1966	IBBY establishes an illustrator's award in honor of Hans Christian Andersen	Often referred to as the "Little Nobel Prize," the Hans Christian Andersen is the highest international recognition given to creators of children's books.
1967	Biennial of Illustration Bratislava (BIB) celebrated for first time.	The biennial event presents the best in international children's illustration and gives artists from countries around the world an opportunity to present their work.
1967	International Children's Book Day (ICBD) celebrated for the first time.	International event that promotes and inspires children's books from around the world.
1967	*Brown Bear, Brown Bear, What Do You See?* published. Written by Bill Martin Jr.; illustrated by Eric Carle.	Eric Carle's first picture book. is probably the most famous predictable pattern narrative.
1968	*Rosie's Walk* published. Written and illustrated by Pat Hutchins.	Often cited for the extreme contradiction between the text and pictures, which created a "third story."

DATE	EVENT	NOTABLE FOR
1969	*The Very Hungry Caterpillar* published. Written and illustrated by Eric Carle.	One of the first books to incorporate a toy format successfully.
1969	*Stevie* published. Written and illustrated by John Steptoe.	Considered to be the first book that realistically portrays a minority character openly and honestly.
1970	*In the Night Kitchen* published. Written and illustrated by Maurice Sendak.	Controversial for the nudity of the protagonist in some scenes in the book. When it first appeared, some children's librarians "dressed" the naked form of Mickey. Critics have applied Marxist and Freudian interpretations to the book.
1970	*Frog and Toad Are Friends* published. Written and illustrated by Arnold Lobel.	A classic example of the beginning reader format with strong verbal and visual narratives.
1971	*Look Again!* published. Conceived and photographed by Tana Hoban.	One of the first picture books to feature photographs as the medium. Prior to this photographs were primarily only seen in informational titles.
1971	Canada's Amelia Frances Howard-Gibbon Illustrator's Award established.	Like other awards that recognize distinction in children's illustration, the Amelia Frances Howard-Gibbon brought attention to Canadian illustrators.
1972	*Alexander and the Terrible, Horrible, No Good, Very Bad Day* published. Written by Judith Viorst; illustrated by Ray Cruz.	A very real boy, portrayed in an honest and forthcoming manner.
1972	*George and Martha* published. Written and illustrated by James Marshall.	The collection of five stories about two of the most endearing friends in literature launched a career filled with energy, fun, spontaneity, and a wonderful cast of characters.
1972	*William's Doll* published. Written by Charlotte Zolotow; illustrated by William Pene du Bois.	In the forefront of writing about personal relationships for the very young, Zolotow struck a blow for ending the stereotypes assigned to the sexes in this groundbreaking book about a boy who wants a doll so he can practice being a father.
1974	Coretta Scott King Medal awarded to an illustrator for the first time.	Acknowledged the work of African American illustrators, who were often overlooked by other award committees.

DATE	EVENT	NOTABLE FOR
1978	*Freight Train* published. Written and illustrated by Donald Crews.	A striking example of graphic art techniques in a picture book.
1979	*The Garden of Abdul Gasazi* published. Written and illustrated by Chris Van Allsburg.	Introduces the talented Chris Van Allsburg.
1979	<u>Max and Ruby</u> series introduced. Written and illustrated by Rosemary Wells.	The first four titles in the series—*Max's First Word, Max's New Suit, Max's Ride*, and *Max's Toys*—earned Wells the distinction of creating the modern board book.
1980	*Hiroshima no Pika* published. . Written and illustrated by Toshi Maruki.	An early sophisticated picture book that explored the horror of the bombing of Hiroshima in a form traditionally intended for younger readers.
1982	*I Hate My Teddy Bear.* Written and illustrated by David McKee.	An early sophisticated picture book with experimental forms and structures that created intentional friction between the reader and the artist.
1983	IBBY (International Board on Books for Young People) founded by Jella Lepman in Zurich, Switzerland.	Today IBBY has more than 65 chapters, promoting children's books in every nook and cranny of the world.
1983	*Reading Rainbow* premiered. Hosted by LeVar Burton.	The television program's dynamic, magazine-style format features on location shoots and an animated version of the featured picture book; it promoted books and reading.
1985	*The Polar Express* published. Written and illustrated by Chris Van Allsburg.	Winner of the Caldecott Medal in 1986, the book was destined to become a Christmas classic
1989	*Chicka Chicka Boom Boom* published. Written by Bill Martin, Bill and John Archambault; illustrated by Lois Ehlert.	An innovative alphabet look that set the standard for future alphabet books. Ehlert's trademark graphic art accompanies the spontaneous and rambunctious narrative.
1989	*The True Story of the 3 Little Pigs* published. Written by Jon Scieszka; illustrated by Lane Smith	Introduced the talented trio that includes designer Molly Leach. The first book to parody fairy tales, a trend that has not ceased.
1990	*Black and White* published. Written and illustrated by David Macaulay.	Not only did *Black and White* win the Caldecott medal in 1991, it also introduced the new type of postmodern picture book.

DATE	EVENT	NOTABLE FOR
1991	Lee & Low Books, an independent children's book publisher specializing in multicultural books, founded.	The company, which published its first list in spring 1993, is one of the only publishers to specialize in multicultural children's literature.
1991	*Brother Eagle, Sister Sky* published. Illustrated by Susan Jeffers.	Controversial for its depiction of Native American culture.
1993	*Mr. Lunch Takes a Plane Ride* by J.otto Seibold published.	The first picture book created entirely on a computer, in this case, a Macintosh.
1993	*The Stinky Cheese Man and Other Fairly Stupid Tales.* Written by Jon Scieszka; illustrated by Lane Smith.	Notable for deconstructing the parts of a picture book.
1997	*Nappy Hair* published. Written by Carolivia Herron; illustrated by Joe Cepeda.	Set off a firestorm of controversy when a New York City teacher was fired after angry parents protested.
1997	Fiftieth anniversary of publication of Margaret Wise Brown's *Good Night Moon.*	This classic example of language, story, art, and design merging reflects how children view the world.
2000	ipicturebooks.com founded.	The first attempt to create a market for digital picture books. The company was defunct as of 2002.
2001	Curious George celebrates his sixtieth birthday!	It took almost a decade after its initial publication in 1941 for *Curious George* to capture the attention that would result in the character's lasting fame.
2007	*Flotsam* (2006) by David Wiesner wins the Caldecott Medal.	Wiesner wins the Caldecott Medal for the third time; the only other individual to do so is Marcia Brown.
2007	*Gallop! A Scanimation Picture* published. Conceived, written, and illustrated by Rufus Butler Seder.	Sold nearly 800,000 copies its first year in print. Introduced a new type of interactive format to picture books.
2008	*The Invention of Hugo Cabret* (2007) by Brian Selznick wins the Caldecott Medal.	The first time a novel was awarded the Caldecott Medal.
2008	Lookybook founded.	Lookybook picks up where ipicturebooks.com left off, with patented technology. The company digitized 1,000 books in 2008.

Appendix C: Sources

Agosto, Denise E. 1999. "One and Inseparable: Interdependent Storytelling in Picture Storybooks." *Children's Literature in Education* 30, no. 4: 268–280

Alderson, Brian. 1986. *Sing a Song for Sixpence: The English Picture Book Tradition and Randolph Caldecott.* Cambridge University Press.

American Library Association. 2007. *And Tango Makes Three tops ALA's 2006 List of Most Challenged Books.* Available at http://www.ala.org/ala/pressreleases2007/march2007/mc06.cfmml (accessed July 2008).

Anderson, Nancy A., and Janet C. Richards. 2003. "What Do I See? What Do I Think? What Do I Wonder? (STW): A Visual Literacy Strategy to Help Emergent Readers Focus on Storybook Illustrations." *The Reading Teacher* 56, no. 5: 442–443.

Arizpe, Evelyn, and Morag Styles. 2003. *Children Reading Picture: Interpreting Visual Texts.* RoutledgeFalmer.

Armbruster, Bonnie B., Fran Lehr, and Jean Osborn. 2003. *A Child Becomes a Reader: Birth through Preschool.* 2nd ed. RMC Research Corporation.

Aronson, Mark. 2001. "Slippery Slopes and Proliferating Prizes: Questions about the Creation of Three Book Awards Based on Race or Ethnicity." *Horn Book* 77, no. 3: 271–278.

Aronson, Mark. 2003. "Where Does Controversy Come From? A Publisher's Perspective." *Journal of Children's Literature* 29, no. 1: 76–81.

Bader, Barbara. 1976. *American Picture Books from Noah's Ark to the Beast Within.* Macmillan.

Bancroft, Colette. 2003. "A Master Who Made It Look Easy." *St. Petersburg Times.* July 6.

Bang, Molly. 2000. *Picture This: How Pictures Work.* SeaStar.

Braxton, Barbara. 2007. "Read-Alouds: Choosing the Right Book." *Teacher Librarian* 34, no. 3: 52–53.

Britton, Jason. 2002. "A New Day for Design: Five Art Directors Discuss the Evolving Field of Children's Book Design." *Publishers Weekly* 249, no. 43: 28–32.

Buccieri, Lisa Rojany, and Peter Economy. 2005. *Writing Children's Books for Dummies: The ABCs of Writing for Chidren.* Wiley.

Burton, Virginia Lee. 1943. "Making Picture Books." *Horn Book* 19, no. 4: 228–232.

Cai, Mingshui. 2002. *Multicultural Literature for Children and Young Adults: Reflections on Critical Issues.* Greenwood.

Carlson, Ann D. 1996. "Concept Books and Young Children." In *Ways of Knowing*, edited by Kay E. Vandergrift, 185–202. Scarecrow Press.

Carr, Kathryn S., et al. 2001. "Not Just for Primary Grades: A Bibliography of Picture Books for Secondary Content Teachers." *Journal of Adolescent & Adult Literacy* 45, no. 2: 146–153.

Cech, John. "The Dance of Words and Pictures." *Words and Pictures an Over-View for Teachers.* Christopher Chandler, ed. The Chicago Humanities Festival, 2001.

"Charges of Racism Stun Nappy Hair Author and Teacher." 1999. *School Library Journal* (January): 13.

Cianciolo, Patricia J. 2000. *Informational Picture Books for Children.* American Library Association.

Clair, Kate. 1999. *A Typographic Workbook.* Wiley.

Collen, Lauren. 2006. "The Digital and Traditional Storytimes Research Project: Using Digitized Picture Books for Preschool Group Storytimes." *Children & Libraries* 4, no. 3: 12–18.

Cooper, Ilene. 1998. "Something Smells Fishy Here." *Booklist* 95, no. 1: 126.

Cortes, Oralia Garza de. 1992. "United States: Hispanic Americans." In *Our Family, Our Friends, Our World,* edited by Lyn Miller-Lachmann. Libraries Unlimited.

Cotton, Penni. 2005. "Visual Narratives across Cultures: Devising a Course on Reading Picturebooks." *Bookbird* 43, no. 2: 39–45.

"Crews, Donald 1932– ." 1994. In *Something About the Author.* Vol. 76, 41–45. Gale.

Cummins, June. 2004. "Accessing the International Children's Digital Library." *The Horn Book* 80, no. 2: 145–151.

Dalby, Richard. 1991. *The Golden Age of Children's Book Illustration.* O'Mara Books Limited.

Darton, Harvey. 1988. *Children's Books in England.* 3rd ed. Revised by Brian Alderson. The British Library.

Dondis, Donis A. 1973. *Primer of Visual Literacy.* MIT Press.

Dooley, Patricia. 1991. "Brother Eagle Sister Sky." *School Library Journal* 37 (November): 288.

Doonan, Jane. 1993. *Looking at Pictures in Picture Books.* Thimble Press.

Dresang, Eliza T. 2003. "Controversial Books and Contemporary Children." *Journal of Children's Literature* 29, no. 1: 20–31.

Drew, Ned. 2005. *By Its Cover: Modern American Book Cover Design.* Princeton Architecture Press.

Druin, Allison. 2005. "What Children Can Teach Us: Developing Digital Libraries for Children with Children." *The Library Quarterly* 75, no. 1 (January): 20–41.

Eddy, Jacalyn. 2006. *Bookwomen: Creating an Empire in Children's Book Publishing, 1919–1939.* University of Wisconsin Press.

"Ehlert, Lois 1934–." 2007. In *Something About the Author.* Vol. 172: 75–82. Gale.

Engelhardt, Tom. 1991. "Reading May Be Harmful to Your Kids: In the Nadirland of Today's Children's Books." *Harper's* 282: 55–62.

Engen, Rodney K. 1988. *Randolph Caldecott: Lord of the Nursery.* Bloomsbury.

Essa, Eva L. 2006. *Introduction to Early Childhood Education.* 5th ed. Delmar.

Fang, Zhihui. 1996. "Illustrations, Text, and the Child Reader: What Are Pictures in Children's Storybooks For?" *Reading Horizons* 37: 130–142.

Feelings, Tom. 1991. "Transcending the Form." In *Multicolored Mirror: Cultural Substance in Literature for Children and Young Adults,* edited by Merri V. Lindgren. Highsmith.

Fingerson, Julie, and Erlene Bishop Killeen. 2006. "Picture Books for Young Adults." *Teacher Librarian* 33, no. 4: 32–34.

Fiore, Carole D. 1999. "Entice Readers to Poetry." *CBC Features* 52, no. 1. Available at http://www.cbcbooks.org/ppw/articles/fiore.html (accessed July 2008).

"Fleming, Denise 1950– ." 2007. In *Something About the Author.* Vol. 173: 50–54. Gale.

Freeman, Evelyn, and Barbara Lehman. 2001. *Global Perspectives in Children's Literature.* Allyn and Bacon.

Galda, Lee. 1993. "Visual Literacy: Exploring Art and Illustration in Children's Books." *The Reading Teacher* 46, no. 6: 506–516.

Gill, Sharon Ruth. 2007. "The Forgotten Genre of Children's Poetry.Ó The Reading Teacher 60, no. 7: 622–625.

Golden, Joanne M. 1990. *Narrative Symbol in Childhood Literature: Explorations in the Construction of Text.* Mouton.

Goldstone, Betta P. 1999. " Traveling in New Directions: Teaching Non-Linear Picture Books." *The Dragon Lode* 18, no. 1: 26–29.

Gralley, Jean. 2006. "Liftoff: When Books Leave the Page." *Horn Book* 82, no. 1: 35–40.

Hade, Daniel. 2002. "Storyselling: Are Publishers Changing the Way Children Read?" *Horn Book* 78, no. 5: 509–517.

Hamer, Russell D. 1990. "What Can My Baby See?" *Parents' Press* 11, no. 2. Available at www.ski.org/vision/babyvision.html.

Hansen, Cory Cooper, and Debby Zambo. 2005. "Piaget, Meet Lilly: Understanding Child Development through Picture Book Characters." *Early Childhood Education Journal* 33, no. 1: 39–45.

Hearn, Michael Patrick. 1996. *Myth, Magic, and Mystery: One Hundred Years of American Children's Book Illustration.* Roberts Rinehart.

Hearn, Michael Patrick. 2000. "Foreign Goods: An Essay." *Riverbank Review* 3, no. 3: 4–7.

Hearne, Betsy. 1991. "Coming to the States: Reviewing Books from Abroad." *Horn Book* 67, no. 5: 562–569.

Hearne, Betsy. 1993a. "Cite the Source: Reducing Cultural Chaos in Picture Books, Part One." *School Library Journal* (July): 23–27.

Hearne, Betsy. 1993b. "Respect the Source: Reducing Cultural Chaos in Picture Books, Part Two." *School Library Journal* (August): 33–37.

Hearne, Betsy, and Deborah Stevenson. 1999. *Choosing Books for Children: A Commonsense Guide.* 3rd ed. University of Illinois Press.

Hirano, Cathi. 1999. "Eight Ways to Say You: The Challenges of Translation." *Horn Book* 75, no. 1: 34–39.

Honig, Alice Sterling. 2004. "Sharing Books with Babies." *Scholastic Early Childhood Today* 18, no. 4: 25–27.

Horning, Kathleen T. 1997a. "Board Books Go Boom." *The Horn Book* 73, no. 1: 155–160.

Horning, Kathleen T. 1997b. *From Cover to Cover: Evaluating and Reviewing Children's Books.* HarperCollins.

Jalongo, Mary Renck. 2004. *Young Children and Picture Books.* 2nd ed. Washington, DC: NAEYC.

Johnson, Charlotte, and William Harroff. "The New Art of Making Books." Net Connect Spring (2006): 8–12

Kobayashi, Miki. 2005. "Which US Picturebooks Get Translated into Japanese?" *Bookbird* 43, no. 2: 5–12.

Kohl, Herbert. 1995. *Should We Burn Babar: Essays on Children's Literature and the Power of Stories.* The New Press.

Kruse, Ginny Moore. 1992. "No Single Season: Multicultural Literature for all Children." *Wilson Library Bulletin* 66, no. 6: 30–33.

Lacy, Lyn Ellen. 1986. *Art and Design in Children's Picture Books.* American Library Association.

Larrick, Nancy. 1965. "The All-White World of Children's Books." *Saturday Review* 48: 63–65, 84–85.

Lee, Marshall. 2004. *Bookmaking: Editing, Design, Production.* 3rd ed. W. W. Norton.

"Letters." 1991. *School Library Journal* 37 (November): 86, 88.

Lindgren, Merri. 1991. *The Multicolored Mirror: Cultural Substance in Literature for Children and Young Adults.* Highsmith.

Lindsay, Nina. 2006. "Bringing Home the World." *School Library Journal* 52, no. 2: 36–37.

Litowinsky, Olga. 2001. *It's a Bunny-Eat-Bunny World: A Writer's Guide to Surviving and Thriving in Today's Competitive Children's Book Market.* Walker.

MacDonald, Margaret Read, and Brian W. Sturm. 2001. *Storytellers Sourcebook: A Subject, Title, and Motif Index to Folklore Collections for Children, 1983–1999.* Gale.

Malarte-Feldman, Claire-Lise, and Jack Yeager. 1998. "Babar and the French Connection: Teaching the Politics of Superiority and Exclusion. In *Critical Perspectives on Postcolonial African Children's and Young Adult Literature,* edited by Meena Khorana. Contributions in Afro-American and African Studies, No. 187. Greenwood Press.

Manghan, Shannon 2007. "Way Cool: Marketing and the Internet." *Publishers Weekly* 254, no. 8: 58–61.

Marciano, John Bemelmans. 1999. *Bemelmans: The Life and Art of Madeline's Creator.* Viking.

"Marshall, James. 1942–1992." 1988. In *Something About the Author.* Vol. 51: 109–121. Gale.

Martin, Michelle H. 1999. "Never Too Nappy." *Horn Book* 75, no. 3: 283–288.

Maughan, Shannon. 2001a. "A 'revolution' waiting to happen." *Publishers Weekly* 248, no. 5: 30–32.

Maughan, Shannon. 2001b. "Time Warner Acquires Ipicturebooks.com." *Publishers Weekly* 248, no. 8: 9

"McCarty, Peter 1966–." 2008. In *Something About the Author.* Vol. 182: 151–153. Gale.

McGillis, Roderick. 1996. *The Nimble Reader: Literary Theory and Children's Literature.* Twayne.

McNair, J. C. 2003. " 'But The Five Chinese Brothers Is One of My Favorite Books!' Conducting Sociopolitical Critiques of Children's Literature with Preservice Teachers." *Journal of Children's Literature* 29, no. 1: 46–54.

Metzger, Phil. 2001. *The Artist's Illustrated Encyclopedia: Techniques, Materials, and Terms.* North Light.

Meyer, Susan. 1997. *A Treasury of Great Children's Illustrators.* Abrams.

Midori, Todayama. 2007. "Revival of an Old Image: The Story of Little Black Sambo in Japan." *Bookbird* 45, no. 1: 23–30.

Minkel, Walter. 2000. "Make Way for E-picture Books." *School Library Journal* 46, no. 7: 15–16.

Minkel, Walter. 2003. "New Kids' E-Books Site Disappoints." *School Library Journal* 49, no. 1: 22.

Mitchell, W. J. T. 1995. *Picture Theory: Essays on Verbal and Visual Representation.* University of Chicago Press.

Moebius, William. 1986. "Introduction to Picturebook Codes." *Word & Image* 2, no. 2: 141–158.

"Nappy Hair Author Defends Teacher Removed from Class." 1998. *Associated Press*, November 25.

Nikolajeva, Maria, and Carole Scott. 2001, 2006. *How Picturebooks Work.* Garland.

Nodelman, Perry. 1990. *Words About Pictures: The Narrative Art of Children's Picture Books.* University of Georgia.

Nodelman, Perry, and Mavis Reimer. 2002. *Pleasures of Children's Literature.* 3rd ed. Addison Wesley Longman.

"NYC Removes Teacher Over *Nappy Hair* Book." 1998. *Boston Globe*, November 25.

Odean, Kathleen. 2003. *Great Books for Babies and Toddlers.* New York: Ballantine.

Odean, Kathleen. 2004. "Building a Board Book Collection." *Booklist* 101, no. 2: 252–253.

O'Sullivan, Emer. 2006. "Translating Pictures." In *The Translation of Children's Literature,* edited by Gillian Lathey. Multilingual Matter.

Pantaleo, Sylvia. 2005. " 'Reading' Young Children's Visual Texts." *Early Childhood Research & Practice* 7, no. 1. Available at http://ecrp.uiuc.edu/v7n1/pantaleo.html (accessed July 2008).

Pinkney, Andrea Davis. 2001. "Awards That Stand on Solid Ground." *Horn Book* 77, no. 5: 535–540.

"Pinkney, (Jerry) Brian." 2004. In *Something About the Author.* Vol. 148: 186–191. Gale.

Pitz, Henry Clarence. 1963. *Illustrating Children's Books: History, Technique, Production.* Watson-Guptill.

Public Library Association. 2001. *Parent's Guide to Emergent Literacy.* Available at http://www.ala.org/ala/pla/plaissues/earlylit/parentguidebrochures/parentguide.cfm (accessed July 2008).

Rawlinson, Nora K. 2000. "Why Not Judge a Book by Its Cover?" *Publishers Weekly* 247, no. 6: 8.

Reid, Calvin. 1998. "Nappy Hair Flap Spurs Book Sales." *Publishers Weekly* 245, no. 49: 16.

Robinson, Lolly. 2000. "The Newest Medium: Illustrating with Save and Undo." *Horn Book* 76, no. 6: 667–680.

Robyak, Anya A., T. Masiello, C. Trivette, N. Roper, and C. Dunst. 2007. "Mapping the Contemporary Landscape of Early Literacy Learning." *CELLnotes* 1, no. 1. Available at http://www.earlyliteracylearning.org/cellreviews/cellreviews_v1_n1.pdf (accessed July 2008).

Rochman, Hazel. 1993. *Against Borders: Promoting Books for a Multicultural World.* American Library Association.

Rose, Jacqueline. 1993. *The Case of Peter Pan: Or the Impossibility of Children's Fiction.* University of Pennsylvania Press.

Roxburgh, Stephen. 2004. "The Myopic American." *School Library Journal* 50, no. 1: 48–50.

Salisbury, Martin. 2004. *Illustrating Children's Books.* Barron's.

Salisbury, Martin. 2006. "No Red Buses Please: International Co-Editions and the Sense of Place." *Bookbird* 44, no. 1: 5–11.

Sawyer, Walter. 2003. *Growing Up with Literature.* 4th ed. Delmar.

Saylor, David. 2000. "Look Again: An Art Director Offers Some Pointers on Learning to See." *School Library Journal* 46, no. 1: 37–38.

Schickedanz, Judith A. 2001. *Much More Than the ABCs: The Early Stages of Reading and Writing.* NAEYC.

Schmitz, Terri. 2007. "Can We Change That? Yes We Can!" *Horn Book* 83, no. 2: 159–170.

Schwarcz, Joseph H. 1982. *Ways of the Illustrator: Visual Communication in Children's Literature.* Chicago: American Library Association.

Schwarcz, Joseph H., and Chava Schwarcz. 1991. *The Picture Book Comes of Age: Looking at Childhood Through the Art of Illustration.* Chicago: American Library Association.

Scieszka, Jon. 1998. "Design Matters." *Horn Book* 74, no. 2: 196.

Scott, Carole. 2005. "A Challenge to Innocence: Inappropriate Picturebooks for Young Readers." *Bookbird* 43, no. 1: 5–12.

Seale, Doris. n.d. "Books to Avoid: Brother Eagle, Sister Sky." Oyate. Available at www.oyate.org/books-to-avoid/bro_eagle.html (accessed July 2008).

Seale, Doris, and Beverly Slapin. 2005. *A Broken Flute: The Native Experience in Books for Children.* AltaMira.

Selden, Raman, Peter Widdowson, and Peter Brooker. 1997. *A Reader's Guide to Contemporary Literary Theory.* 4th ed. Prentice Hall.

Sendak, Maurice. *Caldecott & Co.: Notes on Books & Pictures.* Farrar, 1988.

Shamir, Adina, and Ofra Korat. 2006. "How to Select CD-ROM Storybooks for Young Children: The Teacher's Role." *The Reading Teacher* 59, no. 6: 532–543.

"Shannon, David 1959–." 2005. In *Something About the Author*. Vol. 152: 220–227. Gale.

Short, Kathy G., and Dana L. Fox, eds. 2003. *Stories Matter: The Complexity of Cultural Authenticity in Children's Literature*. NCTE.

Shulevitz, Uri. 1997. *Writing with Pictures: How to Write and Illustrate Children's Books*. Watson-Guptill.

Silvey, Anita. 1995. *Children's Books and Their Creators*. Houghton Mifflin.

Simpson, Mary Jett. 1986. *Reading Resource Book*. Humanics.

Sims Bishop, Rudine. 1997. "Selecting Literature for a Multicultural Curriculum." In *Using Multiethnic Literature in the K-8 Classroom*, 1–20. Christopher-Gordon.

Sims Bishop, Rudine. 2003. "Reframing the Debate About Cultural Authenticity." In *Stories Matter: The Complexity of Cultural Authenticity in Children's Literature*, edited by Kathy G. Short and Dana L. Fox, 25–37. NCTE.

Singer, Dorothy G., and Tracey A. Revenson. 1996. *A Piaget Primer: How a Child Thinks*. Plume.

Sipe, Lawrence R. 1998. "How Picture Books Work: A Semiotically Framed Theory of the Text Picture Relationships." *Children's Literature in Education* 29, no. 2: 97–108.

Sipe, Lawrence R. 2001. "Picturebooks as Aesthetic Objects." *Literacy Teaching and Learning* 6, no. 1: 23–42.

Sipe, Lawrence R., and Carolyn E. McGuire. 2006. "Picturebook Endpapers: Resources for Literary and Aesthetic Interpretation." *Children's Literature in Education* 37, no. 4: 291–304.

Smith, Elizabeth Bridges. 1997. "Reflections and Visions: An Interview with Rudine Sims Bishop." *Journal of Children's Literature* 23, no. 1: 62–65.

"Steptoe, John, 1950–1989." 1988. In *Something About the Author*. Vol. 63: 157–67. Gale

Stewig, John Warren. 1995. *Looking at Picture Books*. Highsmith.

Sutherland, Zena. 1997a. "Fables. Myths and Epics." In *Children and Books*. 9th ed. Longman.

Sutherland, Zena. 1997b. "Folktales." In *Children and Books*. 9th ed. Longman.

Sutton, Roger. 1999. "Now, Why's He Got to Come Back to That?" *Horn Book* 75, no. 3: 260–261.

Tal, Eve. 2004. "Beneath the Surface: The Untranslated Uri Orlev." *The Looking Glass* 8, no 2. Available at http://www.the-looking-glass.net/rabbit/v8i2/jabberwocky.html (accessed July 2008).

Thomas, Susan Gregory. 2007. *Buy, Buy Baby: How Consumer Culture Manipulates Parents and Harms Young Minds*. Houghton Mifflin.

Tisdale, Sallie. 1999. "A Sardine's Story." *Salon*. Available at http://www.salon. com/mwt/tisd/1999/02/11tisd.html (accessed July 2008).

Townsend, John Rowe. 1992. *Written for Children: An Outline of English-Language Children's Literature*. 4th ed. New York: HarperCollins.

Underdown, Harold, and Lynne Rominger. 2001. *The Complete Idiot's Guide to Publishing Children's Books*. Alpha Books.

"Van Allsburg, Chris 1949–." 2005. In *Something About the Author*. Vol. 156: 174–180. Gale.

Wade, Nicholas, and Michael Swanston. 2001. *Visual Perception: An Introduction*. Psychology Press.

Walsh, Maureen. 2003. "'Reading' Pictures: What Do They Reveal? Young Children's Reading of Visual Texts." *Literacy* 37, no. 3: 123–130.

Weinstein, Amy. 2005. *Once Upon a Time: Illustration from Fairytales, Fables. Primers, Pop-ups, and Other Children's Books*. Princeton Architectural Press.

Whitehead, Jane. 1996. "This Is Not What I Wrote! The Americanization of Children's Books, Part 1." *Horn Book* 72, no. 3: 687–694.

Whitehead, Jane. 1997. "This Is Not What I Wrote! The Americanization of Children's Books, Part 2." *Horn Book* 73, no. 1: 27–35.

Williams, T. Lee. 2007. "Reading the Painting: Exploring Visual Literacy in the Primary Grades.Ó The Reading Teacher 60, no. 7: 636–642.

Woolfolk, Anita. 2004. *Educational Psychology*. 9th ed. Allyn and Bacon.

Young, Terrell A., ed. 2004. *Happily Ever After: Sharing Folk Literature with Elementary and Middle School Students*. International Reading Association.

A Comprehensive Glossary of Picture Book Terms

abstract: Artwork in which the subject matter is stated in a brief, simplified manner, with emphasis on form, color, and concept; little or no attempt is made to represent images realistically, and objects are often exaggerated or distorted.

acrylic: Paint with a synthetic base that dissolves in water. Colored pigments are added for an opaque finish. Acrylic paint dries faster than oil paint and has a different texture and finish. It is similar to oil but more durable, and it dries faster. Acrylic paint does not crack over time.

additive colors: Colors produced by light; the more light produced, the brighter the colors. A model in which the RGB (red/green/blue) colors are added and combine to reproduce a broad array of colors. *See also* **RGB; subtractive colors**

analogous: Analogous colors are next to each other on the color wheel; for example, the colors to the left and right of one of the primary colors. Analogous palettes are calming and peaceful because the colors do not fight for attention and instead complement one another.

artist's or author's notes: Background information about the origins or process involved in creating the story or illustrations. Often found in books with a historical setting or an adaptation of a folk or fairy tale.

assemblage: A three-dimensional composition in which a collection of objects is unified in a sculptural work.

asymmetry: A balance of parts on opposite sides of a perceived midline, giving the appearance of unequal visual weight. If two sides of an object are different but appear balanced, it has asymmetrical balance. *See also* **symmetry**

atmospheric perspective: Also called aerial perspective. Refers to the use of bluer, lighter, and duller colors for distant objects in a two-dimensional work of art.

background: The part of the picture plane that seems to be farthest from the viewer. Includes shapes or objects that make up the background of a picture. *See also* **foreground; middle ground**

balance: An arrangement of parts in a composition so that they are equal, creating a feeling of equilibrium in an artwork. The three types of balance are symmetry, asymmetry, and radial. One of the principles of design.

blot: To use an absorbent material (like a cloth) to soak up or dry excess paint or water.

255

blues: The final plates for a book. Used by editors for final checks. If changes are needed, they have to be made to the film, which is expensive.

book jacket: The cover of the book, also called dust jacket. More than just a protection of the book, the book jacket is a vehicle of communication. *See also* **dual-image cover; single-image cover; wraparound cover**

borders: Frames used to enclose text or illustrations. Borders can be simple lines or elaborate and detailed artwork that provides additional information about the story. Borders, as do panels and vignettes, provide balance and variety in picture books.

brushes: Tools used to apply paint and ink to a surface (paper or canvas), made of hair or bristles, which are held in place by a metal ring or cap attached to a handle.

canvas: One of the most commonly used supports for painting. Tightly stretched strong unbleached cloth, usually of hemp or flax, is fixed over a wooden framework.

cartoon art: Art representative of cartoons strips in newspapers. Pictures are silly and goofy, and the artist makes little attempt to make the art appear realistic.

chalk: When applied to drawing, refers to various natural substances that are somewhat soft and crumbly, formed into sticks for the purpose of drawing. White chalk is limestone-based. Chalk comes in many colors, but is often pastel, with color mixed with white.

charcoal: Wood that is bound together and carbonized in an airtight container to prevent it from turning to ash. Fragile and friable, charcoal allows the artist to sketch with the edge for a fine line or to use the broad side, which produces thick strokes. It is most suited for broad, rapid, preliminary sketches.

character: An imaginary representation of a persona in a work of fiction. Characters may be humans, animals, or inanimate objects. They can be round or flat and dynamic or static.

CIP data: Cataloging in publication, is a bibliographic record prepared by the Library of Congress (LOC) before it is published. It includes subject headings assigned by the Library of Congress. The CIP data are usually printed in the verso of the title page.

CMYK: Cyan, magenta, yellow, and black, the four inks used for full-color printing. "K" stands for "key" color, which is black. Also known as the four process colors. *See also* **RGB**

collage: Three-dimensional design created by gluing flat elements such as newspaper, wallpaper, fabric, wood, photographs, cloth, string, etc., to a flat surface. The word is derived from the French word *coller*, meaning "to paste."

color: The result of a pigment's ability to absorb, transmit, and reflect light. Sometimes referred to as hue, color is the name, such as red. The three characteristics of colors are hue, intensity, and value. One of the elements of art. *See also* **primary colors; secondary colors; tertiary colors**

color relationships: Also called color schemes or harmonies, they refer to the relationships of colors on the color wheel. Basic color schemes include monochromatic, analogous, and complementary.

color separation: The process through which the four (CMYK) process printing colors are separated into their primary colors to create negatives and printing plates. *See also* **CMYK**

color wheel: A visual representation of the color spectrum; an aid to color identification, choosing, and mixing.

complementary colors: Colors opposite one another on the color wheel. Red/green, blue/orange, and yellow/violet are complementary colors.

composition: The plan, placement, or arrangement of the elements of art and principles of design in a work. The organization of elements in a work of art.

continuous narrative: One character or object portrayed in two or more places on the same page or page spread.

contour: The outline or visible edges of an object or a figure. *See also* **line; outline**

contrast: Differences between two or more elements (e.g., value, color, texture) in a composition; juxtaposition of dissimilar elements in a work of art. Also, the degree of difference between the lightest and darkest parts of a picture. One of the principles of design.

conventional sign: Sign that requires readers to have a code to decipher meaning. For instance, the word "tree" is meaningless unless readers have the code, in this case, an understanding of the English language.

cool colors: Colors that are calming and soothing; blue, green, and violet are cool colors.

copyright page: Page found in the beginning of the book, usually on the back of the title page. Includes ISBN number, brief summary of story, Library of Congress subject designations (CIP Data), publisher, and copyright date.

crayon: Dry color mixed with oily, greasy, or waxy binding media for drawing on paper. Crayons are soft and can be blended and smudged.

curvature: The act of curving or bending; one of the characteristics of line.

curvilinear: Formed or enclosed by curved lines.

cut paper: Two-dimensional images achieved by strategically cutting and arranging cut paper.

delineate: To draw or trace the outline of an object

depth: The three-dimensional appearance of an artwork. The illusion of space and depth can be created using color, line, and shape.

design: The plan, conception, or organization of a work of art; the arrangement of independent elements (of art and design) to form a coordinated whole.

design principles. *See* **principles of design**

dimension: A measure of a piece of art. The width, height, depth, or length.

display: To present or exhibit artwork.

dominance: The importance of the emphasis on one aspect in relation to all other aspects of a design.

double-page spread: Illustrations that spread across both sides of an open book.

double narrative: Two scenes with different characters or settings on the same page or page spread.

drawing: Use of lines to depict shapes and forms on a surface such as paper. A drawing can be an initial sketch or a completed illustration.

dual-image cover: Illustrations on the front and back of the cover that are complementary to but different from one another. Often by studying these different illustrations, clues to the story reveal themselves.

dummy: A manuscript laid out in book form, with sketches of illustrations.

dust jacket. *See* **book jacket**

easel: A stand that supports canvases or paper for artists.

elements of art: The basic components used by the artist creating a work of art. The elements are color, line, perspective, shape, space, texture, and value. See individual entries for details. Also called principles of art.

emphasis: Special stress given to an element to make it stand out. One of the principles of design.

endpapers: The glued pages inside the cover of the book. Endpapers are intended to enhance the mood or setting of a book. They are often decorated with a design or motif that complements the story or with one color that is dominant in the illustrations.

etching: Printmaking method in which lines and image areas are created by coating a plate with an acid-resistant substance, followed by scratching through the substance with a sharp tool such as a needle, and finally immersing the plate in acid, which leaves depressions in the exposed areas.

expressionism: A style of art that emphasizes emotion, as felt by the artist and experienced by the subject primarily through color and gestural lines or strokes. Expressionistic art has the appearance of reality, but facial expressions or structural lines are exaggerated or distorted.

field of action: The page or page spread.

fixative: A type of spray used on artwork created with charcoal, chalk, pencil, or crayons to prevent smudging.

flaps: Part of the book jacket. The front flap contains a brief summary of the story, price, and age designations. The back flap has brief bios of the author and illustrator, reviews of previous titles, and publisher information.

focal point: The place in a composition that draws the eye, usually because an element is emphasized in some way; the part of a picture that one looks at first.

folded and gathered (F&G): A sheet or sheets from a print run, folded, cut, and ready for binding. Picture book F&Gs are often sent to review journals.

folk art: A style dependent on traditional techniques and content. Folk artists usually have little or no formal training.

foreground: Part of a two-dimensional artwork that appears to be closest to the viewer or in the front. Middle ground and background are the parts of the picture that appear to be farther and farthest away.

form: Three-dimensional objects that is, they have height, width, and depth. A square is a shape (two-dimensional), but a cube (three-dimensional) is a form. *See also* **shape; three-dimensional; two-dimensional**

format: The physical makeup of a book. Includes size and shape (square, rectangular, horizontal, or vertical), as well as binding (paperback or hardcover). Nontraditional formats include pop-up books, books with partial pages, flap books, board books, and bathtub books.

framing: Technique used by illustrators in which a figure or object enters or leaves a frame to create a sense of time and movement.

freehand: Drawn by hand without the aid of tracing paper or drafting tools.

front matter: The pages after the endpapers and before the first page of the story. The half title page, title page, copyright page, and dedication are found in the front matter.

four-color process. *See* **CMYK**

galley: An advance copy of a book.

genre: A term used in literature to designate a type of literature with shared characteristics or to indicate story content, for example, mystery, adventure, romance, history, folklore, fairy tales, and biographies.

geometric: Any form (sphere, cone, cube, cylinder, pyramid) or shape (rectangle, circle, square, oval, and triangle) derived from principles of geometry. Geometric designs are typically made with straight or curved lines. *See also* **organic**

gesture drawing: The drawing of lines quickly and loosely to show movement in a subject.

glossy: Having a smooth, shiny finish.

gouache: (pronounced gwash) A French term used to describe a type of watercolor paint. The word is derived from the Italian *guazzo*, which means a watering place. Pigments used are ground in water and mixed with gum. The finish of gouache is opaque. The appearance of gouache is quite different from the finish of watercolor or tempera.

gradation: Transition of light to dark or dark to light on a tonal scale.

graphic art: Visual arts, often linear in character, such as drawing, engraving, and printmaking, used in conjunction with lettering and typography.

graphite: A form of carbon available in powder, stick, and other forms. Carbon is fine and dense. Pencils are made from graphite.

gutter: The open space between the pages where the pages form the spine. Illustrators and designers must plan for the gutter, otherwise illustrations may "disappear" into the gutter.

half title page: The half-title page is the first page of the book and contains only the title of the work and the name of the publisher.

halftone: An image that has been photographed through a screen to create small dots of varying size or more/fewer dots per inch (dpi) so that it can be reproduced on a printing press.

harmony: The principle of design that creates unity within a work of art. One of the principles of design.

horizon line: An imaginary line where the earth meets the sky.

hue: The exact shade or tint of a color. There are six pure colors: red, orange, yellow, green, blue, and violet. The name of a color.

iconic sign: A sign that is a direct representation of an object. For instance, a picture of a tree is iconic.

illustrated book: A book with more text than illustrations. Small illustrations are used to add to the story or emphasize particular story elements.

illustration: The artistic interpretation of an idea through various techniques, such as drawing, painting, or printmaking.

implied lines: Lines one cannot see, but they are felt through composition.

imposition: A plan for pages on a printing sheet. When folded, the pages are in the correct sequence.

impressionism: A style that captures the moment as it happens, with an emphasis on how light affects objects. Bright colors and swift brush strokes often mark impressionist art.

imprint: A part of a publishing company with a distinct identity, name, and staff. For example, Blue Sky Press is an imprint of Scholastic.

ink: A pigmented liquid used for writing, drawing, and printing.

intensity: The brightness or pureness of a color. A bright color has high intensity and a dull color has low intensity. Color intensity can be changed by adding black, white, gray, or an opposite color on the color wheel. Also called saturation.

intermediate colors. *See* **tertiary colors**

ISBN (International Standard Book Number): A unique 10-digit number internationally assigned to books for the purposes of identification and inventory control. ISBNs have four identifiers: group or country, publisher identifier, title identifier, and the check digit.

ISBN-13: In 2007, the book industry began begin using 13-digit ISBNs to identify all books to expand the numbering capacity of the ISBN system. ISBN-13 has the same identifiers as ISBN-10, except that it has a three-digit identifier preceding the group/country identifier.

layout: The overall design of a picture book, including the text, illustrations, book jacket, and trim size.

legends: Stories based on historical figures or events that embellish the acts of a real person. The facts and adventures of the person are exaggerated, making the individual legendary for his or her deeds. Compare with myths.

library edition: A version of a book that is specially formatted, reinforced to stand up to multiple uses. Library editions feature archival paper (which lasts longer than standard paper), hard covers, and reinforced spines, which make them popular with librarians and media specialists. Library editions are assigned separate ISBNs. *See also* **ISBN; trade edition**

line: A point moving in space. Lines can vary in width, length, curvature, color, or direction. Lines can be straight, curved, bent, angular, thin, thick or wide, or interrupted (dotted, dashed, broken). Line defines a space, creating an outline or contour; it creates patterns, movement, and the illusion of volume. Lines can be two-dimensional or implied (the edge of a shape or form). One of the elements of art. *See also* **contour; outline**

line direction: Horizontal, vertical, or diagonal.

line quality: The unique character of a drawn line as it changes lightness/darkness, direction, curvature, or width.

linear: A painting technique in which importance is placed on contours or outlines.

linear narrative: Writing with a beginning, middle, and end that is read from left to right and top to bottom.

linear perspective: The illusion of depth and volume on a flat surface. Closer objects appear larger and smaller objects appear far away.

linocuts or linoleum cuts: Similar to woodcut illustrations except that wood, which is a natural medium, has natural grains in the wood that show through the carvings, whereas linoleum, which is made by humans, is flat and allows artists greater freedom to create their own patterns. *See also* **monotype; woodcuts**

lists: Semiannual (or more frequent) groups of books produced by a publisher, announced and placed in a catalog together. They include the backlist (previously published books), the front list (new books for the year or season), and the midlist (books with reliable but not outstanding sales).

mass: The outside size and bulk of a form, such as a building or a sculpture; the visual weight of an object; the area occupied by a form.

mass market: Books sold through retail outlets, such as grocery and department stores. They are generally inexpensive paperbacks with mass appeal.

matte: A dull, often rough finish.

media: Plural of *medium*.

medium: The material used to make the artwork, such as oil, watercolor, acrylic, or charcoal, to name just a few. The plural is *media*.

metamerism: When two colors appear to match under one condition but not under another.

middle ground: Area of a two-dimensional work of art between the foreground and background.

mixed media: A technique involving the use of two or more artistic media and combined in a single composition.

monochromatic: A color scheme involving the use of only one hue, which can vary in value or intensity.

monotype: A form of printmaking in which no element of the print is repeatable.

mood: The state of mind or feeling communicated in a work of art, frequently through color.

motif: A unit repeated over and over in a pattern. The repeated motif often creates a sense of rhythm.

movement: The application of design that deals with the creation of action. One of the principles of design.

multiple narrative: Multiple scenes with different characters or settings on the same page or page spread.

naïve art: Paintings having a very childlike quality, identifiable by the flat, two-dimensional quality they possess. There is little detail and limited regard for anatomy.

narrative: Picture books communicate through two narrative forms, the verbal (words) and the visual (images), often diverging into multiple split narratives. *See also* **continuous narrative; multiple narrative; split narrative**

negative: Shapes or spaces that are or represent the areas unoccupied by objects.

neutral colors: Black, white, gray, and variations of brown. They are included in the color family called earth colors.

nonlinear: Can be perceived from any number of starting points, as opposed to linear, with a beginning, middle, and end.

nonobjective: Having no recognizable object as an image. Also called nonrepresentational.

oil: Paint created from mixing colored pigments with an oil base. The thickness of oil paint can vary. It dries slowly and must be added to the painting in layers, creating a rich, glossy finish that is reminiscent of the art of old masters. Painting with oil paint allows previous layers to show through as more are applied. Compare with acrylic.

one-point perspective: A way to show three-dimensional objects on a two-dimensional surface. Lines appear to go away from the viewer and meet at a single point on the horizon, known as the vanishing point.

OP (out of print): The publisher does not have copies in stock and does not plan to reprint it.

organic: Refers to shapes or forms having irregular edges or to surfaces or objects resembling things existing in nature.

outline: A silhouette, made with one line defining the perimeter of a form; flat and two-dimensional. *See also* **contour; line**

overlap: Where parts of a picture lie on top of other parts.

packager: A company specializing in creating books up to the printing stage or the distribution stage; marketing and distributing the book is handled by the publisher. The packager's name may appear on the copyright page, but the publisher's name appears on the spine.

paint: Colored pigments combined with liquid (called vehicles), including a binder that causes it to adhere to a surface. For example, linseed oil is a vehicle for oil paint. Types of paint include acrylic, gouache, oil, tempera, and watercolor.

painterly: A technique in which forms are created by manipulating color and tone. Media used for the painterly technique include, acrylic, gouache, oil, tempera, and watercolor. *See also* **drawing**

pallet knife: A tool, the working end of which is flat and is used especially for mixing and/or applying paint.

palette: A board an artist uses to mix paint. It also refers to the array or range of color an artist uses in a particular work or on a consistent basis. Claude Monet, a nineteenth-century impressionist artist, used only eight colors in his palette.

panels: Illustrations that are broken apart for effect. Panels add to the story by allowing the illustrator to achieve artistic statements not possible in a single- or double-page spread. Panels, as do vignettes and borders, provide balance and variety in picture books.

paperback: An edition with a soft cover, usually a light cardboard. Spines are glued rather than sewn or stitched as is the case with hardcover editions. A trade paperback is usually the same size as a hardcover book and printed to the same standards. Mass market paperbacks are smaller and printed on cheaper paper.

pastels: Pigments that are formed into manageable sticks. Pastels can be either soft or hard, which will affect the final images. Similar to crayon but not as greasy; similar to chalk, but not as dry. They can be rubbed and altered for effect.

pattern: A repeated line or shape in a predictable combination.

pen and ink: A medium that can stand alone or be used with other media to create detail. Pen and ink is often mixed with water to create what is known as "wash" drawing. Using pen and ink allows the artist to create shadows and light with a process known as cross-hatching.

perspective: A technique artists use to create a three-dimensional illusion on a two-dimensional surface. Perspective creates a sense of depth and space. One of the elements of art.

picture book: A book that depends on illustrations to help relate the story. The amount of text is equal to or less than the number of illustrations. Compare with picture story book and illustrated book.

picture story book: A book with illustrations that complement the text but are not relied upon to relate the story. Longer texts, such as folktales, are often illustrated with single-page illustrations. Compare with picture book and illustrated book.

pigment: The element in paint that provides its color. Pigments can be made of a wide variety of materials, including minerals and natural and synthetic dyes.

Plasticine®: Brand name for an oil based modeling clay that does not dry out and can be melted and cooled repeatedly. Plasticine will not harden beyond its original state, which makes it easy to manipulate or mold with fingertips.

point of view: The angle from which the viewer see the objects or scene.

portrait: A likeness of a particular person or animal. Also used to describe vertical orientation.

positive: Shapes or spaces that are or represent solid objects.

PP&B: Paper, printing, and binding. The cost of producing a finished book.

press kit: A packet of promotional materials sent to media outlets.

primary colors: Red, yellow and blue. All other colors are created from the primary colors.

principles of art. *See* **principles of design**

principles of design: The arrangement of visual elements in an illustration. These include balance, contrast, emphasis, harmony, movement, rhythm, and unity. Also called principles of art. See individual entries.

printmaking: The transfer of an inked image from one surface (from the plate or block) to another (usually paper).

proofs: The typeset pages of a book before it is printed.

proportion: The size relationships of one part to the whole and of one part to another regarding size, quantity, or degree.

pure color: A color that has not been mixed with another color.

realism: Subjects are portrayed with accuracy, shown as they would be in real life. Subjects and objects in realistic paintings are recognizable, and pictures have a lot of detail. Sometimes called representational.

recto: A right-hand page of a book, as opposed to a verso, which is a left-hand page.

remainders: Surplus books sold at a steep discount. Publishers sometimes sell off all their stock when putting them out of print, or sell surplus copies to reduce their stock.

render: The way an artist uses his or her tools and medium to achieve the desired result.

representational: An artistic rendering that is very close to the way an object or person looks in life. Also called realism, or photo-realism (which is so close to reality that it looks as though it is a photograph).

review copies: Copies of a book sent to reviewers, usually before publication, and often in the form of bound galleys or F&Gs.

RGB: Red/green/blue, the three colors used by computer monitors to display images. 100 percent of RGB will produce white. *See also* **CMYK**

running story: Objects or picture elements that recur throughout the picture book. Sometimes a secondary character or picture element will be repeated but not referred to in the main storyline.

rhythm: Intentional, regular repetition of lines, shapes, or colors to achieve a specific effect or pattern. One of the principles of design.

romanticism: Emphasizes the opulent atmosphere around the subject, in the style of European artists of the eighteenth and nineteenth centuries. The minute detail and rich color palette are dark and haunting. The romantic style is often applied to folklore and fairy tales.

saturation: How pure a color is. Low saturation looks light and transparent. Saturation can be compared to the process watercolors go through. They start with solid, opaque color (high saturation), but as water is added the color is diluted, giving a low saturation.

scale: Relative size, proportion; used to determine measurements or dimensions within a design or artwork.

scratchboard: A process that includes scratching the illustration in the black paint covering a white board. Colors may be underneath the black paint.

sculpture: Three-dimensional artwork that is either in the round (to be viewed from all sides) or bas relief (low relief, in which figures protrude slightly from the background).

secondary colors: Colors made by mixing two primary colors (red, blue, yellow) to make green, orange, and violet.

shade: A pure color to which black has been added. *See also* **pure color**

shape: A two-dimensional area or plane that may be open or closed, free-form, or geometric. Shapes, found either in nature or made by humans, have height and width, but not depth. One of the elements of art.

signature: A printed press sheet of printed pages, folded to size (e.g., a large press sheet folded in half, fourths, eighths, sixteenths, or thirty-seconds).

single-image cover: One image appears on the front of this type of cover. The back of the book may contain another small illustration or a solid color that blends with the cover.

single-page illustration: An illustration confined to one page. Text is often opposite a single-page illustration.

sketch: A drawing or painting often made as a preliminary study; not the final artwork.

space: The distance or area between, around, above, below, or within things. It can be two or three dimensional, negative or positive. Shapes and forms are defined by the space around and within them, just as spaces are defined by the shapes and forms around and within them. One of the elements of art.

split narrative: Two episodes in the same setting with different characters on the same page or page spread.

storyboard: An illustrator's plan for a book, thumbnails of all pages on one sheet.

structure: The way in which parts are arranged or put together to form a whole.

style: A set of characteristics of the art of a culture, a period, or school of art. It is the characteristic expression of an individual artist.

submissions: Manuscripts sent to a publisher by an author or agent. Submissions can be exclusive, multiple, or simultaneous.

subordination: Making an element appear to hold a secondary or lesser importance within a design or work of art.

subtractive colors: Cyan, magenta, yellow, and black (CMYK). Combined equally, the three colors (CMY) produce black, while in unequal amounts they create all the other colors. *See also* **additive colors; CMYK**

support: The material or surface upon which an artist applies the medium.

surrealism: Represented by imaginative details and startling or bizarre images.

symbolism: Figures and symbols are purposely distorted to express an idea. In picture books, symbols are often imbedded in the illustrations and are not hinted at in the story.

symmetry: A kind of balance in which both sides of a design are exactly alike. Humans have symmetrical balance. *See also* **asymmetry**

tempera: Similar to watercolors, except pigments are mixed with a sticky base, such as egg yolk. Tempera paint dries very quickly. Compare with gouache and watercolors.

tertiary colors: A combination of one primary color and one secondary color: red/orange, yellow/orange, yellow/green, blue/green, blue/violet, and red/violet.

text: The printed words in the book. When used in discussion, usually refers to the narrative story. Distribution and organization of the text affect the reader's overall experience.

text layout: The position and placement of text, an integral part of picture book design. Where and how the text is placed on a page effects the mood and tone of the story. Includes line spacing and line length.

texture: The surface quality of materials, either actual (tactile) or implied (visual). One of the elements of art.

theme: The overall idea of the story; a common thread running through the story. In picture books, the illustrations, book design, and story are integral parts of the theme.

three-dimensional: Objects that have height, length, and width. A doll is three-dimensional; paper dolls are two-dimensional. Also called 3-D.

thumbnails: An illustrator's rough sketches, called thumbnails because of their small size.

tint: A pure color to which white has been added, as opposed to a shade, which is a color to which black has been added, and tone, which is a color with gray added to it. *See also* **pure color**

title page: The next right-hand page following the half title page; it contains the full title and subtitle (if any), the author's name, any editors or translators, and the name and locations of the publisher. In picture books, the title page is usually illustrated with a vignette illustration that hints at a theme in the plot.

tone: Color with gray added to it. *See also* **shade; tint**

tools: Items an artist or illustrator uses, such as brushes, pencils, paint, canvas, paper, and palette.

toy books: Books that can be manipulated physically and used as playthings. Types of toy books include board books, pull-tab books, flap books, pop-up books, cloth books, and plastic books (bathtub books). Toy books can be simple or very complex. Also called novelty books.

trade edition: A version of a book that is formatted for the general public as opposed to a targeted market. Publishers sell them to bookstores and libraries. Distinct from library editions, which are reinforced for multiple uses. Trade editions are generally cheaper than library editions. They have separate ISBN numbers. Trade cloth editions are hardbound books and trade paperback editions are oversized softcover books. *See also* **ISBN; library edition**

trim size: The overall size of a book; the size of the pages, book jacket, and cover. Because size is very important to the overall design of the book, attention and consideration are given to the trim size of a picture book. Horizontal or vertical page orientation contributes to the size considerations.

two-dimensional: Having height and width but not depth; flat. Paper dolls are two-dimensional; a doll is three-dimensional. Also called 2-D.

two-point perspective: A system to show three-dimensional objects on a two-dimensional surface. The illusion of space and volume utilizes two vanishing points on the horizon line.

typeface: The type or lettering used for the text. Typeface is an integral part of the design of the book, and much consideration is given to which typeface is used in a picture book. The choice of typeface may reflect the setting of a book or simply the need for legibility.

unity: A principle of design that connects a variety of elements of art and principles of design into a work of art with harmony and balance. One of the principles of design.

value: The lightness or darkness of any color. A color to which black has been added is called a shade and has a darker value. A color to which white has been added is called a tint and has a lighter value. Value can suggest depth, volume, and mood. A value scale shows the range of values from black to white. One of the elements of art.

vanishing point: In perspective drawing the point at which receding lines seem to converge.

variety: The combination of one or more elements of art in different ways to create interest. One of the principles of design.

verbal: Communication through words. The text in a picture book is verbal.

verso: A left-hand page of a book, as opposed to a recto, which is a right-hand page.

vignettes: Small inset illustrations that can be integrated into double-page illustrations or isolated and balanced against text. Vignettes, as do panels and borders, provide balance and variety in picture books.

visual: Communication through images. The pictures in a picture book are visual.

visual elements. *See* **elements of art**

visual interest: Illustrators create visual interest through the use of framing, pacing, drama, and picture sequence.

visual literacy: Includes thinking and communicating with images. Visual thinking is the ability to transform thoughts and information into images; visual communication takes place when people are able to construct meaning from the visual image.

volume: The space within a form (e.g., in architecture, volume refers to the space within a building).

warm colors: Colors that are bold and energetic; red, yellow, and orange are warm colors

wash: A very thin coat of paint, often with the appearance of transparency.

watercolors: Finely ground-up pigments of color with a natural or chemical base that are mixed with water. Watercolors come in pans, tubes, or bottles. Compare with gouache and tempera.

woodcuts: Woodcuts are made from illustrations carved into wood with chisels and knives and then printed on a surface such as paper. An artist draws an image onto a block of wood and carves away the area around the image. A raised portion remains on the block, which is then covered with paint or ink and pressed to another surface, usually paper. The natural grain of the wood is allowed to enhance and contribute to the illustration. Woodcuts are an example of relief printing. *See also* **linocuts or linoleum cuts; monotype**

wraparound cover: A cover on which artwork begins on the front and wraps around to the back. When removed, the jacket can be laid flat and examined for details about the story and clues to the characters.

Bibliography

Aardema, Verna. *Bringing the Rain to Kapiti Plain*. Illustrated by Beatriz Vidal. Dial, 1980.

———. *Koi and the Kola Nuts: A Tale from Liberia*. Illustrated by Joe Cepeda. Atheneum, 1999.

———. *Why Mosquitoes Buzz in People's Ears*. Illustrated by Leo Dillon and Diane Dillon. Dial, 1975.

Ackerman, Karen. *Song and Dance Man*. Illustrated by Stephen Gammell. Knopf, 1988.

Adler, David A. *Lou Gehrig: The Luckiest Man*. Illustrated by Terry Widener. Gulliver, 1997.

Agee, Jon. *Milo's Hat Trick*. Illustrated by the author. Hyperion, 1998.

Ahlberg, Allan. *Each Peach Pear Plum*. Illustrated by Janet Ahlberg. Viking, 2004.

Alarcon, Francisco X. *Laughing Tomatoes and Other Spring Poems = Jitomates risuenos y otros poemas de primavera*. Illustrated by Christina Gonzalez. Children's Book Press, 1997.

Alborough, Jez. *Hug*. Illustrated by the author. Candlewick, 2000.

Allen, Pamela. *Mr. McGee and the Big Bag of Bread*. Illustrated by the author. Viking, 2004.

Ancona, George. *Harvest*. Photographs by the author. Marshall Cavendish, 2001.

Anholt, Catherine, and Laurence Anholt. *Tiddlers*. Walker, 1993.

———. *Toddlers*. Candlewick, 1993.

Arnold, Tedd. *Parts*. Illustrated by the author. Dial, 1997.

Auch, Mary Jane. *Beauty and the Beaks: A Turkey's Cautionary Tale*. Illustrated by the author. Holiday House, 2007.

Aylesworth, Jim. *The Folks in the Valley: A Pennsylvania Dutch ABC*. Illustrated by Stefano Vitale. HarperCollins, 1992.

———. *Old Black Fly*. Illustrated by Stephen Gammell. Holt, 1992.

Baker, Jeannie. *Home*. Illustrated by the author. Greenwillow, 2004.

Bang, Molly. *Ten, Nine, Eight*. Illustrated by the author. Greenwillow, 1983.

———. *When Sophie Gets Angry-Really, Really, Angry . . .* Illustrated by the author. Scholastic/Blue Sky, 1999.

Bannerman, Helen. *The Story of Little Babaji*. Illustrated by Fred Marcellino. HarperCollins, 1996.

————. *The Story of Little Black Sambo*. Illustrated by the author. HarperCollins, 1899, 1990.

Barry, Robert. *Mr. Willowby's Christmas Tree*. Illustrated by the author. Doubleday, 1963.

Barton, Byron. *Dinosaurs, Dinosaurs*. Illustrated by the author. HarperCollins, 1989.

Base, Graeme. *Animalia*. Illustrated by the author. Abrams, 1986.

Becker, Bonny. *An Ant's Day Off*. Illustrated by Nina Laden. Simon & Schuster, 2003.

Bemelmans, Lugwig. *Madeline*. Illustrated by the author. Simon & Schuster, 1939.

Beneduce, Ann Keay. *Jack and the Beanstalk*. Illustrated by Gennady Spirin. Philomel, 1999 .

Berenstain, Stan, and Jan Berenstain. *The Berenstain Bears and the Blame Game*. Illustrated by the author. Random 1997.

————. *The Berenstain Bears and the In-Crowd*. Illustrated by the author. Random 1989.

Bierhorst, John. *Doctor Coyote: A Native American Aesop's Fable*. Illustrated by Wendy Watson. Macmillan, 1987.

————. *The Woman Who Fell from the Sky: The Iroquois Story of Creation*. Illustrated by Robert Andrew Parker. Morrow, 1993.

Billout, Guy. *Something's Not Quite Right*. Illustrated by the author. David Godine, 2002.

Birdseye, Tom. *Soap! Soap! Don't Forget the Soap!* Illustrated by Andrew Glass. Holiday, 1993.

Bishop, Claire Huchet. *The Five Chinese Brothers*. Illustrated by Kurt Wiese. Coward-McCann, 1938.

Bishop, Gavin. *Kiwi Moon*. Illustrated by the author. Random, 2005.

Blake, Quentin. *Cockatoos*. Illustrated by the author. Jonathan Cape, 1992.

Blake, Robert J. *Swift*. Illustrated by the author. Philomel, 2007.

Borden, Louise. *The Little Ships: The Heroic Rescue at Dunkirk in World War II*. Illustrated by Michael Foreman. McElderry, 1997.

Bowen, Betsy. *Antler, Bear, Canoe: A Northwoods Alphabet*. Illustrated by the author. Houghton Mifflin, 2002.

Boynton, Sandra. *Fuzzy Fuzzy Fuzzy!* Illustrated by the author. Little, Simon, 2003.

Bradbury, Ray. *The Homecoming*. Illustrated by Dave McKean. HarperCollins, 2006.

Brett, Jan. *The Mitten*. Illustrated by the author. Putnam's 1989.

Briant, Ed. *Seven Stories.* Illustrated by the author. Roaring Brook, 2005.

Brown, Calef. *Tippintown: A Guided Tour.* Illustrated by the author. Houghton Mifflin, 2003.

Brown, Don. *Alice Ramsey's Grand Adventure.* Illustrated by the author. Houghton Mifflin, 1997.

Brown, Marc. *Arthur's Eyes.* Illustrated by the author. Little, Brown, 1979.

———. *Arthur's Teacher Moves In.* Illustrated by the author. Little, Brown, 2000.

Brown, Marcia. *Once a Mouse.* Illustrated by the author. Scribner, 1961.

Brown, Margaret Wise. *Bumble Bugs and Elephants: A Big and Little Book.* Illustrated by Clement Hurd. HarperCollins, 1938, 2006.

———. *Goodnight Moon.* Illustrated by Clement Hurd. Harper, 1947.

———. *The Runaway Bunny.* Illustrated by Clement Hurd. Harper, 1942.

Browne, Anthony. *Gorilla.* Illustrated by the author. Knopf, 1985,

———. *The Shape Game.* Illustrated by the author. Farrar, 2003.

———. *Voices in the Park.* Illustrated by the author. DK, 1998.

———. *Zoo.* Illustrated by the author. Knopf, 1993.

Bruchac, Joseph. *The Great Ball Game: A Muskogee Story.* Illustrated by Susan L. Roth. Dial, 1994.

Bruel, Nick. *Bad Kitty.* Illustrated by the author. Roaring Brook Press, 2005.

———. *Poor Puppy.* Illustrated by the author. Roaring Brook Press, 2007.

Brunhoff, Jean de. *The Story of Babar, the Little Elephant.* Illustrated by the author. Random, 1933.

Bryan, Ashley. *The Night Has Ears: African Proverbs.* Illustrated by the author. Atheneum, 1993.

Byrd, Robert. *Finn MacCoul and His Fearless Wife.* Illustrated by the author. Dutton, 1999.

Bunting, Eve. *Smoky Night.* Illustrated by David Diaz. Harcourt, 1994.

Burningham, John. *Granpa.* Illustrated by the author. Jonathan Cape, 1984.

———. *Mein Opa und Ich.* Illustrated by the author. Parabel, 1984.

———. *Mr. Gumpy's Outing.* Illustrated by the author. Holt, 1971.

Burleigh, Robert. *Goal.* Illustrated by Stephen T. Johnson. Harcourt/Silver Whistle, 2001.

———. *Hercules.* Illustrated by Raul Colón. Harcourt/Silver Whistle, 1999.

———. *Home Run: The Story of Babe Ruth.* Illustrated by Mike Wimmer. Harcourt/Silver Whistle, 1998.

———. *Hoops.* Illustrated by Stephen T. Johnson. Harcourt/Silver Whistle, 1997.

Burton, Virginia Lee. *The Little House*. Illustrated by the author. Harper, 1942.

———. *Mike Mulligan and His Steam Shovel*. Illustrated by the author. Harper, 1919.

Cannon, Janelle. *Stellaluna*. Illustrated by the author. Harcourt, 1993.

Carle, Eric. *1, 2, 3 to the Zoo*. Illustrated by the author. Philomel, 1982.

———. *Today Is Monday*. Illustrated by the author. Philomel, 1993.

———. *The Very Hungry Caterpillar*. Illustrated by the author. Philomel, 1969.

Cendrars, Blaise. *Shadow*. Illustrated by Marcia Brown. Scribner, 1982.

Chen, Kersten. *Lord of the Cranes*. Illustrated by Jian Jiang Chen. North-South Books, 2000.

Child, Lauren. *I Will Not Ever Never Eat a Tomato*. Illustrated by the author. Orchard, 1999.

———. *That Pesky Rat*. Illustrated by the author. Candlewick, 2002.

Chodos-Irvine, Margaret. *Sarah Ella Gets Dressed*. Illustrated by the author. Harcourt, 1996.

Christensen, Bonnie. *The Daring Nellie Bly: America's Star Reporter*. Illustrated by the author. Knopf, 2003.

Chu, Dia. *Dia's Story Cloth*. Illus by Chue and Nhia Thao Cha. Lee & Low, 1996.

Climo, Shirley. *Atalanta's Race: A Greek Myth*. Illustrated by Alexander Koshkin. Clarion, 1995

Cline-Ransome, Lesa. *Satchel Paige*. Illustrated by James E. Ransome. Simon & Schuster, 2000.

———. *Quilt Counting*. Illus by James E. Ransome. SeaStar, 2002.

Clinton, Catherine. *When Harriet Met Sojourner*. Illustrated by Shane E. Evans. HarperCollins/Amistad, 2007.

Cole, Babette. *Prince Cinders*. Illustrated by the author. Putnam, 1987.

Coleridge, Samuel Taylor. *The Rime of the Ancient Mariner*. Illustrated by Ed Young. Atheneum, 1992.

Coles, Robert. *The Story of Ruby Bridges*. Illustrated by George Ford. Scholastic, 1995.

Collard, Sneed B. *Beaks*. Illustrated by Robin Brickman. Charlesbridge, 2002.

Collier, Bryan. *Uptown*. Illustrated by the author. Holt, 2000.

Cooke, Trish. *The Grandad Tree*. Illustrated by Sharon Wilson. Walker, 2001.

Cooney, Barbara. *Miss Rumphius*. Illustrated by the author. Viking, 1982.

Corey, Shana. *Players in Pigtails*. Illustrated by Rebecca Gibbon. Scholastic, 2003.

————. *You Forgot Your Skirt, Amelia Bloomer.* Illustrated by Chelsey McLaren. Scholastic, 2000.

Cox, Paul. *Abstract Alphabet: An Animal ABC.* Illustrated by the author. Chronicle, 2001.

Craft, K. Y., reteller. *Cinderella.* Illustrated by the author. Chronicle, 2000.

Craft, M. Charlotte. *Cupid and Psyche.* Illustrated by K. Y. Craft. Morrow, 1996.

Craft, Mahlon F. *Sleeping Beauty.* Illustrated by K. Y. Craft. Seastar, 2002.

Crews, Donald. *Freight Train.* Illustrated by the author. Greenwillow, 1978.

————. *Ten Black Dots.* Illustrated by the author. Greenwillow, 1986.

Cronin, Doreen. *Click, Clack, Moo: Cows That* Type. Illustrated by Betsy Lewin. Simon & Schuster, 2000.

Crummel, Susan Stevens. *Jackalope.* Illustrated by Janet Stevens. Harcourt, 2003.

David, Lawrence. *Full Moon.* Illustrated by Brian Wilcox. Doubleday, 2001.

Davies, Nicola. *Bat Loves the Night.* Illustrated by Sarah Fox-Davies. Candlewick, 2001.

Dayrell, Elphinstone. *Why the Sun and the Moon Live in the Sky.* Illustrated by Blair Lent. Houghton Mifflin, 1968.

de Paola, Tomie. *Strega Nona.* Illustrated by the author. Simon &Schuster, 1975.

de Vicq de Cumptich, Roberto. *Bembo's Zoo.* Illustrated by the author. Holt, 2000.

Deacon, Alex. *Slow Loris.* Illustrated by the author. Kane/Miller, 2002.

Demi. *Buddha Stories.* Illustrated by the author. Holt, 1997.

————. *King Midas: The Golden Touch.* Illustrated by the author. McElderry, 2002.

Diouf, Sylviane A. *Bintou's Braids.* Illustrated by Shane W. Evans. Chronicle, 2004.

Dixon, Ann. *Blueberry Shoes.* Illustrated by Evon Zerbetz. Alaska Northwest Books, 1999.

Donnelly, Jennifer. *Humble Pie.* Illustrated by Stephen Gammell. Atheneum, 2002.

Drummond, Allan. *Casey Jones.* Illustrated by the author. Farrar, 2001.

Duvoisin, Roger. *House of Four Seasons.* Illustrated by the author. Knopf, 1950.

————. *Petunia.* Illustrated by the author. Knopf, 1950.

Early, Margaret. *Robin Hood.* Illustrated by the author. Abrams, 1996.

————. *Romeo and Juliet.* Illustrated by the author. Abrams, 1998.

Ehlert, Lois. *Color Zoo.* Illustrated by the author. HarperCollins, 1989.

Ehrlich, Amy. *Rachel: The Story of Rachel Carson.* Illustrated by Wendell Minor. Harcourt, 2003.

Emberly, Ed. *Go Away Big Green Monster*. Illustrated by the author. Little, Brown, 1993, 2005.

———. *The Wing on a Flea*. Illustrated by the author. Little, Brown, 2001.

English, Karen. *Neeny Coming, Neeny Going*. Illustrated by Synthia St. James. BridgeWater, 1996.

Ernst, Lisa Campbell. *Little Red Riding Hood: A New Fangled Prairie Tale*. Illustrated by the author. Simon & Schuster, 1995.

———. *The Turn-Around, Upside-Down Alphabet Book*. Illustrated by the author. Simon & Schuster, 2004.

Ets, Marie Hall, and Aurora Labastida. *Nine Days to Christmas*. Illustrated by Marie Hall Ets. Viking, 1959.

Falconer, Ian. *Olivia*. Illustrated by the author. Atheneum, 2000.

———. *Olivia Saves the Circus*. Illustrated by the author. Atheneum, 2002.

———. *Olivia Forms a Band*. Illustrated by the author. Atheneum, 2006.

———. *Olivia's Counts*. Illustrated by the author. Simon & Schuster, 2002.

———. *Olivia's Opposites*. Illustrated by the author. Simon & Schuster, 2002.

Fanelli, Sara. *First Flight*. Illustrated by the author. Jonathon Cape, 2002.

Farmer in the Dell. Illustrated by Ilse Plume. David Godine, 2004.

Feelings, Tom. *Middle Passage Wonder*. Illustrated by the author. Dial, 1995.

———. *Soul Looks Back in Wonder*. Illustrated by the author. Dial, 1993.

Fernandes, Eugenie. *Big Week for Little Mouse*. Illustrated by Kim Fernandes. Kids Can Press, 2004.

Fish, Helen Dean. *Animals of the Bible*. Dorothy Lathrop. Lippincott, 1937.

Flack, Majorie. *The Story About Ping*. Illustrated by Kurt Wiese. Viking, 1933.

Fleming, Candace. *Tippy-Tippy-Tippy Hide*. Illustrated by G. Brian Karas. Simon & Schuster, 2007.

Fleming, Denise. *Barnyard Banter*. Illustrated by the author. Holt, 1994.

———. *Count!* Illustrated by the author. Holt, 1992.

———. *In the Tall, Tall Grass*. Illustrated by the author. Holt, 1991.

Fox, Mem. *Hattie and the Fox*. Illustrated by Patricia Mullin. Simon & Schuster, 1987.

———. *Koala Lou*. Illustrated by Pamela Lofts. Harcourt/Gulliver, 1989.

———. *A Particular Cow*. Illustrated by Terry Denton. Harcourt, 2006.

———. *Possum Magic*. Illustrated by Julie Vivas. Omnibus, 1983.

———. *Where Is the Green Sheep?* Illustrated by Judy Horacek. Harcourt, 2004.

Frampton, David. *Mr. Ferlinghetti's Poem.* Illustrated by the author. Eerdmans, 2006.

Freeman, Don. *Mop Top.* Illustrated by the author. Viking, 1955.

———. *Norman the Doorman.* Illustrated by the author. Viking, 1959.

French, Vivian. *Lazy Jack.* Illustrated by Russell Ayto. Candlewick Press, 1995.

Freymann, Saxton, and Joost Elffers. *Baby Food.* Illustrated by the authors. Scholastic, 2003.

———. *Dog Food.* Illustrated by the authors. Scholastic, 2002.

———. *Food for Thought.* Scholastic, 2005.

Frost, Robert. *Birches.* Illustrated by Ed Young. Henry Holt, 1988.

———. *Stopping by Woods on a Snowy Evening.* Illustrated by Susan Jeffers. Dutton, 2001.

Gág, Wanda. *The ABC Bunny.* Illustrated by the author. Coward McCann, 1933.

———. *Millions of Cats.* Illustrated by the author. Coward-McCann 1928.

Galdone, Paul. *Henny Penny.* Illustrated by the author. Clarion, 1979.

Gallaz, Christophe. *Rose Blanche.* Illustrated by Roberto Innocenti. Creative Education, 1985.

Garland, Michael. *Dinner at Magritte's.* Illustrated by the author. Dutton, 1995.

Gay, Michael. *Night Ride.* Illustrated by the author. Morrow, 1987.

———. *Papa Vroum.* Illustrated by the author. L'école de loisirs, 1986.

Geisert, Arthur. *Pigs from A to Z.* Illustrated by the author. Houghton Mifflin, 1986.

Geraghty, Paul. *The Hunter.* Illustrated by the author. Random, 1994.

Gerson, Mary-Joan. *How the Night Came from the Sea.* Illustrated by Carla Golembe. Little, Brown, 1994.

———. *Why the Sky Is Far Away: A Nigerian Folktale.* Illustrated by Carla Golembe. Little, Brown, 1995.

Giganti, Paul. *Each Orange Had 8 Slices.* Illustrated by Donald Crews. Greenwillow, 1992.

———. *How Many Snails?* Illustrated by Donald Crews. Greenwillow, 1988.

Goble, Paul. *The Girl Who Loved Wild Horses.* Illustrated by the author. Bradbury, 1978.

———. *Iktomi and the Boulder.* Illustrated by the author. Orchard, 1988.

Gomi, Taro. *Everyone Poops.* Illustrated by the author. Kane/Miller, 1993.

Goode, Diane. *The Dinosaur's New Clothes.* Illustrated by the author. Scholastic, 1999.

Graham, Bob. *"Let's Get a Pup," Said Kate.* Illustrated by the author. Candlewick, 2001.

Gramatky, Hardie. *Little Toot.* Illustrated by the author. Putnam, 1939.

Grégoire, Caroline. *Apollo.* Illustrated by the author. Kane/Miller, 2002.

Greenberg, Jan, and Sandra Jordan. *Action Jackson.* Illustrated by Robert Andrew Parker. Roaring Brook Press, 2002.

Greenfield, Eloise. *Honey, I Love.* Illustrated by Jan Spivey Gilchrist. HarperCollins, 2003.

Grifalconi, Ann. *Flyaway Girl.* Illustrated by the author. Little, Brown, 1992.

———. *The Village of Round and Square House.* Illustrated by the author. Little, Brown, 1986.

Grimm, Brothers. *The Bremen Town Musicians.* Illustrated by Lizbeth Zwerger. Minedition, 2007.

———. *Snow White.* Illustrated by Trina Schart. Hyman. Translated by Paul Heins. Little, Brown, 1974.

Guarino, Deborah. *Is Your Mama a Llama.* Illustrated by Steven Kellogg. Scholastic, 1989.

Hale, Sarah Josepha. *Mary Had a Little Lamb.* Illustrated by Salley Mavor. Orchard, 1995.

Haley, Gail E. *A Story, a Story.* Illustrated by the author. Atheneum, 1970.

Hall, Donald. *Ox-Cart Man.* Illustrated by Barbara Cooney. Viking, 1979.

Handforth, Thomas. *Mei Li.* Illustrated by the author. Doubleday, 1939.

Hartung, Susan Kathleen. *One Leaf Rides the Wind.* Illustrated by Celeste Mannis. Viking, 2002.

Henkes, Kevin. *Chrysanthemum.* Illustrated by the author. Greenwillow, 1991.

———. *Julius, the Baby of the World.* Illustrated by the author. Greenwillow, 1990.

———. *Julius's Candy Corn.* Illustrated by the author. HarperFestival, 2003.

———. *Kitten's First Full Moon.* Greenwillow, 2004.

———. *Lilly's Chocolate Heart.* Illustrated by the author. HarperFestival, 2003.

———. *Lilly's Purple Plastic Purse.* Illustrated by the author. Greenwillow, 1996.

———. *Owen.* Illustrated by the author. Greenwillow, 1993.

———. *Owen's Marshmallow Chick.* Illustrated by the author. HarperFestival, 2002.

———. *Sheila Rae, the Brave.* Illustrated by the author. Greenwillow, 1987.

———. *Sheila Rae's Peppermint Stick.* Illustrated by the author. HarperFestival, 2001.

————. *Wemberly Worried*. Illustrated by the author. Greenwillow, 2000.

————. *Wemberly's Ice-Cream Star*. Illustrated by the author. HarperFestival, 2003.

Henry, O. *Gift of the Magi/The Purple Dress*. Illustrated by Chris Raschka. HarperCollins, 2006.

Hepworth, Cathi. *Antics! An Alphabetical Anthology*. Illustrated by the author. Putnam's, 1992.

Herron, Carolivia. *Nappy Hair*. Illustrated by Joe Cepeda. Knopf, 1997.

Hershenhorn, Esther. *Fancy That*. Megan Lloyd. Holiday House, 2003.

Hildegard, H. Swift. *The Little Red Lighthouse and the Great Gray Bridge*. Illustrated by the author. Harcourt, 1942.

Hill, Eric. *Where's Spot*. Illustrated by the author. Putnam, 1980, 2005.

Hoban, Tana. *Black on White*. Illustrated by the author. Greenwillow, 1993.

————. *Look Again*. Illustrated by the author. Greenwillow, 1971.

————. *Look Book*. Illustrated by the author. Greenwillow, 1996.

————. *Look Look Look*. Illustrated by the author. Greenwillow, 1988.

————. *Take Another Look*. Illustrated by the author. Greenwillow, 1981.

————. *26 Letters and 99 Cents*. Illustrated by the author. Greenwillow, 1986.

————. *White on Black*. Illustrated by the author. Greenwillow, 1993.

Hodges, Margaret. *Joan of Arc: The Lily Maid*. Illustrated by Robert Rayevsky. Holiday, 1999.

————. *Saint George and the Dragon*. Illustrated by Trina Schart Hyman. Little, Brown, 1985.

Hoeslandt, Jo. *Star of Fear, Star of Hope*. Illustrated by Johanna Kang. Walker, 1996.

Hofmeyr, Dianne. *The Star-Bearer: A Creation Myth From Ancient Egypt*. Illustrated by Jude Daly. Farrar, 2001.

Hoffman, Mary. *Amazing Grace*. Illustrated by Caroline Binch. Dial, 1991.

Hogrogian, Nonny. *One Fine Day*. Illustrated by the author. Macmillan, 1971.

Holwitz, Peter. *The Big Blue Spot*. Illustrated by the author. Philomel, 2003.

Hong, Lily Toy. *Two of Everything*. Illustrated by the author. Albert Whitman, 1993.

hooks, bell. *Be Boy Buzz*. Illustrated by Chris Raschka. Jump at the Sun, 2002.

————. *Happy to be Nappy*. Illustrated by Chris Raschka. Hyperion, 1999.

Houston, Gloria. *But No Candy*. Illustrated by Lloyd Bloom. Philomel, 1992.

Howard, Elizabeth Fitzgerald. *Aunt Flossie's Hats (and Crab Cakes Later)*. Illustrated by James E. Ransome. Houghton Mifflin, 1991.

Howe, James. *Horace And Morris But Mostly Dolores*. Illustrated by Amy Walrod. Atheneum, 1999.

Howitt, Mary. *The Spider and the Fly*. Illustrated by Tony DiTerlizzi. Simon & Schuster, 2002.

Hutchins, Pat. *The Doorbell Rang*. Illustrated by the author. Greenwillow, 1986.

———. *Rosie's Walk*. Illustrated by the author. Simon & Schuster, 1968.

———. *Shrinking Mouse*. Illustrated by the author. Morrow, 1997.

Hyman, Trina Schart. *Little Red Riding Hood*. Illustrated by the author. Holiday House, 1983.

Isadora, Rachel. *ABC Pop!* Illustrated by the author. Viking, 1999.

———. *Luke Goes to Bat*. Illustrated by the author. Putnam, 2005.

———. *The Princess and the Pea*. Illustrated by the author. Putnam, 2007.

Issacs, Anne. *Swamp Angel*. Illustrated by Paul O. Zelinsky. Dutton, 1994.

Janeczko, Paul B. *A Poke in the I: A Book of Concrete Poems*. Illustrated by Chris Raschka. Candlewick, 2001.

Jeffers, Susan. *Brother Eagle, Sister Sky*. Illustrated by the author. Dial, 1991.

Jenkins, Emily. *Five Creatures*. Illustrated by the author. Farrar, 2002.

———. *That New Animal*. Illustrated by Pierre Pratt. Farrar, 2005.

Jenkins, Steve. *Big & Little*. Illustrated by the author. Houghton Mifflin, 1996.

———. *Biggest, Strongest, Fastest*. Illustrated by the author. Houghton Mifflin, 1995.

Jocelyn, Marthe. *Hannah and the Seven Dresses*. Illustrated by the author. Dutton, 1999.

———. *Over Under*. Illustrated by Tom Slaughter. Tundra, 2005.

Johnson, Crockett. *Harold and the Purple Crayon*. Illustrated by the author. HarperCollins, 1955.

Johnson, Stephen T. *Alphabet City*. Illustrated by the author. Viking, 1995.

Joyce, William. *George Shrinks*. Illustrated by the author. HarperCollins, 1985.

———. *William Joyce's Mother Goose*. Illustrated by the author. Random, 1998.

Kalman, Maira. *Fireboat: The Heroic Adventures of the John J. Harvey*. Illustrated by the author. Putnam, 2002.

———. *Max Makes a Million*. Illustrated by the author. Viking, 1990.

Kasza, Keiko. *My Lucky Day*. Illustrated by the author. Putnam, 2003.

Keats, Ezra Jack. *Over in the Meadow*. Illustrated by the author. Viking, 1971.

———. *The Snowy Day.* Illustrated by the author. Viking, 1962.

———. *Whistle for Willie.* Illustrated by the author. Viking, 1964.

Keens-Douglas, Richardo. *Freedom Child of the Sea.* Illustrated by Julia Gukova. Annick, 1995.

Kellogg, Steven. *Paul Bunyan: A Tall Tale.* Illustrated by the author. Morrow, 1984.

Kennedy, X. J. *Uncle Switch: Loony Limericks.* Illustrated by John O'Brien. McElderry, 1997.

Ker, Barbara Wilson. *Maui and the Big Fish.* Illustrated by Frané Lessac. Frances Lincoln, 2003.

Kitamura, Satoshi. *Comic Adventures of Boots.* Illustrated by the author. Farrar, 2002.

Knock! Knock! Multiple authors and illustrators. Dial, 2007.

Kontis, Althea. *AlphaOops! The Day Z Went First.* Illustrated by Bob Kolar. Candlewick, 2006.

Krauss, Ruth. *The Carrot Seed.* Illustrated by Crockett Johnson. HarperCollins, 1945.

———. *A Very Special House.* Illustrated by Maurice Sendak. Harper, 1953.

Kunhardt, Dorothy. *Pat the Bunny.* Illustrated by the author. Golden Books, 1940.

Kurt, Kemal. *Five Fingers and the Moon.* Illustrated by Aljoscha Blau. North-South, 1994.

Kurtz, Jane. *Rain Romp: Stomping Away a Grouchy Day.* Illustrated by Dyanna Wolcott. Greenwillow, 2002.

Kuskin, Karla. *The Philharmonic Gets Dressed.* Illustrated by Marc Simont. Harper, 1982.

La Fontaine, Jean de. *The Hare And the Tortoise.* Illustrated by Giselle Potter. Translated by Bolt Ranjit. Barefoot Books, 2006.

Lasky, Kathryn. *A Voice of Her Own: The Story of Phillis Wheatley, Slave Poet.* Illustrated by Paul Lee. Candlewick, 2003.

Lawson, Julie. *The Dragon's Pearl.* Illustrated by Paul Morin. Clarion, 1993.

Lear, Edward. *Nonsense!* Illustrated by Valorie Fisher. Atheneum, 2004.

Lee, Jeanne M. *I Once Was a Monkey: Stories Buddha Told.* Illustrated by the author. Farrar, 1999.

Leedy, Loreen. *Follow the Money!* Illustrated by the author. Holiday House, 2002.

———. *Fraction Action.* Illustrated by the author. Holiday House, 1994.

Lehman, Barbara. *The Red Book.* Illustrated by the author. Houghton Mifflin, 2004.

Lemieux, Michéle. *The Pied Piper of Hamelin*. Illustrated by the author. Morrow, 1993.

Lester, Helen. *Hooway for Wodney Wat*. Illustrated by Lynn M. Munsinger. Scholastic, 1999.

Lester, Julius. *John Henry*. Illustrated by Jerry Pinkney. Dial, 1994.

———. *Sam and the Tigers: A New Telling of Little Black Sambo*. Illustrated by Jerry Pinkney. Dial, 1996.

Lewin, Ted. *At Gleason's Gym*. Illustrated by the author. Roaring Brook Press, 2007.

———. *Red Legs: A Drummer Boy of the Civil War*. Illustrated by the author. HarperCollins, 2001.

Lincoln, Abraham. *The Gettysburg Address*. Illustrated by Michael McCurdy. Houghton, 1995.

Lionni, Leo. *Frederick*. Illustrated by the author. Knopf, 1967.

———. *Little Blue and Little Yellow*. Illustrated by the author. Harper, 1959.

———. *Pezzettino*. Illustrated by the author. Knopf, 1975, 2006.

Littlesugar, Amy. *Shake Rag: From the Life of Elvis Presley*. Illustrated by Floyd Cooper. Putnam, 1998.

Lobel, Arnold. *Fables*. Illustrated by the author. HarperCollins, 1980.

———. *Frog and Toad Are Friends*. Illustrated by the author. Harper, 1970.

———. *Frog and Toad Together*. Illustrated by the author. Harper, 1972.

Long, Laurel. *The Lady and the Lion*. Illustrated by Jacqueline K. Ogburn. Dial, 2003.

———. *The Magic Nesting Doll*. Illustrated by Jacqueline K. Ogburn. Dial, 2000.

Long, Melina. *How I Became a Pirate*. Illustrated by David Shannon. Harcourt, 2003.

Longfellow, Henry Wadsworth. *Hiwatha*. Illustrated by Susan Jeffers. Dial, 1983.

———. *Paul Revere's Ride*. Illustrated by Ted Rand. Dutton, 1990.

Lowell, Susan. *Cindy Ellen: A Wild Western Cinderella*. Illustrated by Jane K. Manning. HarperCollins, 2000.

———. *Little Red Cowboy Hat*. Illustrated by Randy Cecil. HarperCollins, 2000.

Macaulay, David. *Black and White*. Illustrated by the author. Houghton, 1990.

———. *Shortcut*. Illustrated by the author. Houghton, 1995.

MacDonald, Suse. *Alphabatics*. Illustrated by the author. Bradbury, 1986.

Maddern, Eric. *Nail Soup*. Illustrated by Paul Hess. Frances Lincoln, 2007.

Mahy, Margaret. *The Seven Chinese Brothers*. Illustrated by Jean and Mou-Sien Tseng. Scholastic, 1990.

Marcellino, Fred. *I, Crocodile*. Illustrated by the author. HarperCollins, 1999.

Marshall, James. *George and Martha*. Illustrated by the author. Houghton Mifflin, 1972.

———. *Goldilocks and the Three Bears*. Illustrated by the author. Dial, 1988.

———. *Red Riding Hood*. Illustrated by the author. Dial, 1987.

Martin, Bill. *Brown Bear, Brown Bear, What Do You See?* Illustrated by Eric Carle. Holt, 1967.

———. *The Maestro Plays*. Illustrated by Vladimir Radunsky. Holt, 1994.

Martin, Bill, and John Archambault. *Chicka Chicka Boom Boom*. Illustrated by Lois Ehlert. Simon & Schuster, 1989.

Martin, Jacqueline Briggs. *Snowflake Bentley*. Illustrated by Mary Azarian. Houghton Mifflin, 1998.

Martin, Rafe. *The Brave Little Parrot*. Illustrated by Susan Gaber. Putnam, 1998.

———. *Foolish Rabbit's Big Mistake*. Illustrated by Ed Young. Putnam, 1985.

———. *The Rough-Face Girl*. Illustrated by David Shannon. Putnam, 1992.

Mathis, Sharon Bell. *Ray Charles*. Illustrated by George Ford. Crowell, 1973.

Matthews, Andrew. *Bob Robber and Dancing Jane*. Illustrated by Bee Willey. Jonathan Cape, 2003.

McBratney, Sam. *Guess How Much I Love You*. Illustrated by Anita Jeram. Candlewick, 1994.

McCarty, Peter. *Fabian Escapes*. Illustrated by the author. Holt, 2007.

———. *Hondo and Fabian*. Illustrated by the author. Holt, 2002.

McCloskey, Robert. *Lentil*. Illustrated by the author. Viking, 1940.

———. *Make Way for Ducklings*. Illustrated by the author. Viking, 1941.

McCully, Emily Arnold. *Beautiful Warrior*. Illustrated by the author. Putnam, 1998.

———. *Mirette on the Highwire*. Illustrated by the author. Putnam, 1992.

McDermott, Gerald. *Arrow to the Sun: A Pueblo Indian Tale*. Illustrated by the author. Viking, 1974.

———. *Raven: A Trickster Tale from the Pacific Northwest*. Illustrated by the author. Harcourt, 1993.

McKissack, Patricia. *Flossie and the Fox*. Illustrated by Rachel Isadora. Dial, 1986.

McLaren, Chelsea. *Zat Cat! A Haute Couture Tail*. Illus by the author. Scholastic, 2002.

McMillan, Bruce. *Going Fishing*. Photographs by the author. Houghton Mifflin, 2005.

McMullan, Kate. *I Stink*. Illustrated by Jim @Ref = McMullan. HarperCollins, 2002.

McNaughton, Colin. *Suddenly!* Illustrated by the author. Harcourt, 1995.

Meddaugh, Susan. *Martha Speaks*. Illustrated by the author. Houghton Mifflin, 1992.

Melmed, Laura Krauss. *New York, New York! The Big Apple from A to Z*. Illustrated by Frané Lessac. HarperCollins, 2002.

Merriam, Eve. *The Inner City Mother Goose*. Illustrated by David Diaz. Simon & Schuster, 1996.

Metcalf, Paula. *Norma No Friends*. Illustrated by the author. Barefoot Books, 1999.

Micklethwait, Lucy. *I Spy: An Alphabet in Art*. Greenwillow, 1992.

———. *I Spy a Freight Train: Transportation in Art*. Greenwillow, 1996.

———. *I Spy a Lion: Animals in Art*. Greenwillow, 1994.

———. *I Spy Colors in Art*. Collins, 2007.

———. *I Spy Shapes in Art*. Greenwillow, 2004.

———. *I Spy Two Eyes: Numbers in Art*. Greenwillow, 1993.

Minarik, Else Holmelund. *Little Bear*. Illustrated by Maurice Sendak. HarperCollins, 1957.

Mochizuki, Ken. *Baseball Saved Us*. Illustrated by Dom Lee. Lee & Low, 1993.

Mollel, Tololwa M. *Rhinos for Lunch and Elephants for Supper!* Illustrated by Barbara Spurll. Clarion, 1992.

Mora, Pat. *Doña Flor: A Tall Tale About a Giant Woman with a Great Big Heart*. Illustrated by Raul Colón. Knopf, 2005.

Mosel, Arlene. *Tikki Tikki Tembo*. Illustrated by Blair Lent. Holt, 1968.

Moss, Lloyd. *Zin! Zin! Zin! A Violin*. Illustrated by Marjorie Priceman. Simon & Schuster, 1995.

Munson, Derek. *Enemy Pie*. Illustrated by Tara Calahan King. Chronicle, 2000.

Myers, Walter Dean. *Jazz*. Illustrated by Christopher Myers. Holiday, 2006.

Nelson, Kadir. *The Village That Vanished*. Illustrated by Ann Grifalconi. Dial, 2002.

Newman, Lesléa. *Heather Has Two Mommies*. Illustrated by Diana Souza. Alyson Wonderland, 1989.

Nikola-Lisa, W. *Magic in the Margins: A Medieval Tale of Bookmaking*. Illustrated by Bonnie Christensen. Houghton Mifflin, 2007.

Noble, Trinka Hakes. *The Day Jimmy's Boa Ate the Wash*. Illustrated by Steven Kellogg. Dial, 1980.

Numeroff, Laura Joffe. *If You Give a Mouse a Cookie*. Illustrated by Felicia Bond. HarperCollins, 1985.

Olaleye, Isaac. *Bitter Bananas*. Illustrated by Ed Young. Boyds Mills, 1994.

———. *The Distant Talking Drum: Poems from Nigeria*. Illustrated by Frané Lessac. Boyds Mills, 1995.

———. *In the Rainfield: Who Is the Greatest?* Illustrated by Ann Grifalconi. Scholastic, 2000.

Old MacDonald Had a Farm. Illustrated by Glen Rounds. Holiday House, 1990.

Onyefulu, Ifeoma. *Chidi Only Likes Blue: An African Book of Colors*. Photographs by the author. Dutton, 1997.

———. *A Triangle for Adaora: An African book of Shapes*. Frances Lincoln, 2000.

Orgel, Doris. *The Lion and the Mouse and Other Aesop's Fables*. Illustrated by Bert Kitchen. DK, 2000.

Orgill, Roxanne. *If I Only Had a Horn: Young Louis Armstrong*. Illustrated by Leonard Jenkins. Houghton Mifflin, 1997.

Ormerod, Jan. *Sunshine*. Illustrated by the author. Viking, 1981, 2004.

Page, Robin. *What Do You Do With a Tail Like This?* Illustrated by Steve Jenkins. Houghton Mifflin, 2003.

Palatini, Margie. *Piggie Pie!* Illustrated by Howard Fine. Clarion, 1995.

Paxton, Tom. *Engelbert Joins the Circus*. Illustrated by Roberta Wilson. HarperCollins, 1997.

Perkins, John. *Perceval: King Arthur's Knight of the Holy Grail*. Illustrated by Gennady Spirin. Marshall Cavendish, 2007.

Perkins, Lynne Rae. *Pictures from Our Vacation*. Illustrated by the author. Grenwillow, 2007.

Perrault, Charles. *Puss in Boots*. Illustrated by Fred Marcellino. Farrar, 1990.

Pfister, Marcus. *The Rainbow Fish*. Illustrated by the author. North-South, 1992.

Pilkey, Dav. *The Paperboy*. Illustrated by the author. Scholastiac, 1996.

Pinczes, Elinor J. *A Remainder of One*. Illustrated by Bonnie MacKain. Houghton Mifflin, 1995.

Polacco, Patricia. *Babushka's Mother Goose*. Illustrated by the author. Philomel, 1995.

———. *Oh, Look!* Illustrated by the author. Philomel, 2004.

Pinkney, Jerry, reteller. *Little Red Riding Hood*. Illustrated by the author. Little, Brown, 2007.

Politi, Leo. *Pedro, the Angel of Olvera Street*. Illustrated by the author. Scribner, 1947.

Poole, Amy Lowry. *The Ant and the Grasshopper*. Illustrated by the author. Holiday House, 2000.

Prelutsky, Jack. *If Not for the Cat*. Illustrated by Ted Rand. Greenwillow, 2004.

———. *Scranimals*. Illustrated by Peter Sís. Greenwillow, 2002.

Radcliffe, Theresa. *Bashi, Elephant Baby*. Illustrated by John Butler. Viking, 1998.

Radunsky, Vladimir. *Manneken Pis: A Simple Story of a Boy Who Peed on a War*. Illustrated by the author. Atheneum, 2002.

Rappaport, Doreen. *John's Secret Dreams: The John Lennon Story*. Illustrated by Bryan Collier. Hyperion, 2004.

———. *Martin's Big Words*. Illustrated by Bryan Collier. Jump at the Sun, 2001.

Raschka, Chris. *Arlene Sardine*. Illustrated by the author. Orchard, 1998.

———. *Charlie Parker Played Be Bop*. Illustrated by the author. Scholastic, 1992.

———. *Charlie Parker Played Be Bop*. [board book ed.] Illustrated by the author. Orchard, 2004.

———. *John Coltrane's Giant Steps*. Illustrated by the author. Orchard, 2002.

———. *Mysterious Thelonious*. Illustrated by the author. Orchard, 1997.

———. *Yo! Yes?* Illustrated by the author. Scholastic, 1993.

Rathmann, Peggy. *Good Night, Gorilla*. Illustrated by the author. Putnam, 1994.

———. *Officer Buckle and Gloria*. Illustrated by the author. Putnam, 1995.

Ray, Jane. *Adam and Eve and the Garden of Eden*. Illustrated by the author. Eerdmans, 2005.

Reid, Barbara. *The Party*. Illustrated by the author. North Winds Press, 1997.

———. *The Subway Mouse*. Illustrated by the author. Scholastic, 2005.

Rey, H. A. *Curious George*. Houghton, 1941.

Richardson, Justin, and Peter Parnell. *And Tango Makes Three*. Illustrated by Henry Cole. Simon & Schuster, 2005.

Ringgold, Faith. *Tar Beach*. Illustrated by the author. Crown, 1991.

Roberts, Brenda C. *Jazzy Miz Mozetta*. Illustrated by Frank Morrison. Farrar, 2004.

Rockwell, Anne. *Only Passing Through: The Story of Sojourner Truth*. Illustrated by R. Gregory Christie. Knopf, 2000.

Rohmann, Eric. *Time Flies*. Illustrated by the author. Crown, 1994.

Rosenthal, Amy Krouse. *One of Those Days*. Illustrated by Rebecca Doughty. Putnam, 2006.

Roth, Susan L. *Hard Hat Area*. Illustrated by the author. Bloomsbury USA, 2004.

Ruepp, Krista. *Anna's Prince*. Illustrated by Ulrike Heyne. North-South, 2006.

———. *Runaway Pony.* Illustrated by Ulrike Heyne. North-South, 2005.

———. *Winter Pony.* Illustrated by Ulrike Heyne. North-South, 2002.

Russo, Marisabina. *The Trouble With Baby.* Illustrated by the author. Greenwillow, 2003.

Ruzzier, Sergio. *The Little Giant.* Illustrated by the author. HarperCollins, 2004.

Sabuda, Robert. *Arthur and the Sword.* Illustrated by the author. Atheneum, 1995.

———. *Blizzard's Robe.* Illustrated by the author. Atheneum, 1999.

———. *Christmas Alphabet.* Illustrated by the author. Orchard, 1994, 2004.

———. *Saint Valentine.* Illustrated by the author. Atheneum, 1992.

Salley, Coleen. *Epossumondas.* Illustrated by Janet Stevens. Harcourt, 2002.

———. *Epossumondas Saves the Day.* Illustrated by Janet Stevens. Harcourt, 2002.

———. *Why Epossumondas Has No Hair on His Tail.* Illustrated by Janet Stevens. Harcourt, 2002.

San Souci, Robert D. *The Faithful Friend.* Illustrated by Brian Pinkney. Simon & Shuster, 1995.

Sanderson, Ruth. *Cinderella.* Illustrated by the author. Little, Brown, 2002.

Say, Allen. *Grandfather's Journey.* Illustrated by the author. Houghton Mifflin, 1993.

———. *Kamishibai Man.* Illustrated by the author. Houghton Mifflin, 2005.

———. *Tea with Milk.* Illustrated by the author. Houghton Mifflin, 1999.

Schachner, Judith. *Skippyjon Jones.* Illustrated by the author. Dutton, 2003.

———. *Skippyjon Jones in the Dog-House.* Illustrated by the author. Dutton, 2005.

Schertle, Alice. *Very Hairy Bear.* Illustrated by Matt Phelan. Harcourt, 2007.

Schnur, Steven. *Autumn: An Alphabet Acrostic.* Illustrated by Leslie Evans. Clarion, 1997.

———. *Spring: An Alphabet Acrostic.* Illustrated by Leslie Evans. Clarion, 1999.

———. *Summer: An Alphabet Acrostic.* Illustrated by Leslie Evans. Clarion, 2001.

———. *Winter: An Alphabet Acrostic.* Illustrated by Leslie Evans. Clarion, 2002.

Schwartz, David. M. *How Much Is a Million?* Illustrated by Steven Kellogg. HarperCollins, 1985.

———. *If You Made a Million?* Illustrated by Steven Kellogg. HarperCollins, 1989.

———. *Millions to Measure?* Illustrated by Steven Kellogg. HarperCollins, 2003.

Scieszka, Jon. *Math Curse.* Illustrated by Lane Smith. Viking, 1995.

———. *The Stinky Cheese Man and Other Fairly Stupid Tales.* Illustrated by Lane Smith. Viking, 1993.

———. *The True Story of the 3 Little Pigs!* Illustrated by Lane Smith. Viking, 1989.

Seder, Rufus Butler. *Gallop!* Illustrated by the author. Workman, 2007.

Seeger, Laura Vaccaro. *Black? White! Day? Night! A Book of Opposites.* Illustrated by the author. Roaring Brook, 2006.

———. *Dog and Bear: Two Friends, Three Stories.* Illustrated by the author. Roaring Brook, 2007.

———. *The Hidden Alphabet.* Illustrated by the author. Roaring Brook, 2003.

Selznick, Brian. *The Invention of Hugo Cabret.* Illustrated by the author. Scholastic, 2007.

Sendak, Maurice. *Chicken Soup with Rice.* Illustrated by the author. Harper, 1962.

———. *Where the Wild Things Are.* Illustrated by the author. HarperCollins, 1963.

Seuss, Dr. *And to Think That I Saw It on Mulberry Street.* Illustrated by the author. Random, 1937.

———. *Cat in the Hat.* Illustrated by the author. Random, 1957.

———. *How the Grinch Stole Christmas.* Illustrated by the author. Random, 1937.

Shannon, David. *David Smells!* Illustrated by the author. Scholastic, 2005.

———. *No, David!* Illustrated by the author. Scholastic, 1998.

———. *Oh, David!* Illustrated by the author. Scholastic, 2005.

———. *Oops!* Illustrated by the author. Scholastic, 2005.

Shaw, Charles B. *It Looked Like Spilt Milk.* HarperCollins, 1947.

Shaw, Nancy. *Sheep in a Jeep.* Illustrated by Margot Apple. Houghton Mifflin, 1986.

Sidman, Joyce. *Butterfly Eyes and Other Secrets of the Meadow.* Illustrated by Beth Krommes. Houghton Mifflin, 2006.

———. *Meow Ruff: A Story in Concrete Poetry.* Illustrated by Michelle Berg. Houghton, 2006.

Simont, Marc. *The Stray Dog.* Illustrated by the author. HarperCollins, 2001.

Sís, Peter. *Dinosaur!* Illustrated by the author. Greenwillow, 2000.

———. *Starry Messenger.* Illustrated by the author. Farrar, 1996.

———. *Tibet Through the Red Box.* Illustrated by the author. Farrar, 1998.

———. *The Wall: Growing Up Behind the Iron Curtain.* Illustrated by the author. Farrar, 2007.

Slobodkina, Esphyr. *Caps for Sale.* Illustrated by the author. Scholastic, 1940.

Souhami, Jessica. *The Little, Little House.* Illustrated by the author. France Lincoln, 2005.

Spirin, Gennady. *Martha.* Illustrated by the author. Philomel, 2005.

———. *The Tale of The Firebird*. Illustrated by the author. Philomel, 2002.

Stamm, Claus. *Three Strong Women: A Tall Tale from Japan*. Illustrated by Jean and Mou-sien Tseng. Viking, 1962, 1990.

Stanley, Diane. *Good Queen Bess: The Story of Elizabeth I of England*. Illustrated by the author. HarperCollins, 2003.

———. *Joan of Arc*. Illustrated by the author. HarperCollins, 1998.

———. *Michelangelo*. Illustrated by the author. HarperCollins, 2000.

Steig, William. *Shrek!* Illustrated by the author. Farrar, 1990.

———. *Sylvester and the Magic Pebble*. Illustrated by the author. Simon & Schuster, 1990.

Steiner, Joan. *Look-Alikes*. Illustrated by the author. Little, Brown, 1998.

———. *Look-Alikes Around the World*. Illustrated by the author. Little, Brown, 2007.

Steptoe, Javaka, ed. *In Daddy's Arms I Am Tall: African Americans Celebrating Fathers*. Illustrated by the editor. Lee & Low, 1997.

Steptoe, John. *Stevie*. Illustrated by the author. Harper, 1969.

Stevens, Janet. *Tops & Bottoms*. Illustrated by the author. Harcourt, 1995.

Stevens, Susan. *Cook-a-Doodle-Doo*. Illustrated by Janet Stevens. Harcourt, 1999.

Stevenson, James. *Don't You Know There's a War On?* Illustrated by the author. Greenwillow, 1992.

Stewart, Sarah. *The Library*. Illustrated by David Small. Farrar, 1995.

Sturges, Philemon. *The Little Red Hen Makes a Pizza*. Illustrated by Amy Walrod. Dutton, 1999.

Taback, Simms. *Joseph Had a Little Overcoat*. Illustrated by the author. Viking, 1999.

———. *There Was an Old Lady Who Swallowed a Fly*. Illustrated by the author. Viking, 1997.

Tafuri, Nancy. *Spots, Feathers, and Curly Tails*. Illustrated by the author. Greenwillow, 1988.

Tang, Greg. *The Grapes of Math*. Illustrated by Harry Briggs. Scholastic, 2001.

———. *Math for All Seasons*. Illustrated by Harry Briggs. Scholastic, 2002.

———. *Math Potatoes: Mind-stretching Brain Food*. Illustrated by Harry Briggs. Scholastic, 2005.

Tarpley, Natasha. *I Love My Hair*. Illustrated by E. B. Lewis. Little, Brown, 1998.

Thompson, Kay. *Eloise*. Illustrated by Hilary Knight. Simon & Schuster, 1955.

Thurber, James. *Secret Lives of Walter Mitty and of James Thurber*. Illustrated by Marc Simont. HarperCollins, 2006.

Titus, Eve. *Anatole.* Illustrated by Paul Galdone. Knopf, 1956, 2006.

———. *Anatole and the Cat.* Illustrated by Paul Galdone. Knopf, 1957, 2006.

Tolstoy, Aleksei. *The Gigantic Turnip.* Illustrated by Niamh Sharkey. Barefoot Books, 1999.

Tresselt, Alvin. *White Snow, Bright Snow.* Illustrated by Roger Duvoisin. HarperCollins, 1947.

Turner, Sandy. *Silent Night.* Illustrated by the author. Atheneum, 2001.

Uchida, Yoshiko. *The Bracelet.* Illustrated by Joanna Yardley. Philomel, 1993.

Van Allsburg, Chris. *The Garden of Abdul Gasazi.* Illustrated by the author. Houghton Mifflin, 1979.

———. *Jumanji.* Illustrated by the author. Houghton Mifflin, 1981.

———. *The Mysteries of Harris Burdick.* Illustrated by the author. Houghton Mifflin, 1984.

———. *Polar Express.* Illustrated by the author. Houghton Mifflin, 1985.

———. *The Stranger.* Illustrated by the author. Houghton Mifflin, 1986.

———. *The Wreck of the Zephyr.* Illustrated by the author. Houghton Mifflin, 1983.

———. *Zathura.* Illustrated by the author. Houghton Mifflin, 2002.

Vesey, Amanda. *The Princess and the Frog.* Illustrated by the author. Atlantic Monthly Press, 1985.

Waber, Bernard. *Lyle, Lyle Crocodile.* Illustrated by the author. Houghton Mifflin, 1973.

Walsh, Ellen Stolls. *Mouse Count.* Illustrated by the author. Harcourt, 1991.

———. *Mouse Paint.* Illustrated by the author. Harcourt, 1989.

Walsh, Melanie. *My Nose, Your Nose.* Illustrated by the author. Houghton Mifflin, 2002.

Walsh, Vivian. *Mr. Lunch Takes a Plane Ride.* Illustrated by J.otto Seibold. Viking, 1999.

———. *Penguin Dreams.* Illustrated by J.otto Seibold. Chronicle, 1993.

Wattenberg, Jane. *Henny Penny.* Illustrated by the author. Scholastic, 2000.

Weatherford, Carole Boston. *Moses: When Harriet Tubman Led Her People to Freedom.* Illustrated by Kadir Nelson. Jump at the Sun, 2006.

Wells, Ruth. *A to Zen: A Book of Japanese Culture.* Illustrated by Yoshi. Simon & Schuster, 1992.

———. *The Farmer and the Poor God.* Illustrated by Yoshi. Simon & Schuster, 1996.

Wesley, Valery. *Freedom's Gifts: A Juneteenth Story.* Illustrated by Sharon Wilson. Simon & Schuster, 1997.

West, Delno C., and Jean M. West. *Uncle Sam & Old Glory: Symbols of America.* Illustrated by Christopher Manson. Atheneum, 2000.

Why Did the Chicken Cross the Road? Multiple illustrators. Dial, 2006.

Wiesner, David. *Flotsam.* Illustrated by the author. Clarion, 2006.

———. *The Three Pigs.* Illustrated by the author. Clarion, 2001.

———. *Tuesday.* Illustrated by the author. Clarion, 1992.

Wild, Margaret. *Let the Celebrations Begin!* Illustrated by Julie Vivas. Orchard, 1991.

Willhoite, Michael. *Daddy's Roommate.* Illustrated by the author. Alyson Wonderland, 1990.

———. *Daddy's Wedding.* Illustrated by the author. Alyson Wonderland, 1996.

Williams, Marcia. *The Adventures of Robin Hood.* Illustrated by the author. Walker, 1995.

Williams, Sherley Anne. *Working Cotton.* Illustrated by Carol Byard. Harcourt, 1992.

Williams, Suzanne. *Library Lil.* Illustrated by Steven Kellogg. Dial, 1997.

Williams, Vera B. *A Chair for My Mother.* Illustrated by the author. Greenwillow, 1983.

———. *More More More, Said the Baby.* Illustrated by the author. Greenwillow, 1990.

Wilson, Karma. *Bear Snores On.* Illustrated by Jane Chapman. Macmillan, 2002.

Winter, Jeannette. *The House That Jack Built.* Illustrated by the author. Dial, 2000.

———. *My Name Is Georgia.* Illustrated by the author. Harcourt/Silver Whistle, 1996.

Wisniewski, David. *Golem.* Illustrated by the author. Clarion, 1996.

Wood, Audrey. *Bright and Early Thursday Evening.* Illustrated by Don Wood. Harcourt, 1999.

———. *The Bunyans.* Illustrated by David Shannon. Scholastic/Blue Sky, 1996.

———. *King Bidgood's in the Bathtub.* Illustrated by Don Wood. Harcourt, 1985.

———. *The Napping House.* Illustrated by Don Wood. Harcourt, 1991.

———. *Piggies.* Illustrated by Don Wood. Harcourt, 1991.

———. *Silly Sally.* Illustrated by the author. Harcourt, 1992.

Wormell, Christopher. *The New Alphabet of Animals.* Illustrated by the author. Running Press Kids, 2004.

Yashima, Taro. *Crow Boy.* Illustrated by the author. Viking, 1955.

Yolen, Jane. *How Do Dinosaurs Eat Their Food?* Illustrated by Mark Teague. Scholastic, 2005.

———. *How Do Dinosaurs Get Well Soon?* Illustrated by Mark Teague. Scholastic, 2003.

———. *How Do Dinosaurs Go to School?* Illustrated by Mark Teague. Scholastic, 2007.

———. *How Do Dinosaurs Say Goodnight?* Illustrated by Mark Teague. Scholastic, 2000.

Yorinks, Arthur. *Hey, Al.* Illustrated by Richard Egielski. Farrar, 1986.

Young, Ed. *Lon Po Po: A Red-Riding Tale from China.* Illustrated by the author. Philomel, 1989.

———. *Moon Mother: A Native American Creation Story.* Illustrated by the author. HarperCollins, 1993.

———. *Seven Blind Mice.* Illustrated by the author. Philomel, 1992.

Zelinsky, Paul O. *Rapunzel.* Illustrated by the author. Dutton, 1997.

Zelver, Patricia. *The Wonderful Tower of Watts.* Illustrated by Frané Lessac. HarperCollins, 1944.

Zemach, Margot. *The Three Little Pigs: An Old Story.* Illustrated by the author. Farrar, 1988.

Zolotow, Charlotte. *Mr. Rabbit and the Lovely Present.* Illustrated by Maurice Sendak. Harper, 1962.

———. *William's Doll.* Illustrated by William Pene Du Bois. Harper, 1972.

Index

About the Author

Denise I. Matulka is librarian in the library and archives at the *Lincoln Journal Star Newspapers* in Nebraska. She has worked in public, academic, and special libraries as an early childhood educator, a youth services librarian, a reference assistant, and an "America Reads" coordinator. She is the author of *Picture This: Picture Books for Young Adults* (Greenwood Publishing Group, 1997). In 1999 she created a Web site dedicated to picture books: www.picturingbooks.com.